Global
Environmental
Crises

An Australian Perspective

Graeme **Aplin**
Peter **Mitchell**
Helen **Cleugh**
Andrew **Pitman**
David **Rich**

Melbourne

OXFORD UNIVERSITY PRESS

Oxford   Auckland   New York

OXFORD UNIVERSITY PRESS AUSTRALIA

Oxford New York
Athens Auckland Bangkok Bombay
Calcutta Cape Town Dar es Salaam Delhi
Florence Hong Kong Istanbul Karachi
Kuala Lumpur Madras Madrid Melbourne
Mexico City Nairobi Paris Singapore
Taipei Tokyo Toronto

and associated companies in
Berlin Ibadan

OXFORD is a trade mark of Oxford University Press

National Library of Australia
Cataloguing-in-Publication data:

Global environment crises: an Australian perspective.

   Bibliography.
   Includes index.
   ISBN 0 19 553600 2.

   1. Environmental sciences. 2. Environmental protection —
   Australia. 3. Environmental protection. 4. Man —
   Influence on nature — Australia. 5. Man — Influence on
   nature. I. Aplin, G. J. (Graeme John).

363.7

Edited by David Meagher
Designed by R.T.J. Klinkhamer
Cover photograph from International Photographic Library
Typeset by Superskill Graphics Pte Ltd, Singapore
Printed through Bookpac Production Services, Singapore
Published by Oxford University Press,
253 Normanby Road, South Melbourne, Australia

PREFACE

EVERYWHERE WE LOOK there is clear evidence that human activity is having enormous impacts on a vulnerable Earth. Whether we think of deforestation in Papua New Guinea and Sarawak, the depletion of tuna stocks in the South Pacific, or the massive pollution and congestion problems of Bangkok, the evidence is manifest. Within Australia, winter smog in our capital cities, pollution of rivers and beaches close to those same cities, salination in the Murray–Darling Basin, logging of old-growth forests around the country's timbered fringe, and soil erosion through much of the semi-arid interior are all clear signs of human impacts on the natural environment.

Humans have hit natural systems with some savage blows in recent times. It is now evident that if the global system is to survive relatively intact, and if humans wish to continue to develop as a species, we will have to change our behaviour. The most successful organisms are the most adaptable ones. With our highly developed thinking and doing skills, we can undoubtedly successfully adapt if we put our collective minds to the task and if we have the will to see a difficult task through.

An important starting point is for all of us to gain a better understanding of the nature of the global environmental crises facing us today. We need to know more about the processes involved, especially about the ways in which human activity causes, alters and accelerates that change. Then we might know more about how we can minimise, control or even completely avoid undesirable impacts.

This book approaches the task from a particular viewpoint. It is dealing with global issues, but from an Australian vantage point. As well as dealing with the nature of the crises that are of concern on a global scale, it looks at their effect on the Australian environment and at Australian efforts to come to grips with them. As well as introducing attempts at global cooperation on environmental matters, it discusses Australia's role in achieving that cooperation and Australia's reactions to international agreements. Priorities in Australia and its region are in many ways different from those in other parts of the world, and those priorities will become evident in this book.

Five themes run through the book:

1 People are the primary cause of the major global environmental crises confronting us, and people hold the key to potential solutions.

2 The Earth's biophysical system is complex, comprising five interacting spheres (atmosphere, hydrosphere, biosphere, lithosphere and cryosphere). Changes in one component of the biophysical system, perhaps induced by humans, often lead to changes in other aspects.

3 There are four key dimensions to the human world system: the economic, the political, the technological and the demographic. These four dimensions, like the five biophysical spheres, interact in very complex ways, and simplistic explanations and solutions are rarely useful. In addition, these dimensions exist within particular cultural contexts in any given nation or region, and that context needs to be considered when seeking understanding or proposing action.

4 The human and biophysical systems interact in extremely complex ways, and any attempt to overcome global crises requires knowledge of, and action in, both the biophysical and human systems.

5 The concept of sustainable development, or that of a sustainable society, must be central to any potential solutions.

Underlying our approach to global environmental issues is the belief that geography and geographers are uniquely placed to contribute to understanding and debate in such areas. We believe this to be the case because geography spans the biophysical and social sciences; because it is, by nature, integrative; and because scale and location (place) are central concerns of the discipline.

These five themes and our geographical approach to them are developed further in Chapter 1. Then follow four chapters dealing with particular types of environment: land and water, forests, cities, and the atmosphere. Each type is clearly of global rather than local concern, although each also has local dimensions to it. Indeed, a subsidiary theme throughout the book is that we need to act on many different scales in tackling environmental problems. Chapter 6 discusses attempts to find global solutions through international co-operation, some more successful than others. Even here, however, the subject matter is seen through Australian eyes. Finally, Chapter 7 deals with some of the key issues that have to be faced if solutions are to be found before it is too late.

This is not a practical manual for fixing the environment, but rather an introduction to the broader issues that underlie environmental problems, and which must equally underlie attempts to overcome those problems. Our goal is to raise awareness and understanding of the global crises confronting us all and to promote an approach to them that will maximise the success of the human race in avoiding catastrophe.

CONTENTS

1 GLOBAL CRISES — AN INTRODUCTION

2 LAND AND WATER

3   FORESTS

4 URBAN ENVIRONMENTS

5 THE GLOBAL ATMOSPHERE

6   INTERNATIONAL CO-OPERATION

7   SOME WAYS FORWARD

FIGURES, PLATES, TABLES AND BOXES

FIGURES

BOXES

ACKNOWLEDGMENTS

Tᴴɪꜱ ʙᴏᴏᴋ has been even more of a collaborative effort than is usually the case, its origins lying in a first-year course, *Global Crises — Technology and Survival*, taught by human and physical geographers in the School of Earth Sciences at Macquarie University. We owe thanks to the more than 2000 students in both geography and resource and environmental management who have taken this course between 1990 and 1994. Whether they knew it or not, their response, or lack of response, to our attempts to grapple with the complexities of environmental change contributed in important ways to the final form of this book. A number of our colleagues have made valuable criticisms, suggestions and other contributions during the development of the course and of this book; we would particularly like to thank Professor Ann Henderson-Sellers for her role in the development and initial teaching of the course.

In preparing the book itself, we gratefully acknowledge permission granted by the CSIRO Office of Space Science and Applications, the Australian Centre for Remote Sensing, and Bryant McAvaney of the Bureau of Meteorology Research Centre to reproduce several of the plates. We also thank the Carbon Dioxide Information Analysis Center for some of the data used in Chapter 5. John Cleasby, Judy Davis and Carol Jacobson all helped prepare the illustrations and we sincerely thank them for their patience and dedication. Finally we would like to thank Jill Lane, David Meagher, Debra Burgess and their colleagues at Oxford University Press for their enthusiasm for the project and for the efficient way in which they have handled it.

While the book has been a team effort involving much consultation and critical discussion, there has inevitably been a division of labour. Individuals have taken prime responsibility for particular chapters: Peter Mitchell for Chapter 2, David Rich for Chapter 3, Helen Cleugh for Chapter 4, Andrew Pitman for Chapter 5, and Graeme Aplin for Chapter 6 and Chapter 7. Graeme and David prepared the index, while Graeme co-ordinated the whole project. That said, it has been a successful co-operative venture from start to finish and we accept joint responsibility for the result.

GLOBAL CRISES — AN INTRODUCTION

O UR SENSES are bombarded daily by images of environmental crises, images gained either through personal experience or through the media. In fact, just about everywhere we look there seems to be evidence of the Earth's vulnerability in the face of human activity. What are the big issues? How serious are they? How are they interrelated? What biophysical and social processes are involved? Are they matters for rich nations to remedy and poor nations to avoid? What is being done about them? What else can be done about them? Do our individual actions matter, or can the questions only be addressed by government and industry, or through international agreements? These are some of the key questions addressed in this book.

Our aim is to help you understand, through a series of case studies, several of the global-scale environmental challenges facing us all, along with possible responses to them. Our choice of issues is not meant to be exhaustive, but to be representative of those that are global in nature. Among our case studies, climate change is clearly global, while deforestation and land degradation are concentrated in particular areas but still have obvious global implications. The adverse effects of urban development are even more localised, in one sense, but their overall impact is undoubtedly being felt around the world. These case studies introduce broad principles applicable to other environmental issues as well. Perhaps the two most important principles are that the various crises are interrelated in complex and often poorly understood ways, and that it is critically important that the challenges be approached through a joint investigation of biophysical and human **systems**.

Two other crucial issues, human population growth and **biodiversity**, are closely linked to almost all global environmental concerns. While these are not treated separately in their own chapters, they are discussed in a number of places throughout the book.

We can begin to capture the complexity of the globe's natural systems by identifying the five major components: the atmosphere, the hydrosphere (oceans and fresh water), the cryosphere (frozen water), the lithosphere (rocks and soil), and the biosphere. The biosphere consists of all living things, from deep below the Earth's surface (or in the deepest oceans) to the top of the atmosphere. In the broadest terms, biophysical systems involve the cycling of matter and energy within the biosphere. Some **cycles** operate on geological time-scales over millennia, while others are more easily related to a human frame of reference, operating over days, weeks or years. Figure 1.1 is a diagrammatic representation of these spheres, but it is highly simplified in two important ways: each sphere is itself a complex combination of sub-systems; and every sphere is connected to every other sphere. Most importantly, there is a continual exchange of energy and materials through space and time, both between spheres and within each sphere. (Section 1.3 discusses two examples of natural cycles that illustrate such exchanges.)

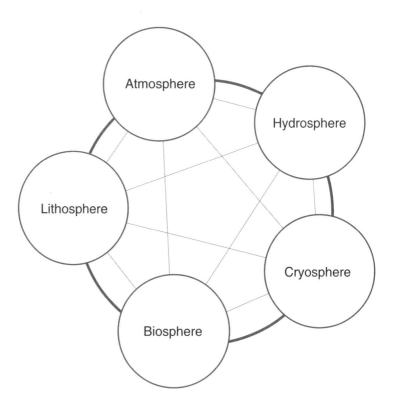

Figure 1.1
The interlinked natural spheres of the Earth's biophysical system.

Human systems involve social, cultural, political, economic and technological dimensions, as well as biophysical ones. People affect biophysical systems by diverting energy and matter (resources) from natural cycles to specifically human uses, as well as by introducing waste energy and matter into the environment. Such interventions extend over a relatively short period (geologically speaking), thus bringing us into conflict with natural systems when our demands for resources are greater than their short-term capacity to supply them, or our introduction of waste exceeds their capacity to absorb them. (The intricacies of the human dimension are introduced in Section 1.4.)

A central theme of this book is that the biophysical and human perspectives must be integrated if we are to understand the global environmental crises confronting us. Furthermore, both human and biophysical factors must be taken into account if we are to mitigate the undesirable consequences of these crises or, possibly, avoid them altogether. We firmly believe that geography and geographers have a key role to play in developing such integrated approaches — a contention discussed in detail in Chapter 1. The remainder of this chapter develops a framework for understanding the global system, encompassing both biophysical and human aspects. This framework is then used for the case studies in later chapters.

AN AUSTRALIAN PERSPECTIVE 1.1

We have adopted an Australian viewpoint throughout this book. But what is it about Australia that gives us a view of the human condition and environmental issues which differs from views held by other people?

Australia is a physically isolated, resource-rich country, located in the 'water hemisphere' of the globe. It has a small, dominantly Caucasian (but increasingly multiracial) population which enjoys a high standard of living and education derived, in part, from large-scale exploitation of its biophysical environment. It has a long Aboriginal prehistory, but only a very short written history beginning with the first known European contact in the seventeenth century. During its prehistory, the indigenous people developed a close spiritual link with the environment, a link from which we all have much to learn. During the European period, Australia has passed from a Stone Age culture to the emergence of **biotechnology** and the information revolution. Many mistakes have been made and, as a result, a huge range of environmental problems now besets Australians. However, given our present economic, political, social and technological status, we should be able to reach agreement about the significance of these problems and do something positive about them. We have already begun to address many of the key issues (the initiatives of the Murray–Darling Basin Commission provide an outstanding precedent for integrated action (Box 1.1)), but much remains to be done.

B O X

1.1

The Murray–Darling Basin Commission: An example of an integrated approach to environmental management

Under the Australian constitution water is a state resource and, although each state has a single department which is supposed to be primarily responsible, management is actually shared by many departments and other bodies, down to the individual irrigator, all operating in an absolute jungle of law and regulation. In New South Wales (NSW) alone more than 60 legal Acts relate to rivers.

The Murray–Darling river system is the country's largest river network (see Figure 2.9). It drains 14 per cent of the continent and carries 60 per cent of the runoff. The main tributaries rise on the inland slopes of the Great Dividing Range and flow through southern Queensland, western NSW and northern Victoria to discharge into the Southern Ocean in South Australia. The basin supports approximately half of the country's sheep, one quarter of the cattle, half of the cropland, three quarters of the irrigated land and 12 per cent of the people. The water resources of this river system are shared by four states and the Australian Capital Territory, and over the past 150 years each state has evolved its own priorities and management systems with, until quite recently, little consideration for downstream users.

Since 1988, environmental management and research within the basin has been co-ordinated by the Murray–Darling Basin Commission (MDBC), which operates under an agreement between all states and the Federal Government. It replaced the River Murray Commission, whose management brief was limited to the supply and distribution of water, without consideration for quality or any other environmental matter.

The MDBC's brief covers the most comprehensive set of environmental management objectives ever agreed to between Australian states. It is to promote and co-ordinate effective planning and management for equitable, efficient and sustainable use of the land, water and other environmental resources of the basin. After detailed investigation of the main problems and widespread community consultation, a series of interstate strategy agreements are being made in which the state departments accept responsibility for remedial action and management, and the Federal Government assists with funding. The two most important agreements established to date are the Natural Resources Management Strategy (NRMS) and the Salinity and Drainage Strategy.

The purpose of the NRMS is to provide a framework for managing a whole range of problems recognised in the basin. These include a decline in native flora and fauna, damage to heritage and cultural values, poor water quality (especially that caused by salinity and blue-green algae) and numerous forms of land degradation.

Of all the problems, salinity and drainage are regarded as the two most important, so the Salinity and Drainage Strategy was established as a priority issue in January 1988. At that time the annual costs attributable to these problems were estimated to total A$102 million. Without management intervention these costs were predicted to rise to A$152 million by the year 2015 when more than 500 000 ha of irrigated land would be out of production. To address these issues, the states agreed to a combination of engineering works to intercept saline waters, more effective on-farm land and water management, and an extensive community involvement program. Funding for major works is provided by all the governments involved, and a large proportion of it has been allocated to approved projects put forward by 'communities of common concern'. Much of the early funding has been spent on survey and field trials, and a number of experiments into new ways of dealing with the issues have been conducted by local people. In the first three years of the NRMS, A$38 million was invested in initial restoration works, which were expected to show a significant reduction in salinity levels in the Murray River within 5 years; the full effects of all management action will not be seen for 30–50 years.

The MDBC is an outstanding example of how disparate groups of managers, political bodies and the community can work together to improve the environment when the scale of the problems is so large that no single group can be effective.

Some objectives of the NRMS

In addition to the objectives listed here, all the programs involve establishing research priorities, different forms of community consultation, and public education operations.

Agricultural land resource management

Map the extent of land degradation and land capability; promote whole farm planning techniques and farm extension services; encourage best management practices within a framework of Total Catchment Management; fund major restoration works; and review policies and practices of all the public organisations involved with land degradation.

Vegetation management

Map special areas of native vegetation, including all riparian zones and mallee areas; review clearing controls; identify groundwater recharge areas for revegetation; and provide assistance and incentives to land managers to undertake better vegetation management through existing programs such as Landcare and the National Soil Conservation Program.

Groundwater management

Map the hydrogeology of the entire basin; establish a groundwater data base and construct a computer model for groundwater management; control recharge of groundwater through vegetation management; develop usable groundwater resources; and assess the impact of evaporation basins.

Flora and fauna management

Develop a basin-wide management plan for the preservation of existing natural communities; review the effectiveness of conservation areas; encourage the integration of flora and fauna management on private lands; and monitor the effectiveness of all such activities.

Aquatic and riverine environment management

Identify and protect priority river environments, especially wetlands, riverine forests and instream ecosystems; develop and implement policies for the allocation of irrigation water to environmental uses such as flooding wetlands; and implement measures to ensure that water released from reservoirs is at an appropriate temperature and level of dissolved oxygen for instream needs.

Water quality management

Improve and maintain water quality for all beneficial uses; monitor quality within river management reaches; and encourage remedial action to control problems related to salinity, turbidity, nutrient loads and blue-green algae.

Water allocation management

Improve water allocation efficiency, especially between the states; promote a market-oriented approach to pricing and efficient use which reflects the real cost of water supply; and develop procedures for the transfer of water rights and the allocation of surplus and dilution flows.

Water use efficiency management

Improve water delivery and use in irrigation areas to reduce seepage losses and associated salinity problems; encourage irrigators to adopt more efficient technology and practices; and make domestic users more aware of water conservation issues.

Riverine region management

This limited area program focuses on the central area of the Murray River valley defined by the extent of the 1956 floods and deals with management of the river corridor and the flood plain with special emphasis on vegetation and water quality, maintenance of scenic qualities and control of visitor access and activities.

Cultural heritage management

Identify, protect, manage and monitor the basin's recorded and unrecorded historic and Aboriginal heritage sites under existing state and federal legislation.

Tourism and recreation management

Manage tourism and recreation within the basin to minimise degradation and improve the natural and cultural environment, while ensuring conservation of the resource base.

(*Source*: Murray–Darling Basin Ministerial Council. Background Papers No 89/1 (1989).)

Australia is also an unusual continent. During the eighteenth and nineteenth centuries, entirely new and unexpected species of plants and animals were discovered; new fossils, rocks, and minerals were unearthed; new climatic patterns noted; and even the indigenous peoples were perceived by Europeans as unexpectedly exotic. Australia was seen as a unique continent where things were fixed in time and where living species, even whole **ecosystems**, were 'fossilised'. Half-truths like this became established myth.

The reality is much more interesting than the myth. Many aspects of Australian ecosystems are unusual, for two reasons: the continent has had a very different geological history in comparison with other continents; and it is presently placed in mid-latitudes and is mostly semi-arid or arid. Because of Australia's geographical isolation over geological time, evolution has taken different paths and **endemism** is very high, not only at the species level but also at the genus and higher levels. The unusual features of Australian ecosystems should be studied not only to better understand the Australian environment, but also to allow possible reinterpretation of conventional scientific wisdom developed in the Northern Hemisphere. We have often found that conventional models are not applicable to Australian conditions; for example, those dealing with the classification and distribution of forests (Section 3.1) and soils. We have also discovered natural processes missed elsewhere and can sometimes see the results of natural 'experiments' which, when interpreted from our perspective, can change conventional paradigms in sciences such as ecology and hydrology. The same may well be true with respect to other environmental matters.

Socially, politically and economically, Australians have a changing view of their place in the world as a small but important power in the Asian and Pacific regions. We maintain close ties with South Pacific nations while developing closer ones with many Asian countries. Australia's trade has become increasingly focused on South-east and East Asia, while links with those regions in such diverse areas as politics, tourism and defence are becoming stronger. More specifically, many Australian biophysical and social scientists have conducted extensive research in Asia and the Pacific. In addition, we have operated scientific research establishments in Antarctica since the early days of exploration, and we have taken an active part in the establishment of international agreements concerning sovereign rights in our surrounding seas and oceans (Chapter 6).

As well as making a very hesitant and often unconvincing start in its own drive toward sustainable development, Australia is endeavouring to contribute to the sustainable development of neighbouring nations through overseas development assistance, through the provision of technical knowledge and appropriate technologies, and through business investment and partnership in enterprises which have undergone **environmental impact assessment**. Australia may be in a position to play a constructive role in the Asia–Pacific region following the Earth Summit in Rio de Janeiro in 1992, and to assist in implementing *Agenda 21* action plans and the requirements of various international conventions. Australians have learnt to be cautious in applying conventional science to practical environmental management, developing instead a range of 'soft' management technologies particularly suited to the region. The lessons learnt have application elsewhere, thus further justifying the discussion of global crises from an Australian perspective.

PLANET EARTH 1.2

An astronomical perspective

As far as we know, the Earth is unique. It is the only planet in our solar system where surface temperatures allow liquid water to exist and where a biosphere has evolved. Elsewhere in our galaxy and beyond, there are so many stars like the Sun, and presumably planets associated with them, that it would be foolish to conclude that the Earth is the only living planet, or that humans are the only form of life to have evolved such a high level of intelligence. But even if we feel certain that life exists elsewhere, we presently have no way of confirming this nor of communicating with extraterrestrial life forms. We are, therefore, 'alone', and if we are to persist on planet Earth we need to make the most of this little 'spaceship', refrain from despoiling its life-support systems, and restore the damage already done.

A geological perspective

There has been interaction between life and the non-living environment throughout the Earth's history. Each has modified the other through feedback (Section 1.3A) and evolution. Sometimes changes have been slow and progressive, sometimes random and directionless, sometimes chaotic. Two examples illustrate the broad types of interconnections that exist. Firstly, the presence of free oxygen in the atmosphere is a function of the evolution of the biosphere. Secondly, past climatic conditions have been quite different from those of the present, and every time major changes occurred in the composition of the atmosphere, the extent of the ocean waters and ice caps, or global climatic patterns, there were accompanying changes in the biosphere, often including periods of rapid species extinction and subsequent **speciation**. It has been estimated, for example, that at the end of the Permian period (225 million years ago), 96 per cent of all marine creatures then living became extinct. Similarly, at the end of the Cretaceous period (65 million years ago), the dinosaurs became extinct, along with large numbers of marine invertebrates and several groups of plants. During the present geological period, the Quaternary (which commenced less than 1.8 million years ago), the Earth has been in another period of mass extinction. Humans have evolved rapidly during this period and, while there has been much debate about their role during earlier centuries, it is undoubtedly true that twentieth-century people have made large numbers of species extinct and that the process is accelerating.

Extinction seems to be the ultimate fate of all species, another sobering thought arising from studying the fossil record. Palaeontologists have calculated that species survive on average for about 2.5 million years. Humans have already been on Earth for roughly twice that period, so why should our fate be any different? It is certainly true that our survival chances have been increased by our superior brain-power, allowing us to adapt to environmental change and to exploit environmental resources. If our survival is to continue, however, we need to use those powers more than ever before, and to work with the environment rather than against it.

The Earth has changed continually over geological time: we must expect it to continue to change. But a geological time-frame dealing in millions of years is meaningless to most people, as well as being inappropriate when dealing with human impacts on the environment in a practical manner. We may plan for the future in terms of months and years, but few of us, including our politicians, have a realistic planning frame which exceeds a decade or extends to the next generation. Nevertheless, just such an extended time-frame is essential if humans are to survive on Earth. Furthermore, it is an essential component of the concept of sustainable development (see Sections 1.5 and 7.8).

A geographical perspective

If we are to fully understand environmental problems, we need to examine them with respect to our interactions with every part of the Earth's systems, biophysical and human. The whole is more important than the parts, but the whole can only be visualised and managed if the parts are understood and seen in the context of one another. A geographical approach to understanding, integrative by nature, does this by taking into account knowledge from many other disciplines and by weaving together the spatial and temporal patterns that describe the total environment. Geographers also have the additional advantage of routinely working with spatial patterns and processes at a wide variety of scales.

Integration

Geography deals with both place and people. In Stoddart's terminology, it also deals with 'Earth's diversity, its resources, man's survival on the planet'.[1] All of these topics are vital to any understanding of global crises or, indeed, local environmental problems. They are certainly all vital in any search for remedies. Furthermore, these topics must be brought together and integrated rather than studied separately, and it is the geographical perspective more than any other that brings about this integration. In addition, relative locations are of crucial importance, as few environmental problems are purely local and specific to one point. So space, location and direction, all central geographical concerns, are also part of the equation.

Stoddart describes the geographer's task as being to:

> identify geographical problems, issues of man and environment within regions — problems not of geomorphology or history or economics or sociology, but geographical problems; and to use [his or her] skills to work to alleviate them, perhaps to solve them.[2]

He goes on to describe a practical application of the integrative ability of geographical work in the storm-prone coastal lands of Bangladesh. The details need not concern us here: what is important is that the breadth of view allows solutions beyond those likely to derive from specialists in narrow discipline areas. Of course, the skills and knowledge of specialists such as engineers, economists, meteorologists and sociologists are needed. The crucial point, however, is that none of these specialists, by themselves, could provide as adequate a solution.

The integrative approach provided by geography must ultimately recognise the integrity of humans as part of nature. Although this book may at times appear to deal with biophysical and human systems as if they were separable, we emphasise that this is merely an artificial means of simplifying the discussion. Indeed, the complexity and integration of Earth systems is a key theme of this book.

Scale

While Stoddart writes of geographical problems being studied within 'regions', this term should not be interpreted narrowly. In fact, geography is very adept at dealing with issues at all scales, from the local to the global. Geographers, above all others, appreciate the importance of scale, and the fact that solutions to problems must be adapted to the particular scale that is most appropriate. Some environmental problems are local and can be dealt with locally. Others are global and need global solutions arrived at through international cooperation (Chapter 3 and 6). Yet there remains much truth in the saying: 'Think globally, act locally'. Perhaps, in some cases, this should be 'Think locally, act globally', for there are certainly crucial local manifestations of global environmental problems, just as local problems accumulate to become global crises.

1.3 BIOGEOCHEMICAL CYCLES AND BIOPHYSICAL SYSTEMS

In order to appreciate the totality of the Earth's dynamic systems, two approaches are commonly used to simplify or model the complexity of all the interactions that we know of between the different biophysical spheres of the planet shown in Figure 1.1. The first approach is to consider the cycling of energy or matter through and between the spheres via biogeochemical cycles; the second attempts to deal with the dynamics and apparent long-term stability of biophysical systems such as **communities** and ecosystems. Both models are extreme simplications of reality. It is also important to acknowledge that people do not operate outside either of them: the elements in our bodies, the energy we use, the matter we divert from our pathways, and the water we need are all parts of both biogeochemical cycles and ecosystems.

Some natural constraints

Within a human time-frame, the Earth's cycles and systems tend to operate around a condition of balance referred to as dynamic equilibrium (Figure 1.2). For example, there are no large fluctuations in the oxygen content of the atmosphere because an overall balance exists between the liberation of oxygen by plants during **photosynthesis** and its consumption by plants, animals and organisms involved in decomposition. Within an ecosystem, the populations of particular organisms may fluctuate in response to local and short-term pressures, but negative feedback mechanisms are usually able to return numbers to an equilibrium level. On the rarer occasions when positive feedback mechanisms dominate a system, **perturbations** may be reinforced rather than dampened out. Such systems can sometimes cross a **threshold** into a new and usually unexpected condition, which itself may turn out to be in dynamic equilibrium under the new conditions.

An example of linked negative and positive feedbacks can be imagined in a population of organisms where numbers are limited by food availability. When food is abundant, more individuals survive and reproduce, and numbers rise. Increased numbers put pressure on the food resource, which in turn means that fewer individuals are able to reproduce and fewer progeny survive, and this negative feedback causes the population to decline. Over time the population is maintained around a mean figure by both positive and negative feedbacks linked to all sorts of factors, both intrinsic (such as life history, age structure and genetics) and extrinsic (such as weather conditions, predation

A

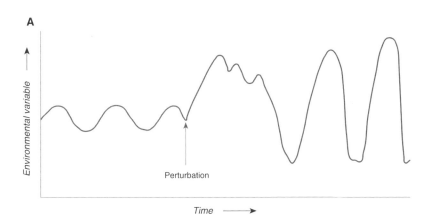

Perturbation

Time

Environmental variable

B

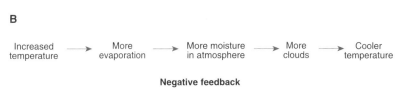

Increased temperature → More evaporation → More moisture in atmosphere → More clouds → Cooler temperature

Negative feedback

C

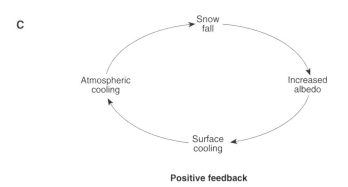

Snow fall

Atmospheric cooling

Increased albedo

Surface cooling

Positive feedback

Figure 1.2
Dynamic equilibrium, perturbations and feedbacks.

and disease), which affect food supply or some other essential part of the organisms' requirements. If any feedback control is overridden by the scale or nature of a particular disturbance, a threshold may be crossed and that organism may become locally extinct. An extreme example can be found in parts of Indonesia where entire rainforest communities have been converted to grassland by the introduction, by people, of frequent fires (see Section 3.4).

It follows that one of the keys to understanding the dynamics of either biogeochemical cycles or biophysical systems, and the interaction of humans with them, is to identify the **disturbance regime** to which they are naturally subject. As long as human manipulation of the cycles or systems remains within the natural disturbance regime, feedback processes will probably balance out these perturbations. But if people impose pressures on the system that are larger than or different from those in nature, catastrophic changes may occur.

All changes in cycles and systems in time and space have some underlying cause. We can sometimes identify these causes, and we can sometimes model the dynamics of ecosystems reasonably accurately, but our understanding always remains limited. This means that wherever possible, environmental management should be conservative and that we should always be prepared for the unexpected. This approach is essentially that embodied in the precautionary principle discussed in Section 7.8.

The two most important biogeochemical cycles are those involving energy and water. These are involved in every other cycle and every important natural system on Earth, as the following simple versions indicate.

The energy cycle

In terms of energy flows, the Earth is an open system with energy inputs entering it and energy outputs leaving it. Virtually all of these flows are driven by solar energy, though there is a small component of **lithospheric energy** available to some living communities in volcanic regions, and humans have tapped this lithospheric source, along with nuclear energy. Nevertheless, people gain most of their non-food energy from burning fossil fuels, which contain 'solar' energy stored millions of years ago when plants used the Sun's energy to build living tissue through photosynthesis.

The consumption of energy and matter is governed by the laws of thermodynamics. When energy is used it is not lost or destroyed, but simply transformed (for example, from mechanical energy to heat). Energy conversions are never 100 per cent efficient, and in time the tendency is for all energy to be degraded and for the system to run down (that is, for **entropy** to increase). Natural systems, however, do not run down because there is a constant resupply of energy from the Sun. This energy enters all the biophysical systems by being absorbed, stored, and transported from place to place in various forms, but most importantly in living plant tissue or water molecules.

Figure 1.3 illustrates the main **fluxes**, **stores** and **sinks** for solar energy on the Earth as a whole. Over time the total incoming energy (solar radiation) balances outgoing energy (thermal infra-red radiation), but while it is within the Earth system this energy drives the biosphere, atmosphere, hydrosphere and cryosphere. Solar energy has

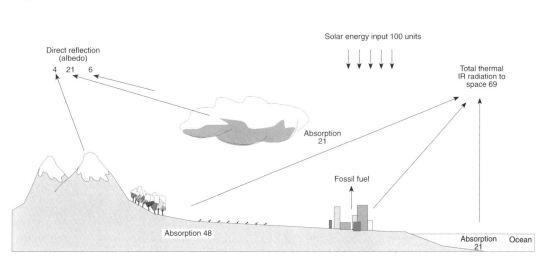

Figure 1.3
A simplified version of the global energy cycle using an arbitrary 100 units of solar energy input. Details of the atmosphere-to-ground counter-radiation, an essential part of the greenhouse mechanism (see Chapter 5), have been omitted.

a less obvious impact on the lithosphere, but it is important in the creation of sedimentary rocks with an organic component; in the generation of fossil fuels, where energy may have a residence (or storage) time of hundreds of millions of years; and in rock weathering and soil formation. The last two processes, in turn, feed back to the biosphere. There are many other feedbacks which operate within this system: for example, the creation of fossil fuels and carbon-based sedimentary rocks removes carbon dioxide from the atmosphere. If this did not happen the Earth could warm too much and become less favourable for plant growth.

The most important ways in which humans have interfered with the global energy balance are by consuming fossil fuels, depleting biospheric stores of organic carbon (by clearing rainforests, for example, as discussed in Chapter 3), and changing surface **albedo** (reflectivity) or energy absorption parameters in agricultural and urban areas (Section 4.4A). These activities are causing changes in the patterns of energy flux and in the composition of the atmosphere, which affect the radiation balance, feed back to the hydrosphere, and in turn change climates and affect the biosphere. (These climatic impacts are discussed in Chapter 5.)

The water cycle

The Earth's system is a closed system for water, virtually all of which takes part in the water (or hydrological) cycle, which in turn is primarily driven by solar energy. The great bulk of the hydrosphere (97.2 per cent) is found in the saline oceans. Of the 2.8 per cent of water which is fresh, and essential for terrestrial organisms, 2.15 per cent is frozen in the cryosphere with a residence time of tens of thousands of years, and 0.62 per cent is stored as groundwater (Figure 1.4). Only a tiny 0.03 per cent of the hydrosphere is readily available in streams and lakes, but fortunately this is in the most active part of the water cycle and water is moved rapidly through the atmosphere and returned to the Earth's surface. But it is also the part of the cycle where human impacts are greatest in the form of extraction, supply depletion, wastage and water pollution. The management of these problems and the provision of adequate supplies of clean water to all people are among our biggest environmental challenges. (They are discussed in Chapters 2 and 4.)

Figure 1.4 illustrates the water cycle and gives an indication of how humans have modified it. The flux of water through these stores, with their different capacities and residence times, is a vitally important part of the Earth's climate system because water has the important physical property of allowing the absorption and release of large quantities of energy when it changes state from ice to water and to water vapour. Water vapour is only a tiny and variable fraction of the gases in

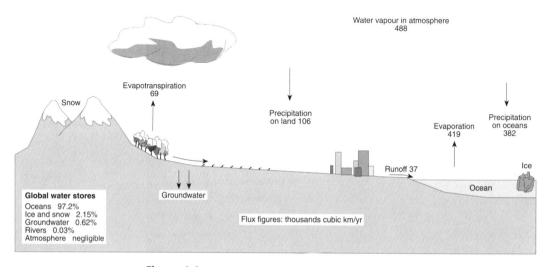

Figure 1.4
A simplified version of the global water cycle. Average annual fluxes are shown in thousands of cubic kilometres per year.

the atmosphere, but it is absolutely fundamental to the operation of all
Earth systems because of its ability to transfer and transport energy.
(Section 4.4 takes up many of these issues in an urban context.)

Understanding the biosphere

Everything on Earth is composed of combinations of the ninety-two
natural elements. In the inorganic world of rocks and minerals, these
combine into about 2000 naturally occurring compounds, most of
which are well understood and all of which have essentially predictable
properties. In the organic world of living things, however, there are
probably between 10 million and 30 million living species, only 1.4
million of which have been named let alone adequately studied. Many
millions more have existed in the past. These are all basically composed of fewer than about twenty-five of the elements; but despite this
seeming simplicity, living things are exceedingly complex and hence
less understood and less predictable than inorganic materials.

The diversity of life forms making up the biosphere is extraordinary
and there are many reasons why we should take steps to preserve
as much of that diversity as possible. (Biodiversity is discussed in
Chapters 2 and 3, and attempts at reaching international agreements
on preserving it are addressed in Chapter 6.) There are several aspects
of the biosphere of which we all should be aware:

- Living organisms are fundamentally different from rocks and minerals because they are subject to evolutionary change, where even a
  small variation at the molecular level (in the genes) can create
  substantial change at the species level. Today we can purposefully
  induce such changes using biotechnology, as well as doing so unin-
  tentionally through, for example, pollution and ozone depletion.
- Like all other systems on Earth, the biosphere is subject to the laws
  of thermodynamics and generally seems to exist in a state of dynamic equilibrium. We need to appreciate what these concepts
  mean and, indeed, whether they have any real validity on human
  time-scales.
- There are various growth limits within the biosphere. There are
  limits to the maximum physical size that individuals of any species
  can become; there are limits to the size of species populations; and
  over longer time spans there are also limits to species diversity.
  These limits do, however, change from time to time as a result of
  feedbacks between species and their environments.
- As far as we know no other animal species has developed the ability
  to deliberately and substantially shift the natural limits in directions
  which favour its growth and development at the expense of other

species to the same extent as *Homo sapiens*. Humans are unique in having a strong **niche**-expansion trait and in having harnessed the powers of technology to achieve it. This niche-expansion is based on consumption of energy, tapping stores built up over millions of years. Since we are using energy far faster than it is being stored, this consumption cannot continue indefinitely.

People and the biosphere

People are part of the biosphere, but they are also different from other organisms in many ways. There is vigorous biological and philosophical debate as to whether this difference is merely one of degree, or something more than that. We are just like all other animals in that we have essential needs for air, water, food, shelter and the opportunity for reproduction, but we are also the species with the most developed brain. Two consequences of our intelligence are that we have developed technologies and harnessed forces that have never been seen on Earth before, and that we have applied them to manipulate the Earth to our own ends. We also have a real appreciation of time that includes the concepts of past, present and future; we can learn from our mistakes; and we possess a sense of right and wrong. The quality of our life and the future condition of the biosphere depend on whether or not we use these attributes wisely.

1.4 HUMAN SOCIETY

The significant environmental challenges now facing the Earth are not merely natural or biophysical: people are the crucial element in contemporary environmental change. Almost every kind of human activity affects the biophysical environment in some way, often destroying an existing equilibrium or accelerating natural rates of change. For example, the time-scales of most human activities are much shorter than those of most natural cycles, and the burden of wastes we are producing is rapidly exceeding natural global fluxes of similar substances. In other words, we are pouring out effluent at a greater rate than the environment can cope with it. We also have the ability to manufacture effluents, such as **chlorofluorocarbons** (CFCs) and polychlorinated biphenyls (PCBs), that are extremely rare or absent in nature, break down extremely slowly, and have the capacity to adversely affect biophysical systems to a considerable degree.

We need to place the natural global systems in their human context and to grasp something of the nature of human activities and the way in which society has evolved if we are to understand both the context and causes of environmental change, to comprehend the origins of global crises, and to begin to explore the scope for human intervention to manage the environment more successfully. Figure 1.5 provides the foundations on which we can build. It is an explicit recognition that the biophysical environment is now being fundamentally affected by human activities of all kinds. It is also a recognition that there are four major dimensions of contemporary human existence that need to be explored in our attempts to understand the origins of global environmental crises and to develop appropriate management strategies. Indeed, Figure 1.5 is in a sense the cornerstone of this book. It reflects the key arguments about the importance of links between natural systems and human activities; it offers scope as a framework for analysing specific global crises; and it reflects key themes about the types of human activity that need to be explored. Some of its implications are considered in this chapter, while more detailed explorations recur throughout the rest of the book.

One fundamental point needs to be made, however: all human activity takes place in a particular cultural context. If we are to successfully address environmental issues, we must be keenly aware of the local cultural contexts in which they occur. While people are grouped

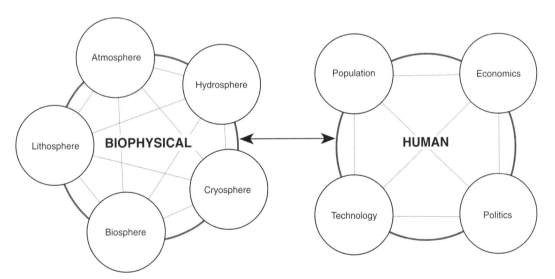

Figure 1.5
The interlinked biophysical and human Earth systems, showing sub-systems within each. The human sub-systems are somewhat arbitrarily defined and are all linked with each other in complex ways that reflect the cultural milieux of particular localities. The biophysical and human systems interact in a similarly complex and dialectical fashion, with clear cause-and-effect relationships being rare.

into local, regional and national societies which to varying degrees share common cultures, it is important to realise that there is no single human culture and hence no single way of viewing the environment. In fact, different societies and cultures relate to their environments in very different ways, ranging from the extremely anthropocentric, exploitative culture of 'European' USA and Australia to the spiritual relationship to the biophysical environment shared by the Australian Aborigines and many other indigenous peoples. Not surprisingly, different people view environmental problems in different ways. We must understand the cultural context of a society if we are to have any chance of understanding environmental issues in that society. Furthermore, it is unrealistic to expect a solution devised in one cultural context to automatically be successful and relevant in another; appropriate solutions must be culturally appropriate as well as economically appropriate. It is also crucial to recognise that, at present, political and economic systems are often imposed from outside, or by a small élite group, and are thus likely to be alien to the majority of the local population, particularly in low-income nations.

Population growth, poverty and environmental change

Figure 1.6 shows that the world's human population increased slowly and almost imperceptibly in earlier times. Population numbers suffered many setbacks, most notably during the so-called Black Death of the fourteenth century. But during the last 300 years both numbers of people and the growth rate have increased sharply. Whereas it took all of human history until about 1800 for the world's population to reach 1 billion (1000 million), the next billion came in only 130 years (1930). Successive increments of 1 billion came in a mere 30 years (3 billion in 1960), 14 years (4 billion in 1974) and the astoundingly brief period of only 12–13 years, global population reaching 5 billion in 1986. By late 1992 the total world population had passed 5.5 billion and 6 billion is expected to be reached in 1997 or 1998.[3] The last billion will have been added in only about 11 years.

During the twentieth century the world's population has grown markedly as annual rates of increase have risen, at least until recent years, especially as better health and nutrition in many countries reduced death rates before compensating falls in birth rates occurred. It now appears that the annual percentage rate of increase has peaked: as Table 1.1 shows, United Nations figures suggest a fall in the rate of annual increase by the second half of this decade (see also Section 7.7).

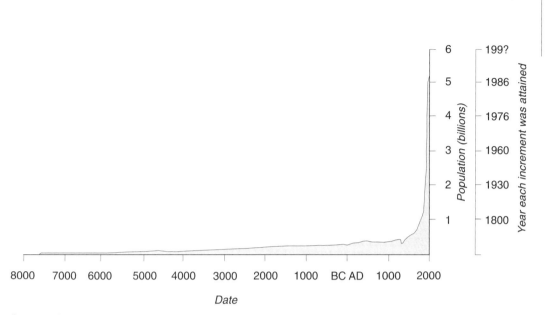

Figure 1.6
World population growth.

Nevertheless, we should bear several important points in mind. Firstly, the absolute numbers being added to the world will go on rising at least until early next century (Table 1.1). An annual growth of 90 million (slightly below the annual average in the early 1990s) means little unless couched in more familiar terms: it is equivalent to almost 250 000 new people every day, or about 27 new 'Sydneys' every year! Secondly, estimates for global population in 2025 are around 8.5 billion, while projections to 2050, within the lifetime of the children of the 1990s, are for the population to be as large as 13 billion, nearly two and a half times the current total. Thirdly, almost all of this massive net growth in population is occurring in particular parts of the world, especially in the low-income nations of Africa, Asia and Latin America. It is also occurring disproportionately in the globe's large cities. Such geographical unevenness has huge implications for the environment, as Chapters 2 and 4, in particular, explore further.

It is self-evident that there could be a close relationship between human population growth and environmental degradation: more

Table 1.1 Global population changes, 1950–2025.

	1950–55	1965–70	1975–80	1985–90	1990–95	1995–2000	2000–25
Av. increase (% p.a.)	1.8	2.1	1.7	1.7	1.7	1.6	1.0
Av. increase (millions p.a.)	47	72	74	88	93	94*	85*

*Medium-variant projections.

Source: United Nations, *World Population Prospects: The 1992 revision*, UN (New York, 1992), 6.

people means more mouths to feed, more space given over to human activities, and more fuel and raw materials consumed to maintain even a subsistence style of living. Brown views it this way:

> . . . poverty drives ecological deterioration when desperate people over-exploit their resource base, sacrificing the future to salvage the present. The cruel logic of short-term needs forces landless families to raze plots in the rain forest, plow steep slopes, and shorten fallow periods. Ecological decline, in turn, perpetuates poverty, as degraded ecosystems offer diminishing yields to their poor inhabitants. A self-feeding downward spiral of economic deprivation and ecological degradation takes hold.[4]

An obvious solution might appear to be to introduce programs of population control in the low-income nations where population growth is highest. However, the picture is a good deal more complicated than that and it is simplistic to state that overpopulation causes poverty and environmental degradation (see Sections 7.3 and 7.7). As an example, it may be rational for small-scale farmers without the capital to buy modern equipment to have a large family that can provide labour to work the land and support them in their old age in the absence of institutionalised social security, even though it increases aggregate population pressure. For many scholars population growth is certainly an important agent in environmental decline, but as Brown hints it is not so much the fundamental cause as an effect of poverty and under-development. Population control without social reform in low-income countries does little to tackle the underlying causes of poverty. For population control to really work, it has to be allied with other programs, notably economic, social and political restructuring, to deal with the causes of poverty and inequality.

In any case, directing population control programs largely to low-income countries may be missing one of the most important aspects of resource depletion and environmental degradation — global inequalities in the use of environmental resources (Table 1.2). One additional person in a wealthy nation such as the USA, Japan or Australia will consume much more of the world's resources and produce much more waste than one born in Bangladesh or Kenya. All this has led some people to argue that population control is a program developed by the wealthy élite in countries like the USA and intended to serve their own interests. The implication is that humanitarian rhetoric cannot mask the fact that the major exploiters of the environment are asking the exploited to control their fertility so that the exploitation can continue. Whether or not such a view is accepted, moves to control population are attacked from at least two directions: from nations where people are seen as the biggest resource, sometimes the key to military security, so that attempts to control population growth

Table 1.2 Some key national indicators, 1990–95.

	GNP per capita ($US) 1991				
	Low-income nations		*Middle-income nations*	*High-income nations*	
	<1000	*1000–5000*	*5000–10 000*	*10 000–15 000*	*>15 000*
Number of nations in:					
Africa/Middle East	31	10	0	0	0
Asia	13	5	3	2	2
Europe	0	5	2	2	13
Former USSR	2	13	0	0	0
North/Central America	5	7	0	0	2
South America	2	10	0	0	0
Oceania	2	1	0	1	1
TOTAL	55	51	5	5	18
Average annual population change 1990–95 (%)	2.71	1.51	1.61	1.32	0.67
Average urban population 1995 (%)	32	59	55	83	79
Average rural population with safe water 1990 (%)	45	55	75	95	99
Average commercial energy use per capita 1991 (gigajoules)	5.9	45.3	109	125	216
Average industrial additions to CO_2 flux per capita 1991 (tonnes)	0.5	3.3	7.8	8.4	11.9
Average overseas development assistance per capita 1991 ($US)	55	43	−23*	41#	−139*

1995 figures are estimates.
* Negative amounts represent net donor countries.
# Includes Israel, the world's highest per capita recipient of ODA.

Source: Data calculated from tables in *World Resources 1993–94: A Guide to the global environment*, Oxford University Press (New York, 1994).

are seen as a plot to undermine that security; and in countries where such programs are contrary to religious beliefs about the sanctity of the family and human life.

Population issues are vitally important in relation to all of the global environmental crises discussed in the chapters that follow. It cannot be stressed too strongly, however, that it is overly simplistic to view population growth as the overriding problem which, if solved, will by extension solve all or most environmental problems. In most cases it may not even be the most important problem. Indeed, it may often be more an effect than a cause, reflecting underlying social, economic and political factors. (The complex population issue is considered explicitly in a number of sections of Chapters 2, 3 and 6, and implicitly in many more sections of those chapters. It is discussed again at some length in Section 7.7.)

Economic factors

If we are to comprehend human impacts on natural systems, we need to consider not only the number of people but also what those people do, how they live, and how they choose to utilise the environment and interact with it. Economic activity is central to these issues. At this stage we can do no more than give several examples of ways in which the economy impinges on natural systems, though this issue will be highlighted further in later chapters.

Economic growth

Most societies in recent human history have sought to increase their level of economic activity through economic growth, and so increase their capacity to provide goods and services. It is common for people and governments in the richer nations to equate progress and development with economic growth and, more particularly, with the type of economic growth that appears to be tied to ever-increasing consumption of resources and creation of wastes. This has meant an acceleration of the flow of matter and energy through the economy. We have used more and more of the globe's natural resources and have had greater adverse impacts on the natural environment as time has passed.

Inequalities

There are marked geographical inequalities in the level of economic activity, both within countries and between countries. International inequalities are commonly measured in terms of gross national product (GNP) per capita. While this measure has many deficiencies (see Box 1.2), it does give some indication of the extent and geographical pattern of such international inequalities. Figure 1.7 shows that high per capita incomes are found in North America, much of Europe, Japan and Australia, as well as a few oil-rich countries. At the other end of the range, many countries in Africa and some in South and South-east Asia register very low GNP per capita figures. While this geographical pattern of inequalities has remained fairly stable in outline

Figure 1.7
Global distribution of gross national product per capita in US$, 1991. [Source of data: *World Resources 1993–94: A guide to the global environment*, Oxford University Press (New York, 1994), 256–7.]

>15 000

10 000 – 14 999

5 000 – 9 999

1 000 – 4 999

<1 000

No data

BOX

1.2

Measuring economic activity and welfare

Economic activity is usually measured as the gross national product (GNP) of a country — the market value in current dollars of all goods and services produced in an economy for final use during a particular year, adjusted for income flows in and out of the country. To better assess whether economic activity is increasing or decreasing, it is normal to correct GNP data for inflation so that the real GNP is measured. For many purposes the important thing is not so much the GNP of the country as a whole (which is a measure of the total size of the economy), but GNP per capita (an indicator of the volume of economic activity per person).

Although GNP-based statistics are commonly used, they are poor measures of the true state of economic activity, poor indicators of the real quality of life experienced by people, and completely inadequate as statements of the impact of economic activity on the natural environment. We can briefly examine some of these problems, concentrating on those particularly relevant in the context of this book.

- Conventional measurements of GNP include as 'good' (producing a higher GNP) many of the 'bads' of modern human existence. For example, money spent on cleaning up a major oil spill is counted in the GNP: so the more we pollute, the higher our GNP. Likewise, human health consequences of environmental pollution cause us to spend more on health care, and this also is taken as a positive value, raising GNP, when it really reflects a negative condition — the adverse effects of pollution on health.

- Depletion of natural resources and degradation of the natural environment are not taken into account in GNP measurements. Thus, a country could exhaust its mineral and energy resources, degrade its soils and waterways, and pollute the atmosphere, with none of this showing up directly as a loss of GNP. In short, a country could increase its *economic welfare* (as measured by GNP) but head rapidly towards *ecological disaster*. In 1989, researchers at the World Resources Institute proposed that depletions of natural resources should be included in the GNP to create a measure of the country's net national product (NNP). Applying this concept to Indonesia, they found that whereas between 1970 and 1984 that country's GNP grew by 7 per cent per annum, the NNP grew by only 4 per cent per annum, taking into account the depletion of forests, soils, water quality and so on. Had they also considered the depletion of coal, minerals and other non-renewable resources, the measured growth rate would have been even lower.

- GNP and similar measures are highly imperfect indicators of the overall quality of life of individuals because they ignore so many factors. American researchers have developed an index of sustainable economic welfare (ISEW). As well as average GNP adjusted for inequalities in income distribution, this index takes into account depletion of non-renewable resources and loss of the natural environment, including estimates of the impact of long-term environmental change such as ozone depletion. Applying this index to the USA shows that, whereas the conventional measure, GNP per capita, has risen reasonably steadily since 1950, the ISEW rose by 46 per cent between 1950 and 1976, but then fell quite sharply, by 12 per cent between 1977 and 1988.

over recent decades, there have been many changes in details. One such change is that GNP per capita levels have stagnated or even fallen in much of Africa in the last 20 years while those in parts of South-east Asia have risen sharply (for example, Indonesia's GNP per capita was lower than Nigeria's in 1965, but by the early 1990s it was three times as high).

Such enormous variations in standards and styles of living imply equally large variations in human interactions with the environment: high GNP per capita levels are associated with high levels of demand for materials and energy and the creation of large volumes of wastes and, consequently, with substantial pressures on the natural environment. On the other hand, such high living standards may make it possible for individuals and societies to make decisions to use natural resources more efficiently and effectively, with a view to minimising those environmental strains. At the other end of the spectrum, people living in the very poorest nations are faced with a serious day-to-day struggle for survival. That struggle may well mean that, while individual consumption levels are tiny compared with those in the wealthiest nations, immediate needs have to take precedence over medium and long-term considerations, such as attempting to use the environment in a sustainable manner. Poverty may thus be associated with acute pressures on the natural environment, especially when associated with rapidly rising populations, as well as posing enormous ethical and humanitarian dilemmas for the rest of the world (see Section 7.3).

A different range of problems occurs between the two extremes, such as those associated with nations adopting strategies to develop their economies at all costs and at the fastest possible rates, almost irrespective of the consequences. Such a policy may be a recipe for

extreme levels of pollution and other forms of environmental degradation. Malaysia and Brazil, for example, both resist outside pressure
to preserve their rainforests by pointing out that wealthy nations
almost all became wealthy in part by exploiting and degrading their
own natural resources, including their forests, and that it is hypocriti-
cal to ask present low-income nations to behave any differently (see
Chapter 3). As another example, the collapse of communist regimes
in Eastern Europe revealed huge levels of environmental degradation
of all sorts, frequently associated with an almost obsessive preoccupa-
tion with industrialisation and material development.

We have grappled with the various terminologies that can be used
for important groups of nations, including the geographically confus-
ing 'North' and 'South' and the politically outdated 'First World' and
'Third World'. Then there is the whole range of terms that depend on
the poorly defined and even misleading concept of development (usually regarded as being synonymous with increasing energy and resource use): undeveloped, underdeveloped, developing, developed,
less developed, and more developed. But this interpretation of development is clearly at odds with the concept of sustainable development
(see Section 1.5 and 7.8) and has a European and North American
bias. We have finally settled on the terms *low-income nations* and *high-
income nations*, a dualism increasingly used in the literature, including
that of international institutions. These terms, based on GNP per
capita, encapsulate much about the lifestyles of the citizens as well as
the place of each nation in the global economy. Of course reality is
never that simple, and very wealthy minorities can inflate average
incomes and partially hide poverty in others (see also Box 1.2).

Table 1.2 contains values for a number of key variables for nations
in each of five GNP per capita groups in the late 1980s. You can see
that there are general relationships between each of these variables
and GNP levels, although the highest income group has a slightly
lower proportion of its population living in urban areas and clearly
donates less in overseas development aid per capita than does the next
highest income group.

International trade

The global economic system of the late twentieth century is built
around international trade in food, raw materials, semi-processed commodities, finished manufactured goods, and a huge variety of services.
Excluding services, this trade is built directly and indirectly upon
exploitation of the natural environment. It provides one important

mechanism whereby environment and economy are linked, as well as one of the major ways in which different locations on the Earth's surface interact with one another. At a very simple level, many of the world's poorest nations have economies based on exploiting raw materials and exporting them in an essentially unprocessed form. At the other end of the spectrum, the roles of high-income nations in the international economy are characterised by processing materials that are often largely imported, turning them into more complex goods, and selling them on the domestic market, to other wealthy nations or to the original raw material suppliers. As we shall see in Chapter 3, there are a whole variety of intermediate stages, often viewed as part of the process of development, which might involve producing nations gradually undertaking more and more processing of raw materials before export. However, the message is clear: the international economy depends on global sourcing of raw materials, so that environmental problems, even in nations with very low living standards, are attributable in part to the demands of the high-income nations.

The international economic system is also built around flows of money. Indeed, one of the major changes of the last decade or so has been a vast increase in the volume and speed of financial flows around the world. Many nations, including Australia, have accrued very large international debts since the 1970s. While this is not necessarily a problem, it has created huge difficulties for poorer nations. The need to pay interest and at least some of the capital owing, together with **International Monetary Fund** (IMF) and **World Bank** demands for economic restructuring, have dramatically restricted the ability of these nations to import goods and also the ability of their governments to provide essential services, such as health and education, as well as environmental management and protection. In many cases the result has been a severe drop in the real standard of living. Moreover, it has led a variety of governments to embark on policies to promote exports, generally of raw materials, to help pay their debts. This has often been at the expense of local food production, but also at the expense of the environment when it has involved rapid exploitation of natural resources such as agricultural lands (Chapter 2), forests (Chapter 3), fisheries (Section 6.2) or mineral deposits. Section 7.4 discusses many of these issues further.

In short, human-induced environmental change is intimately and fundamentally tied to the way we live and to our economic systems. In *Our Common Future* (also known as the Brundtland Report)[5] the World Commission on Environment and Development argues eloquently that if we are to do anything effective about issues like low living standards and poverty we also need to cope with a whole raft of environmental issues (and vice versa): that is, the two cannot be separated. This argument is central to this book, and it is developed in relation to future strategies in Chapter 7, especially Section 7.4.

The economic imperative and the environment

Some of the literature on environmental issues suggests or implies that there is a fundamental conflict between environmental protection and economic development which must be resolved if we are to deal with the problems. Politicians and media commentators also frequently assume there is such a conflict. To the extent that champions of each of the two causes deal with common subjects, though often failing to realise it, and largely ignore one another, there is a very real problem. Neither group has a monopoly on wisdom and both have significant shortcomings in their understanding of the real world. It is clear that one of the steps toward a sustainable future is to achieve a working marriage between environmental concern and economics, but that alone will not be enough to ensure such a future (see also Sections 7.1 and 7.8).

It does seem to be true that economists and proponents of the high-income nations' version of development have ruled the roost globally, as well as within most nations (not only those of the high-income group). These people have certainly set the agenda of the World Bank and the IMF and have steadfastly refused, until very recent times, to diverge from it. It is imperative that this narrowly economistic view of life be balanced by a recognition of environmental and welfare issues. A more humane approach needs to be brought into political debate at all levels. (Section 1.2 argued that the geographical perspective can do much to bring the necessary breadth of vision to analysis and planning, and this whole area of discussion is taken up again in Chapter 7.)

Science and technology

Among the things that differentiate us from other animal species are our continually increasing knowledge of our environment and our invention and extensive use of technologies of all kinds. Both are critical to the way we live and to our standard of living. They are also central to the nature and impact of our interactions with the biophysical environment. Examples abound, from our development of technologies to make paper from wood that are a huge source of environmental destruction and waste today, to our use of transuranic elements with their frightful potential to contaminate the environment for periods longer than human history. Fortunately, another example is our increasing understanding and successful management of many environmental problems.

It is more useful to consider briefly how technologies have evolved than to list more examples of how scientific knowledge and new technologies create new environmental challenges or offer new possibilities for more appropriate and less invasive dealings with our environment. Toffler's idea of the 'three waves' of human history[6] is just one of many possible organising frameworks. In his view, each wave involved the emergence of new technologies that quickly became associated with fundamentally new ways of organising human society and, we might add, new forms of human interaction with the environment. Toffler's three waves are: the agricultural revolution, involving the development of settled agriculture and pastoralism and the emergence of permanent settlements; the industrial revolution, involving the emergence of factory production, global sourcing of raw materials and food, and the consolidation of people into urban areas; and the information revolution, now under way, leading to less emphasis on large-scale production and more on the processing and exchange of information.

Even the briefest reflection should show that many aspects of human interaction with the environment can be related to one or more of these waves. Agriculture and the associated problems of soil degradation and water use can be related to the change from nomadic to settled lifestyles and the need to provide for higher population densities concentrated in towns. Many features of the present global economy can be seen to have originated in the upsurge of global sourcing of food and raw materials that was a consequence of the industrial revolution. While such historical associations might be too simplistic, they often help us to better understand current situations, and understanding is the first step toward finding solutions.

Technology is created by people, and the direction of scientific investigation is chosen by people. Both are intimately related to cultures, political systems and economies — to the way we live and the environment in which we live. While some new scientific discoveries and technologies bring new ways of exploiting the biophysical world, other technologies offer new ways of monitoring, assessing and managing the environment (Section 7.6).

Politics

Political systems must also be incorporated into our attempts to understand the ways in which we deal with the environment. As well, they are central to all our hopes for developing strategies to live less destructively as a species. At this stage, some examples of the importance of politics and political systems will suffice: discussions later in this book about efforts to minimise environmental damage or develop improved strategies for environmental management will involve an unwritten or overt reference to the political dimensions of human activity. Politics and political systems are thus a critical element in our framework for exploring the interaction of human and biophysical systems.

Most obviously, governments and politicians control our exploitation of the natural environment. They may, for example, grant licences for companies to extract minerals or to export woodchips. They may also do many other things that are less obviously environmental but which might have substantial implications for the environment. One example is a country's attitude to foreign investment and its willingness to allow in foreign companies, perhaps to mine, farm, or cut down trees. Furthermore, governments have the power to limit environmental damage, for example, by prohibiting exploitation of particularly sensitive resources or imposing various safeguards. Internationally, governments are increasingly faced with having to negotiate with other governments on environmental issues, leading to events like the Earth Summit of 1992. Chapter 6 takes up this question of international politics at some length.

But politics involves more than simply what governments do. It is also about the actions of individuals within societies and how they deal with other people and their surroundings. Thus, the way in which the world's governments measure national income as GNP (Box 1.2) was a political decision based on an assessment of what human society thought appropriate at the time. A similar decision made now might well pay much greater attention to many of the things ignored earlier, including the environmental costs of increased economic activity. This is an example of an underlying philosophy or ethos in which societies have acquiesced and which could be changed through political processes. People are also environmentally active in many other ways, from sit-ins to protect old-growth forests (see Section 3.4) to education campaigns and changes in purchasing and consuming habits. The outcomes of individual and group political action can, however, have either positive or negative impacts on the environment.

Another very important issue that is central to public debates about our environmental future is the so-called jobs-versus-environment conflict, the idea that modern society can either develop to create jobs and income, or protect its environment, but not both. This is a misguided and simplistic interpretation, based on particular social and political attitudes and an outdated assessment of the potential for human interaction with the environment. In any case, it is an inherently

political interpretation. But any move toward sustainable development, an approach that necessarily brings together the economic and
environmental aspects, also requires decisive political action derived,
in a democracy, from popular opinion.

SUSTAINABLE DEVELOPMENT 1.5

As we have seen, human activities have been largely responsible for
disturbing the global system's dynamic equilibrium. Those activities
appear to be taking many of the Earth's natural systems in directions
that are not sustainable in the long term: we are imposing burdens on
those systems that are too severe for them to accommodate. Human
activities thus need to change if we are to avoid what may be catastrophic responses by those natural systems.

The concept of sustainable development has been put forward as a
framework within which we can balance immediate and long-term
human demands and the health of the environment, both now and in
the future (see Section 7.8). While this concept has been defined in
many different ways and used in many different ways for different
purposes, one of the most appealing definitions comes from *Our
Common Future*. It says that sustainable development is 'development
that meets the needs of the present without compromising the ability
of future generations to meet their own needs'.[7] This definition explicitly involves intergenerational equity (see Section 7.8). In terms of
systems (see Section 1.3), a sustainable economy or society is one that
manages to keep values of key parameters, including consumption of
materials and energy and creation of wastes, within limits and below
thresholds. Perturbations are held to levels that can maintain a dynamic equilibrium and avoid a collapse into catastrophe. Feedback,
especially negative feedback, is crucial, but warning signs from feedback must be heeded and acted on. Societies must be sustainable
socially and politically, as well as economically and physically, so they
must address such issues as poverty and the rights of minorities as well
as the overtly economic or environmental issues. These themes run
implicitly or explicitly throughout this book and through many contemporary discussions of global environmental crises.

CONCLUSION 1.6

This chapter has introduced the major themes of the book, emphasising the complex ways in which the various aspects of the Earth's
biophysical and human systems interact. The global environmental

crises that face us today are neither wholly of the natural world nor wholly of the human world. It is the interaction of people and nature that must be addressed if solutions are to be found. Major changes in people's ways of life will undoubtedly be necessary, changes that will impinge upon the cultural, social, economic, technological and political aspects of our lives.

Chapters 2 to 5 apply these themes to particular components of the world's systems, highlighting a small number of environmental issues. We try to point out linkages between the case studies, but you should always be looking out for them, as well as for examples of interactions between various parts of the human and biophysical systems. As well as being important issues in their own right, the crises covered illustrate the main themes of the book. Another point made continually is that action needs to occur at all levels, from the local to the global. Each chapter mentions aspects of the problem under consideration at various scales, but Chapter 6 specifically discusses moves towards global co-operation on environmental issues. Finally, Chapter 7 contains an explicit and more detailed consideration of crucial components of planning and action that are needed if both people and the environment are to have an assured future. This includes a return to what is perhaps the most important concept of the book, sustainable development.

FURTHER READING

Data Sources/Resource Books

These books are produced frequently, usually annually, and provide both statistical information and short essays on a wide variety of environmental and development issues.

Brown, L.R. (ed.), *State of the World*, Allen & Unwin (Sydney, annually).

Fridtjof Nansen Institute, *Green Globe Yearbook*, Oxford University Press (Oxford, annually).

UN Development Programme, *Human Development Report*, Oxford University Press (New York, annually).

ITM, *Third World Guide*, Instituto del Tercer Mundo (Montevideo, annually).

World Bank, *World Development Report*, Oxford University Press (New York, annually).

World Resources Institute, *World Resources: A guide to the global environment*, Oxford University Press (New York, annually).

Goudie, A., *The Human Impact on the Natural Environment* (4th edn), Blackwell (Oxford, 1993). [A summary of the major forms which human impacts on the biophysical environment have taken, emphasising a physical geography perspective.]

Harrison, P., *The Third Revolution: Population, environment and a sustainable world*, Penguin (Harmondsworth, UK, 1993). [The third global revolution, after the agricultural and the industrial, is seen as being the transition to sustainable development.]

Johnston, R.J., *Environmental Problems: Nature, economy and state*, Belhaven Press (London, 1989).

Lovelock, J., *Healing Gaia: Practical medicine for the planet*, Harmony Books (New York, 1991). [An introduction to the controversial Gaia hypothesis of the planet Earth as a 'mega-organism'.]

Mannion, A.M. and Bowlby, S.R., *Environmental Issues in the 1990s*, Wiley (Chichester, UK, 1990). [A general introduction to the major environmental issues from a Northern Hemisphere perspective.]

Myers, N. (ed.), *The Gaia Atlas of Planet Management: For today's caretakers of tomorrow's world*, Pan Books (London, 1985). [A highly pictorial introduction to global environmental crises and possible action: the Gaia hypothesis, disputed by many, underlies the book.]

Pickering, K.T. and Owen, L.A., *An Introduction to Global Environmental Issues*, Routledge (London, 1994). [A general, profusely illustrated introduction to the major environmental issues.]

Ponting, C., *A Green History of the World*, Penguin (Harmondsworth, UK, 1991). [A new look at world history, stressing human–environment interactions and the importance of both changing technologies and changing attitudes.]

Turner, B.L., et al. (eds), *The Earth as Transformed by Human Actions: Global and regional changes in the biosphere over the past 300 years*, Cambridge University Press (Cambridge, UK, 1990). [A very large, comprehensive and detailed collection of essays.]

White, R.R., *North, South, and the Environmental Crisis*, University of Toronto Press (Toronto, 1993). [Another introduction to global environmental issues, but stressing the differing perspectives of the low-income nations and the high-income nations.]

World Commission on Environment and Development, *Our Common Future* (Australian edition), Oxford University Press (Melbourne, 1990). [The Brundtland Report: see Section 6.6 of this book for its historical context.]

Australia

ABS, *Australia's Environment: Issues and facts*, Australian Bureau of Statistics (Canberra, 1992).

ABS, *Striking a Balance! Australia's development and conservation*, Australian Bureau of Statistics (Melbourne, 1992). [These two compilations contain a wealth of statistics covering many aspects of the Australian environment and also act as a guide to sources for further investigation.]

Beder, S., *The Nature of Sustainable Development*, Scribe Publications (Newham, 1993). [An accessible introduction to sustainable development written from an Australian perspective and including a number of case studies.]

Graetz, R.D., Fisher, R.P. and Wilson, M.A., *Looking Back: The changing face of the Australian Continent, 1972–1992*, CSIRO Office of Space Science and Applications (Canberra, 1992). [A very useful and revealing collection of remote-sensing images with informative commentaries.]

Mercer, D., *A Question of Balance: Natural resource conflict issues in Australia*, Federation Press (Sydney, 1991). [A thorough and scholarly introduction to this subject with many case studies from the Australian experience.]

NOTES

1 Stoddart, D.R., 'To claim the high ground: geography for the end of the century', *Transactions of the Institute of British Geographers* **NS12** (1987), 331.

2 Ibid, 327–36.

3 Bissio, R.R. et al. (eds) *Third World Guide 1993–94*, Instituto del Tercer Mundo (Montevideo, 1993), 31.

4 Brown, L.R. (ed.) *State of the World 1990*, Allen & Unwin (Sydney, 1990), 144–5.

5 World Commission on Environment and Development, *Our Common Future* (Australian edition), Oxford University Press (Melbourne, 1990).

6 Toffler, A., *The Third Wave*, Pan Books (London, 1980).

7 World Commission on Environment and Development, *Our Common Future* (Australian edition), Oxford University Press (Melbourne, 1990), 87.

LAND AND WATER

INTRODUCTION 2.1

TEN OR TWELVE THOUSAND years ago people in many parts of the world took a major step toward 'modern' lifestyles by domesticating plants and animals, thereby increasing food and raw materials production while reducing labour inputs. The change from hunter-gatherer lifestyles to settled agriculture and pastoralism led to profound changes in society, enabling the establishment of urban centres and an increased emphasis on trading and manufacturing. These changes provided the framework upon which industrialised and urbanised economies and societies are based, leading indirectly to a range of environmental problems.

Agriculture as environmental exploitation

Agriculture and pastoralism have also had more direct negative impacts on the biophysical environment. Soil erosion, soil and water pollution, water supply and species extinction have all become important issues. While impacts were initially small-scale and local, they increased in extent and severity as agricultural systems became more industrialised and less in tune with natural ecosystems, processes, and cycles. In fact, large-scale, artificial ecosystems with greatly modified and controlled processes and cycles became the norm in many nations. Such agricultural and pastoral systems rapidly extended their geographical coverage so that much of the Earth's surface is now affected by them. As a result, land and water degradation, together with water supply problems, now deserve to be thought of as global crises.

This chapter reviews the extent and significance of these problems in rural areas; Chapter 4 deals with similar issues in the urban context. We will concentrate on the specific problems of land and water use and abuse. As with all global crises, they are complex issues involving both biophysical and human aspects. It has been the changing nature of the interaction of people with their environment, as outlined in Section 2.2, that has led to the crises, often because of ignorance about the real impacts of human action on biophysical systems. It would therefore be unrealistic to expect biophysical or technological approaches alone to provide solutions. Clearly, the economic, cultural, social and political implications also need to be addressed.

Although the basic focus of this chapter is on land and water, there is also considerable discussion of the production of food and raw materials to supply the world's people. It is the search for increased production that has fuelled developments in agriculture, leading indirectly to the environmental crises. Furthermore, falling levels of production may well be one of the most important consequences of continuing degradation.

Scale and geography of supply problems

Land and water degradation affect the Earth's potential to supply adequate food and water to all people. How successful are we at meeting these demands now? Are there important regional differences? What roles do human systems play in enhancing or reducing our ability to meet basic demands for all? Can we reach solutions simply by applying 'big' technology, or are there other issues that must be addressed as well?

Every year more than 40 million people die from hunger and about 500 million people are seriously undernourished. These two figures have increased steadily since 1950, and 600 million people (10 per cent of the global population) are expected to be malnourished in the year 2000. This is despite the increased area of cultivated land, the increased number of domestic animals, and the **Green Revolution** of the 1960s and 1970s which doubled grain yields. It is also despite the fact that, during the 1980s, we produced sufficient basic food to feed the entire human population plus 1500 million more people. This last point needs to be placed in its global context.

Success in feeding regional populations varies markedly. North America, Western Europe, Japan, Australia and New Zealand all produce food surpluses, while Eastern Europe and the former USSR produce enough basic supplies to feed their own people and have the potential to produce more (though internal distribution is a major problem). China has achieved a miracle in that it now feeds 21 per cent of the total human population from only 6.6 per cent of the world's cropland. Among low-income regions, Latin America and Asia break even, while Africa is rapidly losing the race. However, the simple diversion of food surpluses to populations in need, even if possible, would not be enough to redress this imbalance, because such 'food aid' encourages subsidised agriculture in countries which are already over-producing (and where environmental damage often occurs) and discourages recipient countries from becoming self-sufficient. In any case, the infrastructure for food aid distribution does not exist in many places where famine and civil unrest are increasingly common.

A similar story can be told about access to fresh water. Water is something people must have every day of the year. Furthermore, it must be clean, safe water, free from pollutants, salt, silt, organic matter, bacteria and viruses — the sort of water taken for granted in Australian cities when delivered to kitchen taps for ridiculously low prices (about 32 cents per household per day in Sydney in 1993). While the basic minimum requirement of fresh water to maintain human life is about 5 litres per person per day, the ease and cheapness of supply in these cities, along with affluent lifestyles, has led to an average daily consumption (not including industry) of about 500 litres per capita. Such high consumption is typical of cities in high-income countries and stands in marked contrast with poorer parts of the world where 15–20 litres is the most available.

Fresh water is globally abundant, but there are real problems of supply in many areas. The volumes required militate against extensive redistribution from one catchment to another, so there is little trade in water (although this may change in the future; for example, proposals to transfer Canadian water to the west coast of the USA have a long history). Meanwhile, local or temporal scarcity and poor quality cause the annual deaths of 6 million children, and 1 billion people suffer heavy internal parasite infestations spread through insanitary living conditions. In Australia, Aborigines living in outback communities provide a shameful example of how an inadequate water supply affects community health even in an affluent country. The Aboriginal infant mortality rate is three times that of other Australians, and eye diseases such as trachoma, which are related to a lack of sufficient water for personal cleanliness, affect 38 per cent of Aborigines compared with only 1.7 per cent of non-Aborigines living in the same districts.

Different standards of water quality are required for different end uses. Stock water supplies can be more saline than human supplies; irrigation water can carry some sediment, but not if also used to generate hydroelectricity; and power station cooling water can have high levels of dissolved salts or organic matter. Most large water-supply schemes are established for multiple uses, and therefore the highest standards (usually those for domestic consumption) need to be met even if they are necessary for only a small portion of the end use. Of all the water stored in Australia, 74 per cent is used in irrigation, 8 per cent for other rural uses, 8 per cent for industry, and 10 per cent for domestic purposes. Two-thirds of this water is consumed in the Murray–Darling Basin, the location of the nation's biggest irrigation areas. Virtually all the water is used once only. By contrast, in the high-income countries of the Northern Hemisphere perhaps 90 per cent of the industrial and domestic water is reused at least once, and often many times, downstream. In crowded cities in low-income nations, water may be used repeatedly for all sorts of incompatible purposes, and the quality is often appalling. (Chapter 4 discusses the urban aspects of these issues further.)

There are obviously serious problems with food and water supply on a global scale, but these are not absolute shortages as much as inequalities in distribution. Many people live in climatically marginal environments and are subject to floods, droughts or pestilence. Large-scale irrigation and water-supply schemes often have undesirable social, economic and environmental impacts, and in some low-income countries they have failed outright. Extensive agriculture and **rangeland** management are having enormous impacts on soil resources in all countries where they are practised. In poor countries many people have neither the means of production (land) nor the money to purchase food supplies, and yet surplus food production occurs in developed nations at a cost higher than poor countries can afford.

2.2 ORIGINS AND IMPACTS OF AGRICULTURE AND WATER USE

The development of agriculture has involved the domestication of animals and plants by humans in a complex set of **mutualistic** relationships. All the species involved have interacted in an evolutionary sense, and a situation has developed where our plant and animal breeding strategies have produced new varieties that have higher yields but are no longer viable in the wild. The following brief summary of the development of agriculture and grazing highlights the changing nature of the human relationship with the biophysical environment, as well as introducing some of the major environmental problems relating to land and water.

Four idealised historical types of agricultural development can be recognised: hunter-gatherer communities; simple agricultural settlement in villages; grazing systems; and modern systems of agriculture.

Each of these has enabled an increase in human population to occur and has affected the environment to a greater extent than simpler systems. But it is extremely important to note that no sequence from one type to the next is implied, and elements of all or several types can exist concurrently in the one region or nation. Present-day Australia is a good example: some Aboriginal groups still practice a partial hunter-gatherer lifestyle; most of the semi-arid zone of the continent is loosely managed as an open rangeland; Western-style agriculture has reached peaks of technological 'efficiency'; and we have scientists playing a leading role in the development and application of tomorrow's **biotechnology**.

Hunter-gatherer communities

For several million years of prehistory, the co-evolution of plants, animals and humans was fairly straightforward because people supported themselves in hunter-gatherer communities. Populations were small and their impact is often assumed to have been limited, but we know only a little about the economies of such groups. The experience of the Australian Aborigines, however, can give us some insights into the environmental impacts associated with this lifestyle.

There are two common clichés purporting to describe Aboriginal lifestyles: one is of the noble savage living in harmony with the environment, and the other is of an unchanging people in an unchanging land. Both of these are erroneous. Any harmony that existed at the time of first European settlement in 1788 had evolved over more than 40 000 years of Aboriginal occupation. That a human population persisted for so long is itself evidence that a sustainable, but not necessarily unchanging, relationship between the people and the land had been attained.

With such a long history of occupation, the Aborigines undoubtedly had important impacts on the Australian environment. But were they in any major way responsible for the vegetation changes associated with the late Pleistocene climatic shifts (**Ice Ages**) and the extinction of the large marsupials? Archaeologists and others have been asking these questions about indigenous people everywhere for more than a century. Many hypotheses have been erected arguing cases for a human role in landscape change and the Pleistocene mass-extinction, but all are difficult to prove because it seems impossible to untangle human impacts from climatic impacts over this time period.

If early humans were responsible for change, was it the direct result of uncontrolled hunting pressure? Was it an indirect consequence of other changes, such as a shift from woodlands to grasslands induced by the use of fire? Or was it, perhaps, a more subtle combination of factors, both human and climatic, including seemingly unconnected things like the introduction of dogs and rats to areas where they were previously absent? These are all legitimate questions to which there are no certain answers, but strong circumstantial evidence from sediment cores in north Queensland and the Southern Tablelands of NSW suggests at least partial human involvement in such changes in Australia.

Environmental exploitation leading to species extinction, however, was not inevitable in hunter-gatherer societies. Social evolution also occurred in human populations and a variety of conservation strategies were adopted as taboos or religious practices, having the effect of limiting exploitation of species and protecting environments. There is even some evidence that social groups in harsher environments with sparser resources were more conscious of the need for conservation than groups living in areas with abundant resources. Examples include the seasonal harvest of certain animals or plants; limitations on the size of a kill or the quantity taken; recognition of sacred sites where hunting, food collecting and fire were not allowed; the use of peripheral environments rather than core environments whenever seasonal conditions allowed; randomisation of hunting sites through some sort of divination process; and, universally, a close spiritual identity with the land and the **biota**. In other words, a form of environmental management occurred.

Simple agricultural settlement in villages

Three main centres of domestication of plants and animals are generally recognised: South-east Asia as early as 13 000 **BP** (years before present); the Middle East by 11 000 BP, with irrigation by 7000 BP; and Central America by 7000 BP (Figure 2.1). Today the total number of domesticated foodstuffs in use is very small: we gain about 95 per cent of global food from 30 kinds of plants, and 75 per cent is derived from just eight crop types. There have been contributions to this larder, however, from most parts of the world, although several major **biomes**, including all of those in Australia, have contributed very little. There must be hundreds of species with a commercial potential in this country and others with extensive but little-known natural environments, such as the rainforests (see Section 3.3). In purely economic terms, this is a very good reason for maintaining **biodiversity** and preserving viable conservation areas around the world (see Section 6.6).

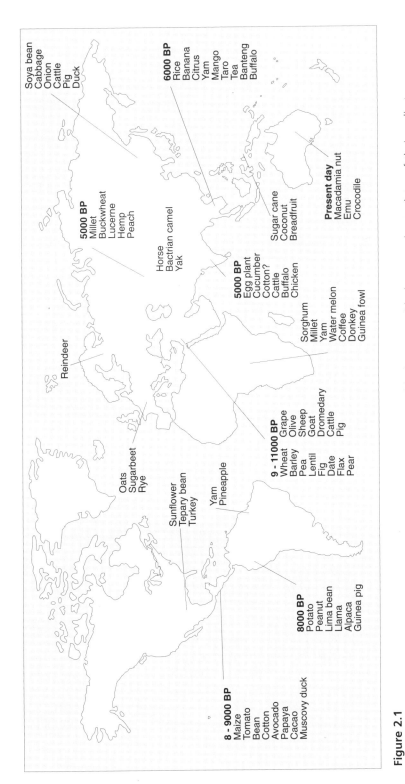

8 - 9000 BP
Maize
Tomato
Bean
Cotton
Avocado
Papaya
Cacao
Muscovy duck

8000 BP
Potato
Peanut
Lima bean
Llama
Alpaca
Guinea pig

9 - 11000 BP
Wheat   Grape
Barley   Olive
Pea   Sheep
Lentil   Goat
Fig   Dromedary
Date   Cattle
Flax   Pig
Pear

Oats
Sugarbeet
Rye

Sunflower
Tepary bean
Turkey

Yam
Pineapple

Reindeer

5000 BP
Millet
Buckwheat
Lucerne
Hemp
Peach

Horse
Bactrian camel
Yak

5000 BP
Egg plant
Cucumber
Cotton?
Cattle
Buffalo
Chicken

Sorghum
Millet
Yam
Water melon
Coffee
Donkey
Guinea fowl

Soya bean
Cabbage
Onion
Cattle
Pig
Duck

6000 BP
Rice
Banana
Citrus
Yam
Mango
Taro
Tea
Banteng
Buffalo

Sugar cane
Coconut
Breadfruit

Present day
Macadamia nut
Emu
Crocodile

Figure 2.1
Centres of domestication of the most important plants and animals used by humans, with the approximate dates of their earliest appearance in archaeological deposits.

Australian Aborigines had a domesticated dog, the dingo, but did not develop an agricultural economy, although some of their uses of fire, food-gathering practices and patch settlements can be regarded as agricultural precursors, and there were established gardens on the Torres Strait Islands at the time of European contact. In the Highlands of Papua New Guinea, however, real agriculture, in the sense of culti-vated crops, has been in existence for more than 10 000 years. People entered this region about 52 000 BP, and the first certain evidence of their impact was forest clearance with heavy stone axes about 40 000 BP. It is speculated that this clearance was small-scale and only intended to favour the plants already growing in canopy gaps — a plant-promotion strategy rather than true forest gardens. By 9000 BP, however, drained swamps and extensive food plantations were estab-lished in the Highlands, almost as soon as the post-glacial climates were suitable.

Throughout South-east Asia the cultivation of rice as a staple grain resulted in even more extensive landscape change through the construction of terraced paddy fields with their associated water-distribution systems so characteristic of Luzon, Java and Bali. Some of these agricultural engineering works date back at least 2500 years and may be older.

Grazing systems

The earliest evidence for the domestication of grazing animals is found rather later than the first signs of agriculture, but it is likely that humans had been nurturing wild herds for thousands of years before controlling their breeding and selecting improved stock. It is also very likely that pastoralism as a land use has always been marginal to agriculture, just as it is today, because the business of grazing is to convert bulky, poor-quality fodder into meat, milk, fibre and leather. Goats, sheep, cattle, horses, camels, buffalo and llamas do this well and all are native to relatively arid environments where agriculture would not normally be possible.

Nomadic pastoralism was the normal form of grazing land use because available fodder and water was usually limited in any given area. In the last few centuries, however, sedentary range management as practised in high-income nations has become more common, with the result that animal pressures on rangelands have increased, causing greater damage. This is not to say that range condition under other forms of pastoral management is necessarily better. It often is not, especially where cultural norms recognise grazing stock as visible wealth and herd sizes increase in parallel with human populations to the point where neither people nor stock can be supported in poor years.

The key to range management is to balance stock numbers with available forage and water supplies and prevent a decline in range condition. In arid or semi-arid rangelands, forage production depends on rainfall, but it may be weeks or months between the rain and the availability of adequate feed. Rainfall is typically unreliable, and extremes of drought and above-average rain both have profound effects on the composition and quantity of available forage.

Nomadic pastoralists and **transhumant** graziers can maintain a safe balance between stock numbers and available feed if the seasons are reasonably regular; if they are free to move without political or social restrictions; if they do not attempt to carry excessive numbers of stock at any time; and if there are not large numbers of competing herbivores. Modern graziers operating on limited areas have to buy or sell stock to adjust to varying range conditions. This is difficult to do because stock prices are inevitably low as the range enters drought, but high after good rains. Graziers therefore adopt a compromise strategy whereby a minimum number of breeding stock are carried through all conditions. Economics force them to increase productivity through the provision of artificial watering points, fencing for better herd control, pasture improvement by burning or the introduction of new species, and possibly the provision of supplementary feed. Improvements cost money, which the graziers try to recoup by carrying more stock.

In marginal conditions, this is a recipe for extensive land degradation. Rangeland is eroded by wind and water as vegetation cover is depleted, soil compaction by trampling occurs around watering points, groundwater supplies may be depleted, and natural patterns of runoff may be altered. All of these changes in turn affect the native biota: some species become extinct, most decline in number, and a few may be favoured by habitat change to the extent that they increase in number and become pests (some kangaroos, for example). Many exotic species are favoured by change and can also become pests, as did rabbits in Australia. The spread of woody weeds on Australian rangelands provides a good example of the types of problems that can arise (Box 2.1).

We know what the major land-degradation problems in the Australian rangelands are and we know how to deal with them, but the value of the land and the levels of production from it are so low that individual graziers cannot possibly afford to do very much restoration work. It is possibly time for a complete reappraisal of land use in the semi-arid areas of Australia; some scientists suggest a much greater emphasis on 'farming' native species, especially kangaroos and emus.

Woody weeds on Australian rangelands

BOX 2.1

About three-quarters of Australia is arid or semi-arid and has been used for 100–150 years as rangeland for sheep and cattle. All of the problems mentioned above are now evident and it is estimated that at least 30 per cent of the range is moderately to severely degraded. Degradation was evident within the first 20 or 30 years of settlement of the rangeland and was exacerbated by extreme drought conditions. The degradation continues, albeit at a slower rate, and new problems are becoming evident. For example, there has been a spread of native woody weeds on more than 20 million ha of the Western Division of NSW and on large semi-arid areas in other states since the 1950s. These native shrubs have increased in density because of reduced fire frequency and their inedibility, crowding out annuals and edible perennials and competing for soil moisture. The dense scrub makes mustering difficult, lowers **carrying capacity**, lowers lambing percentages, increases stock losses and lowers land values. Because the woody weeds are native species, there is little opportunity for **biological control**, and herbicides are too expensive.

One control technique that is cheap enough to use and which has been partly successful is to burn the shrub-infested country after a good season when there is sufficient dry grass to carry a hot fire. Grass represents income to the grazier, and so this is a desperate management act which, in another few decades, may simply encourage the survival and growth of the fire-resistant shrubs, perhaps exacerbating the problem. Large-blade ploughs have been used to mechanically clear woody weeds in Queensland since 1993, but this technique is expensive, not always successful, and can have other undesirable impacts on the environment. Their use in NSW has been resisted by conservationists.

Modern systems of agriculture and water use

Agriculture

Modern agriculture of the type common in high-income nations is characterised by high levels of investment in technology, machinery, chemicals and genetics; a very extensive scale of operation, extending agriculture to marginal environments and often involving irrigation; a dominance of **monocultures**; and constant change. Indeed, change is

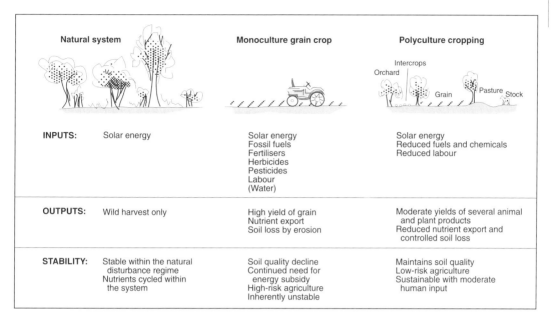

Figure 2.2
Comparative advantages and disadvantages of natural ecosystems,
monocultures and polycultures.

so much a part of modern farming that it is difficult to describe a
typical farming enterprise. Animal and human labour have been
replaced by machines and fossil fuels; natural cycles of soil fertility
have been replaced by the use of chemical fertilisers; monocultures
have replaced complex **polycultures**; and weed and pest control are
dominated by commercial chemicals (Figure 2.2). Most of these changes
have been developed as technological responses to management
problems. When an innovation is adopted there is usually a brief
period of increased yield until a new problem is recognised which, in
turn, is countered by another change.

The geography of modern agriculture reflects climate and soil quality modified by human ingenuity and technology. Agriculture, however, is still a high-risk enterprise which depends on soil quality, weather
extremes, water availability and the occurrence of pests and diseases.
All these factors have to be considered in farm management, along
with the economics of markets, social and political pressures influencing the selection of crop types, and the farmer's access to knowledge
and technology. Modern agriculture is undertaken on such a large
scale and is so industrialised that it can change the landscape. Across
southern Australia, for example, more than 16 million ha of woodland
and scrub have been cleared for the cultivation of grain crops since
1870. In Britain 200 000 km of hedgerows have been removed since

1945 to make larger fields that are suitable for tractors. In extreme cases, such as factory farming, beef feedlots and hydroponic horticulture, the 'farm' is so industrialised as to be almost unrecognisable, forming a completely artificial environment.

The greatest levels of food and fibre production occur in the high-income countries, where they are heavily subsidised by inputs of fossil-fuel energy and capital. These countries dominate international trade in food, supply virtually all the food aid donated to poorer nations, and still have surpluses that are stockpiled or dumped. Low-income countries have much larger proportions of their populations engaged in agriculture and, despite simpler technology and small-scale enterprises, their traditional forms of production are ecologically sounder than those used in high-income nations. Traditional agriculture of the simpler, non-mechanised type is often a polyculture which is ecologically more sensible than the extensive monocultures which have replaced it.

If agriculture is to be sustainable, a balance between these two broad approaches must be achieved, whereby social and environmental impacts are mimimised while production is optimised. If agriculture is to be sustainable, and not propped up by inputs of fuel and nutrients, we have much to learn from the subsistence gardens of the world, especially those in the tropics where plant diversity can be so great it rivals the diversity we admire in rainforests.

Water supply

Agriculture is very often the most important and extensive land use within river catchments. It is also the reason for the construction of irrigation schemes with their big dams on major rivers and extensive networks of canals delivering water to distant farms. Grand water-supply schemes always look attractive to politicians, as they are able to spend money in their electorates and are seen to be doing something about 'developing' the country's 'untapped riches'. The bigger the scheme, the more attractive it becomes to development-oriented politicians, bureaucrats, and engineers, so we see an endless succession of ideas for turning rivers inland and shifting 'surplus' water — from Canada to California, from the Ord River to Perth, or to by-pass the Sudd marshes with the Jonglei Canal in the Sudan.

Big dams, however, do not always live up to their promises, and all over the world we are now recognising that the social, economic and environmental costs of big dams may well be greater than their benefits. This is particularly true in the tropics, where an increase in waterborne diseases is an important social cost. Examples from China and India illustrate very well the inadvisability of a race for large-scale, 'Western'-style development projects proposed or carried on without adequate planning to take into account adverse environmental and social effects.

In China, a proposed dam on the Three Gorges section of the Yangtze River would impound waters for 600 km upstream. It is intended primarily for flood control and, secondarily, for hydro-electricity generation. On the debit side, it would involve the displacement of 1 million people from the land and the loss of 108 heritage sites. Full accounting of these losses does not seem to have been carried out and there is growing Chinese and international opposition to the project, to the extent that the **World Bank**, a traditional supporter of 'mega-dam' schemes (see Section 7.4), was reported to be 'worried about its involvement', and by 1994 had dramatically reduced its involvement in such projects.

India has been one of the busiest dam builders this century, with more than 1600 large dams constructed for irrigation and hydro-electric power, twin 'holy grails' of development in that nation. Few of these dams have paid economic returns, the capital costs of the projects cannot be recovered, and in most cases even running costs are not covered. Electricity transmission losses are twice those in developed countries and the cities take much more than their fair share of power at the expense of rural areas. Despite all the dams, major flooding still causes loss of life and reduces agricultural production, and the extreme erosion rates caused by overgrazing in the hilly catchments raise the rate of **siltation** of reservoirs to as much as ten times that predicted at the design stage. Some dams consequently have effective lives of only decades. Many of the dams are in the foothills of the Himalayas — one of the most seismically active regions of the world — and it is well known that big dams increase the occurrence of small earthquakes. They also have the potential to trigger large earthquakes and subsequent dam collapse: there is at least one such Himalayan example on record associated with the filling of the Koyna Dam in 1967, when 200 people were killed. In late 1993 the World Bank withdrew support for the Namarda Dam project in India, partly because of earthquake fears but also because of a lack of serious and just resettlement schemes for the thousands displaced.

Water quality is another catchment management issue with a geographical twist. Rivers are commonly used as a convenient urban waste-disposal system, as well as collecting polluting runoff from agricultural areas, and people downstream get all the upstream wastes. In rivers which cross state and national boundaries, the control of this pollution presents difficult international political problems. International disagreement also arises over supply problems, as in the Middle East, parts of Africa, and between the USA and Mexico. The last gave rise to the bilateral Colorado River Agreement, a negotiated international treaty between the USA and Mexico signed in 1973 and leading to the Colorado River Basin Salinity Control Act enacted in the USA in 1984.

To summarise, the most important agricultural problems are those which deplete the capital of the soil and genetic resources used in production. The most important water-related problems are controlling pollution and other environmental degradation, reducing wastage, and ensuring that everyone has reasonable access. These problems are encapsulated in the sometimes emotive terms of 'land degradation' and 'water degradation', the topics of Sections 2.3 and 2.4 respectively.

2.3 LAND DEGRADATION

Land degradation is not just soil erosion: the term includes any change in the condition of the land which reduces its productive potential. Soil erosion, although sometimes spectacular, may not even be the worst form of degradation. Paradoxically, the most obvious forms of erosion such as gullies and landslides have less impact on production than the almost unseen stripping of topsoil by wind or water. Another cause of loss of productive land, not treated in this section, is encroachment by non-agricultural, usually urban, activities (see Sections 4.3 and 4.6).

Few areas of the world have reliable land degradation statistics, NSW being an exception. A 1988 survey[1] found the following problems in that state of 80 million ha (Figure 2.3);

- soil erosion affecting 48 million ha (water erosion on 28 million ha and wind erosion on 20 million ha);
- induced soil acidity affecting 8 million ha;
- soil structural decline affecting 15 million ha;
- woody shrub infestation of 23 million ha;
- a lack of tree regeneration on 39 million ha;
- mass movement (for example, landslides) on 3 per cent of the land;
- and salinity on 2.2 per cent.

This catalogue of woes indicates something of the magnitude of the problems involved and is not by any means atypical; other mainland states of Australia are comparable, and similar figures could be expected in southern Africa, India and the drier regions of North and South America. Land degradation is a truly global crisis.

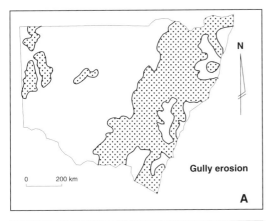

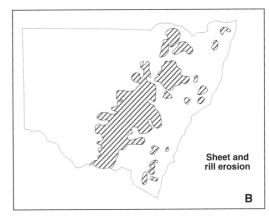

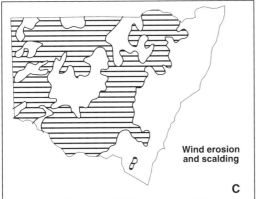

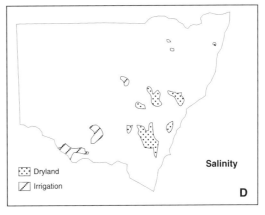

Figure 2.3
Generalised distribution of some types of land degradation in New South
Wales, 1987–88. (a) Gully erosion is most common on either side of the
Great Dividing Range. (b) Sheet and rill erosion are found on the extensive
grain fields of the western slopes. (c) Wind erosion and scalding are common
in the grain fields and in the semi-arid rangelands of the Western Division.
(d) Dryland salinity occurs on the central and southern tablelands, and
irrigation salinity is most significant in the Murray, Murrumbidgee and
Macquarie valleys.

Soil erosion

The global extent of soil erosion is uncertain because it is difficult to
measure. Most research is conducted over short periods and may not
take account of major climatic events. There are many variables to
consider, none of which is independent, and the majority of erosion
studies have been done on lands managed in a particular way, while
few studies have been done using the same measurement techniques
on equivalent natural lands.

When it comes to comparing erosion rates with the rates of soil
formation, the situation is worse because the time-scale involved is at

least two or three orders of magnitude different. Soil formation cannot be directly measured and has to be interpreted from geological or geomorphological situations where soil parent materials (rock or sediments) can be shown to be of a certain age and the degree of soil development on them can be assessed. Climatic change is involved in this time-frame of thousands of years, and the entire story of soil development and erosion rates is thus further complicated.

Figure 2.4 summarises some key erosion processes. On natural lands erosion rates 'average' about 0.05–2.0 mm/yr (approximate thickness of topsoil removed).[2] Under cultivation this increases to about 5–10 mm/yr, and on bare soil to more than 25 mm/yr and often more than 100 mm/yr. (An erosion rate of 1.0 mm/yr is equal to an annual soil loss of 1.0–1.5 tonnes/km², but thickness is easier to visualise). Accepting these figures as a rough global average, they suggest that erosion rates will increase dramatically under any management regime which depletes vegetation cover and disturbs the soil. Data on rates of soil formation are even less reliable than the erosion data, but a typical global 'average' figure would be something less than 0.1 mm/yr. If we accept some erosion as an inevitable natural process, we should aim to keep our losses at about the level of the natural rate. There are very few examples of land management where this has been achieved.

It has been estimated that the USA is losing 5 billion tonnes of topsoil per year. Water erosion accounts for 80 per cent of this, and wind for the remainder. Much of the waterborne sediment enters river systems, changing their dynamics and form and often increasing flood problems and hindering navigation.

Loss of soil fertility

Soils are usually considered to be fertile if they contain sufficient basic nutrients, including trace elements, for plant growth. Nutrients must be replaced if they are lost by erosion or taken from the soil in plant or animal products. This is an easy task using chemical fertilisers provided that a balance is maintained and that the nutrient status of the soil is properly monitored.

It is also very easy for soil nutrients to become unbalanced, and simply adding more of the required compounds sometimes produces negative effects. One example of such an effect is off-site pollution when excess fertiliser is washed into farm dams, streams and water-supply reservoirs. Another is the induced soil acidity in Australian grain-growing areas that has occurred as a consequence of repeated applications of superphosphate and nitrogen fertilisers and the use of

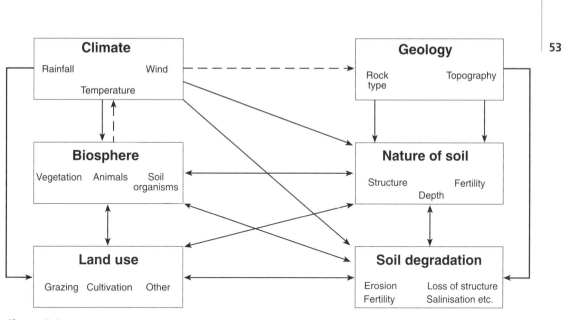

Figure 2.4
The relationships between the main factors of soil formation and
degradation.

legume-based pastures. These changes were all introduced between
1920 and 1960, and by the 1980s it was recognised that soil **pH** had
fallen from near-neutral to as low as 3.0 or 4.0. At this level of acidity,
yields decline dramatically because aluminium and manganese, which
are usually abundant in soil, are released in solution and thus become
toxic to plants. The situation can be reversed by heavy applications of
lime, but that is difficult and expensive.

Strategies for restoring chemical fertility are available to Australian
farmers because they can expect the increased yield to pay for the
fertilisers. They are not so readily available for an African or Indian
farmer facing the same problems but without money to buy fertiliser.
But continued dependence on chemicals is not the only way to maintain fertility. Copying nature's nutrient cycle by incorporating organic
matter into the soil is a practice as old as cultivation itself, and more
relevant today after decades of neglect than it has ever been. The
organic matter used can be anything than will break down into **humus**
and support a diverse soil biota. Crop residues and animal dung are
ideal. So are human wastes, a resource which the high-income world
shuns, but the safe use of which might also alleviate disposal problems
in urban areas (see Section 4.3).

54 | Soil structural change

Soil fertility, in a broader sense, is not just a question of organic matter and nutrient supply. Plant roots also need access to soil water and air, and there are many positive reactions between plants and the soil biota which contribute to plant growth. These aspects of fertility are less understood than the chemical ones, but we certainly know that damaging the structure of soils reduces diversity and abundance in the soil biota and that crop yields decline.

Soil structural damage seems to be worst in high-income countries, where it is caused mainly by the use of heavy machinery. Plough pans of compacted soil at a shallow depth limit the penetration of plant roots. They also change the pattern of water infiltration, which can increase erosion. In low-income countries, soil structural decline and nutrient loss go together because organic matter is lost when all of the crop is harvested or grazed and even animal dung is collected for use as fuel. Nutrients returned through artificial fertilisers do not solve this problem: the only answer is to break the cycle of abuse and get more organic material back into the soil.

Salinisation

There are two common forms of soil salinity (Figure 2.5). Irrigation salinity arises from poor irrigation practices, while dryland salinity is caused by changing the vegetation cover in sub-humid hill country.

Irrigation salinity, caused by excessive application of water to arid-zone soils which have large amounts of salt stored in the subsoil or groundwater, first became evident when the irrigation-based civilisations of Mesopotamia began to fail as salt accumulated in the surface soil. The farmers initially responded by shifting from wheat to barley, a more salt-tolerant crop: in 3500 BC the proportions of these two crops were equal; by 2400 BC wheat was only 20 per cent of the total crop; and by 2100 BC only 2 per cent. After that time there was no choice, and by 1700 BC farmers had abandoned saline lands.

Exactly the same problem is evident today in almost every large-scale flood-irrigation project in the world. If the land is dry enough to require irrigation, there is a very high probability that salt is present deep in the soil. If excessive volumes of water are used, groundwater levels will rise, creating the twin problems of waterlogging and salinisation. Estimates are that today 50 per cent of the irrigated land in Iraq and Syria, 30 per cent in Egypt, 25 per cent in India, 23 per cent in Pakistan and 15 per cent in Iran is saline or waterlogged.

Before clearing, grazing, and cropping:

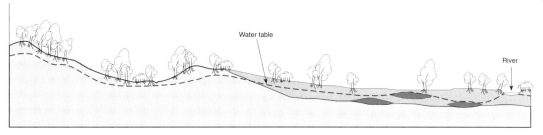

After 50 years of intensive land use:

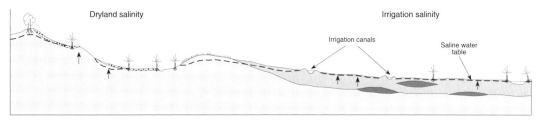

Figure 2.5
The development of soil salinity. Soluble salts stored in the ground under a natural regime are brought to the surface when groundwaters rise because of reduced evapotranspiration after clearing or increased recharge by flood irrigation. Surface waterlogging also occurs and affects plant growth.

In Australia, irrigation salinity developed within 20 years of the first water application in the lower Loddon Valley of Victoria, where there are now more than 100 000 ha of salinised land. Similar problems are evident in the other irrigation areas of Victoria and NSW; the resultant annual loss of production in NSW is estimated at A$30 million. The saline water drained from the irrigation areas also causes other environmental and economic losses downstream in the Murray Valley: Adelaide relies on the Murray River for 80 per cent of its water supply in dry years, the very time when water quality is at its worst.

Dryland salinity is more typically a problem of pasture lands than of agricultural lands, and is most common in sub-humid areas where a change of vegetation cover and land use has allowed more rainfall to enter the soil on upper hillslopes and flush salt down to the valley margins. The hydrology of these systems is complex; although it is not fully understood, part of the story may relate to salt accumulation under different climatic conditions in the past. Clearing or ringbarking woodlands and heavily grazing native pastures are part of the cause, because a good tree cover can move five to ten times more water by transpiration than a grazed pasture. Less ground cover also allows more soil erosion to occur. It is estimated that 5.3 million ha of Australian pastoral land in all states have been ruined by dryland salinity this century. Salt can find its way into local streams: the greatest increases in salt load recorded in Australia's rivers following clearing for agriculture have been in Western Australia — by a factor of nineteen in the Dale River and fifteen in the East Collie River.[3]

Soil pollution

Yet another way in which arable soils can be degraded is by polluting them. The polluting agent might be excess fertilisers, a build up of salt, the accumulation of pesticides in the soil, industrial or other pollution by heavy metals or toxic chemicals (for example, the dioxin cloud that escaped from a factory at Seveso in Italy, or the use of Agent Orange in Vietnam), or nuclear fallout from accidents such as Chernobyl in the former USSR. The last is a good example of the potentially far-reaching affects of industrial pollution on agricultural land and production.

In April 1986, one reactor of the nuclear power station at Chernobyl suffered a partial meltdown and a cloud of radioactive matter drifted west and north-west across Europe. Most attention has focused on the evacuation of people and the later clean-up and encasement of the plant in concrete, but there is also a soil pollution problem of uncertain dimensions. One published estimate suggests that 150 km² in the immediate vicinity of the plant may be so contaminated that it will not be farmed again for decades. Further afield, millions of dollars worth of agricultural produce across Europe was destroyed because of contamination, although some exporters attempted to circumvent these controls. Experts criticised the European policy of crop destruction as an overreaction, but analysis of the disaster policy implemented in Britain suggests, in hindsight, that it may have been the most economical approach.

The Chernobyl event provided a dramatic lesson on the risks of nuclear power, but it would be wrong to overemphasise its importance when more subtle soil pollution continues daily, particularly in the Northern Hemisphere, from acid rain (Box 4.1). Acid rain has been extremely damaging to lake ecosystems and forests and must also be affecting soils, particularly those with a naturally neutral or slightly acid pH and a low **buffering** capacity. The dying forest may be a symptom of a soil problem; but while it is easy to apply lime to a lake and correct its pH, it is rather more difficult to apply it in large quantities to an extensive land area.

Other examples of industrial soil pollutants include large concentrations of lead in the soils adjacent to busy roads, and heavy metal particulates downwind of large mines and smelters. All of these are sometimes serious problems, but they tend to be localised rather than important on a global scale. However, the local occurrences are frequent enough to add up to a problem of worldwide concern.

Desertification

The word **desertification** is a value-laden term widely used in the media, as well as by many involved in environmental debates. It is not well-defined and includes many distinct land degradation problems, most of which have already been discussed in this chapter, but it is generally only applied to the arid and semi-arid parts of the world which seem to be becoming effectively drier as a consequence of human use. Global estimates by the United Nations (UN) are that 60 per cent of the 3.3 billion ha of agricultural land outside the humid regions is threatened by desertification. The Sahel region of northern Africa is the classic example. This region of savanna grasslands between Senegal and Ethiopia has an average annual rainfall of 200–400 mm. Like most arid areas it is sensitive to slight changes in rainfall or human pressure, and in the 1960s it was subject to repeated drought and severe wind erosion at a time when the human population was growing rapidly, animal herds were increasing, pasture and fuelwood were being depleted (see Section 3.4) and famine became the norm. All of these pressures reduced protective vegetation cover and allowed desert sand dunes to advance into formerly marginal agriculture lands.

At the insistence of low-income nations, particularly those in Africa, desertification became a key issue at the Earth Summit in Rio de Janeiro in 1992. Subsequent meetings have gone some way toward achieving international agreement on the nature of the problem and possible ways of mitigating its effects (see Section 6.5).

WATER DEGRADATION 2.4

Virtually all human activities take place within river catchments and have the potential to alter the water cycle, affecting water quality and quantity or feeding back into different aspects of land degradation, such as soil erosion. The scale of these problems is now so large that water degradation caused by some types of land use deserves separate discussion here. (The impacts on urbanisation are dealt with in Chapter 4.)

Impacts of forestry

Timber harvesting from native forests can be one of the least disturbing ways in which we use natural resources, but even at the level of low-intensity selective logging the hydrological regime of forested catchments is changed, soil is eroded and floods are exacerbated (see Section 3.3).

Australian forests also face another problem, generally less common overseas — the presence of intense wildfires. The effects of fire on catchment hydrology are not easy to predict, except that they are almost always deleterious. The same effects as produced by partial clearing are common, to which must be added the phenomenon of a large volume of sediments and dissolved nutrients moving down streams in the runoff from the first rains after a fire. Few studies have been done, but data from Lake Burragorang after fires in the Blue Mountains of NSW in 1968 show that the increased phosphorus washed into the reservoir was responsible for an algal bloom which tainted domestic water supplies. Repeated events of this nature can lead to an accumulation of phosphorus and other nutrients in a lake, and eventual **eutrophication**.

Impacts of agriculture and grazing

The agricultural or pastoral use of catchments produces all the effects on runoff quantity and quality mentioned above with respect to forests, but the total impact is greater and the pollution loads include more nutrients and manufactured chemicals. A large proportion of the fertilisers applied to crops and pastures reaches streams and lakes, where it contributes to eutrophication. In the summer of 1991, a toxic blue-green algae bloom, caused by excess phosphorus combined with high temperatures and low-flow conditions, polluted more than 1000 km of the Darling River in NSW. In intensive agricultural areas, especially cattle feedlots, the volume of nitrates entering shallow groundwater has become a serious problem, and in the USA it is estimated that at least 5 per cent of all the pesticides used in agriculture end up in surface waters.

Groundwater depletion and pollution is also serious in more arid parts of the world and in several major cities such as Perth, Bangkok and Mexico City, all of which rely on groundwater for urban supplies. The best-documented example of excessive water extraction for agriculture is from the Ogallala aquifer under the southern High Plains of Kansas and Nebraska, tapped for irrigation supplies during the 1970s. In 1972 Nebraska had 441 ha of land under irrigation, but by 1976 it had 525 000 ha. Water levels declined, and by the 1980s so many wells had dried up that integrated control across several states had to be imposed.

A lesser-known example of groundwater abuse, on which there is conflicting opinion and little firm data, involves the Great Artesian Basin of Australia (Figure 2.6). This is the primary source of stock water supply to 1.76 million km² of semi-arid rangeland in NSW, Queensland and South Australia. The basin has numerous management problems, such as overextraction, wastage, declining yield, unlicensed bores and some cases of increasing salinity. Wastage is the most important issue. We do not fully understand the geology or hydrology of this system, but we certainly know that the water is a finite resource. Daily extraction rates are about 1220 megalitres, of which 90 per cent soaks into the ground or evaporates. This large wastage becomes of even more concern when it is realised that some data suggest this rate of extraction is three times faster than the rate of recharge.

Irrigation

Irrigation deserves special mention because it is not only our largest form of water use but also the least efficient, and has the associated land degradation problem of salinisation discussed in Section 2.3. The following four technologies are available for irrigation. The one we use most (flood irrigation) is the least efficient and causes the greatest problems, but we continue to use it because the price of water is too low wherever government supplies the capital for its storage and delivery.

FLOOD IRRIGATION. This involves diverting water directly from a river or artificial channel. It is one of the oldest forms of water reticulation and still the most common form of irrigation. The huge volumes of water involved usually require complex engineering works which are expensive to construct and maintain in terms of capital or labour (or both). In low-income tropical countries these may consist of traditional water-supply and drainage networks connected to paddies; in arid environments they may be the interconnected wells of a *qanat* system tapping groundwater in alluvial fans; and in high-income nations (or as aid projects in low-income nations) they may involve large dams and delivery systems carrying water hundreds of kilometres to large-scale irrigation areas. Almost all of these systems have high seepage losses and present waterlogging, drainage and salinity problems, especially in arid areas. Very large volumes of water are used, but at only 30–60 per cent efficiency as far as the growing plants are concerned.

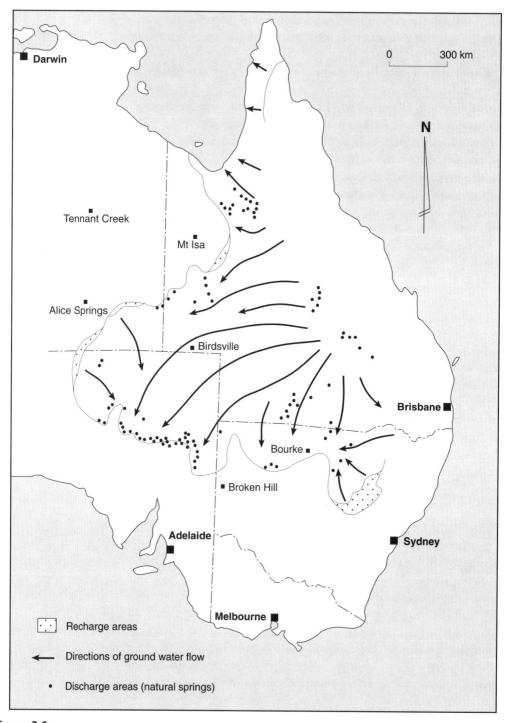

Figure 2.6
The Great Artesian Basin of Australia. Computer modelling of declining yields
from water bores indicates that water withdrawals probably exceed recharge.

SPRINKLER IRRIGATION. This is more efficient in water use than flood irrigation (60–80 per cent) but involves a higher capital cost to the farmer. It presents fewer problems with drainage and salt, and on light-textured soils slightly saline water can be used for some crops.

TRICKLE IRRIGATION. This relatively new technique was developed for use in glasshouses and for market-garden crops, then extended to a much greater range of crops (but not broad-acre crops) because mass production of the plastic pipes and fittings reduced installation costs. Trickle systems have the highest water-use efficiency (90 per cent) and least salt problems of any systems. Fertilisers in the irrigation water can be applied directly to the plants, and the system is also suitable for use with sewage as a water and nutrient source.

RUNOFF IRRIGATION. This was developed in the Sinai Desert 2000–3000 years ago by the Nabatean people.[4] This system of runoff/runon irrigation is a form of water harvesting which taps flow from local storms and directs it to small areas of arable land on the valley floors. The system has been re-established in Israel in the Negev Desert, and a few examples exist in Australia. (These include five properties in the Cobar-Byrock region of NSW, which increased sheep-carrying capacity twentyfold, and the experimental catchment treatment on Kalabity Station in South Australia, which increased runoff by two to three times.) It has considerable potential for increasing food and forage production in all arid and semi-arid environments.

Impacts of industry

Industry is a major source of a great range of water pollutants. This source of pollution is now being better controlled in most high-income countries, but it is still extremely bad in low-income nations where environmental legislation and enforcement often take a back seat to the push for development. Even in high-income nations where 'clean-ups' have been effective in the past 20 years, pollution from reworked, contaminated river sediments may continue for decades after a factory discharge has been eliminated. Rivers downstream of former base-metal mine sites, such as Mount Lyell in Tasmania, Nairne in South Australia and Rum Jungle in the Northern Territory, are classic examples of this occurring despite expensive site restoration works.

Loss of amenity: rivers, wetlands and wildlife

Rivers, swamps and lakes are more than just convenient sources of water for people. They are also discrete ecosystems which support complex communities of wildlife. We sometimes regard these features as an asset, sometimes as breeding grounds for pests and diseases. We very often interfere with their natural operation by allowing them to be polluted or abused: swamps are drained for agriculture, while rivers and lakes are used for waste disposal or dredged as sources of minerals, sand and gravel.

Of all the changes we make to water bodies which affect their amenity and wildlife values, 'river management' is probably the most controversial. River management has developed as an engineering art form in which all sorts of things are done to the channel. Engineers use a number of euphemistic terms for these activities: river improvement, river maintenance, river training, river control, restoration, rehabilitation, desnagging and bank protection, to name but a few. Every one of these terms really means 'engineering works', and most have a flimsy theoretical basis and can often be shown to be actually damaging to the river environment, especially the biotic environment, rather than improving it. Desnagging, for example, is justified on the basis that it will result in improved bank stability, increased channel capacity and easier flow, but until very recently none of these 'improvements' had ever been seriously considered from an ecological viewpoint. In one major reversal, attempts are under way to restore the 'natural' characteristics of the Rhine River's channel and adjacent flood plain in the limited areas where this is possible.

In Australia, natural flow regimes in our rivers are twice as variable as those in the rivers of the Northern Hemisphere, and the big flow events are the most important in modifying the beds and banks. Our engineering designs, however, tend to overlook this fact and use parameters more appropriate to the Northern Hemisphere. In recent years, questions about these issues have been raised and policies on river management have shifted away from the river to consider the catchment. This is where the management process should always have been focused, because water quality and quantity questions all relate to management of the land surface in the catchment, a lesson which needs to be applied all over the world. This approach is embodied in **total catchment management** (TCM), discussed in Section 2.6.

2.5 FUTURE DIRECTIONS

What does all this mean? In the face of rising human populations in the next 30 years, people have to achieve at least five things:
1 doubling the production of food and fibre;
2 placing agriculture on a firm ecological footing by balancing the budgets of energy and nutrient input and output;

3 reducing erosion losses and restoring damaged landscapes to viable
   production and regional stability wherever possible;
4 providing safe water supply and waste disposal systems for 10 billion
   people; and
5 achieving all of the above while living with the 'wildcard' of
   changing climates under enhanced greenhouse conditions (see
   Chapter 5).

Doubling production

It is predicted that the total human population will reach 10 billion in
the 2030s, no matter what family planning programs are used. The
greatest growth will occur in Africa and, less dramatically, in Asia and
Latin America, and all of these people will require adequate supplies
of food and water. To provide these, we must double food and fibre
production. There are three immediate routes toward this goal which
do not involve putting more land under the plough: improving weed
and pest control, reducing post-harvest losses, and sensibly using the
benefits of biotechnology and **genetic engineering**.

In the last 20 years the rate of increase in the production of all foods,
and particularly cereals, has kept ahead of population growth. This has
been due largely to the Green Revolution, through which dwarf hybrid
varieties of rice and wheat have been adopted in many low-income
nations. Increased yield depends on substantial artificial fertiliser and
water inputs. This can be achieved if the farmers are given adequate
training and education and can sell part of the crop surplus to pay for
the inputs. When small-scale farmers see that it works, the rate of
adoption of new methods is staggering. In one foreign aid project in
Ghana, for example, 40 test farms were established in 1986; the next
year 1600 farmers took up the new methods, and in 1988 more than
20 000 did so.

In 1985 India donated 100 000 tonnes of wheat as food aid to
Ethiopia, an achievement nobody would have thought possible a decade earlier. Along with high-yield crop varieties, land reform and other
changes in rural society have sometimes been necessary, as in Kerala,
India, where the changes included the establishment of a local-area
food distribution system through subsidised 'fair-price shops'. Malnutrition has been beaten and foreign aid is no longer required in that
region. Kerala is unusual, however, in not having gone through the
'economic rationalist' restructuring so often imposed by the World
Bank and the **International Monetary Fund** (IMF) (see Section 7.4).

On the negative side, people starve in Bangladesh and parts of
Africa because food spoils in transit or storage and because there is no
adequate method of distributing it over large areas, but also because

land has been given over to growing export crops rather than food for local consumption. Bangladesh has generally good soils and enough arable land to feed all its people, but 2 million tonnes of food aid — 20 per cent of the global total — has been supplied to that country every year since independence in 1971. There are numerous accounts of aid not reaching the needy villagers because of poor transport networks and a deliberate government policy of feeding the military, police and urban middle class before the villagers.

Advances in weed and pest control

Weed or pest management is an exercise in species population control, but instead of attempting to eliminate the problem species we should be seeking to minimise the **propagules** carried into the next season. Although they are effective, the use of artificial chemicals generally should be a last resort because they have unwanted side effects and because plant and animal species rapidly develop tolerance when frequently exposed to a single control agent. We learnt this lesson 30 years ago with DDT but have been slow to apply it to comparable modern circumstances. A large range of alternative control methods is available, those most appropriate being best identified after studying the life cycle of the problem species. For some weeds, cultivation or grazing at a particular stage may be effective, others may be reduced by a timely irrigation or burn, and yet others, especially exotics, may be best dealt with by some form of biological control.

No single technique is necessarily best and the real answer is to undertake integrated pest management (IPM) (Figure 2.7), in which different methods are used at different times in a season according to the scale of the problem, the species involved and the expected level of damage.[5] For effective IPM, the farmer needs access to sound information and, sometimes, expert advice. In high-income countries this is now provided by consultants and is also becoming available in the form of **expert system** computer programs written for particular crops and environments. Transferring this technology and knowledge in suitable forms to low-income nations presents a real challenge.

Reducing post-harvest losses

Post-harvest losses due to damage, decay and pests in fruit and vegetables are variously estimated at 25–80 per cent of total production in both high-income and low-income countries. Losses in stored grain in Asia probably average 10 per cent, and can be as high as 50 per cent in some years. If these figures could be reduced, the food saved would clearly make a substantial contribution to feeding the world.

Research scientist:

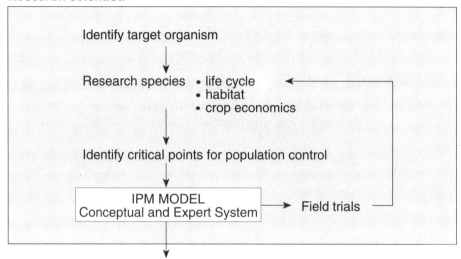

Farmers:

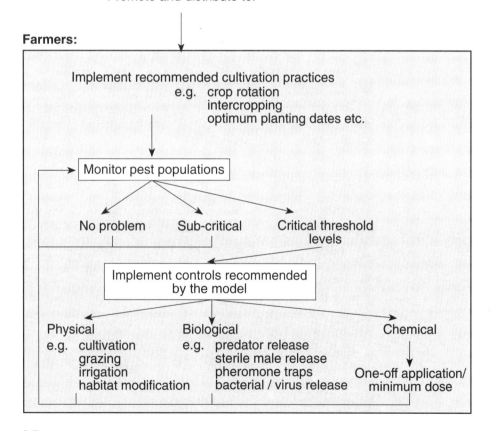

Figure 2.7
The role of research scientists and farmers in the development and use of integrated pest management (IPM) practices.

There are already technical answers to the problem of improving the storage life of foodstuffs. Perhaps the most important technology that could be applied to improve food access in low-income countries is the controlled drying of staple grains and the control of insects and rodents in grain stores. Numerous pesticides are available for this purpose, but these present some management problems such as pest resistance and the risk of human poisoning, and they are expensive. Pesticide use in stored grain, however, can be almost eliminated by silo aeration. Simply blowing cool air through the grain reduces grain temperature, assists drying, slows the rate of breakdown of any pesticides which are used and, most importantly, reduces the rate of insect reproduction. All these factors will improve grain quality and lengthen the storage life.

There are some special problems in storing and drying grain in the tropics. Ambient air temperature and humidity are high, computer-controlled technology is out of reach for the small-scale farmer, and bulk handling is only just beginning. One possible answer lies in the use of small, solar-powered air-cooling systems with desiccant beds of silica gel. During the night, cool air is passed over the desiccant bed and into the silo; during the day the bed is regenerated by solar drying. This system has been shown to work, is simple to manufacture and operate, and is appropriate to the needs of the small-scale farmer. Making it available is another question, but it is an excellent example of the need to find appropriate technology suited to conditions in developing nations (see Section 7.6).

Making the most of biotechnology

Biotechnology is part of the evolving human – plant – animal mutualism which was discussed earlier, but it is a part which is sometimes moving a long way from the soil and our usual view of agriculture, and into industry. Today, biotechnology and genetic engineering promise enormous and rapid changes in the nature of the biosphere into the next century: black violets already exist, blue roses are not far away, **transgenic** animals are entering commercial production, and the limits of this creativity seem only constrained by ethics and imagination.

Originally our manipulation of the form and lifestyle of other organisms only involved the breeding and nurturing of plants and animals, but about 7000 years ago people 'invented' wine, beer and leavened bread using single-celled organisms (yeasts) in the preparation of new foods. The invention was probably accidental but the realisation of the potential of the new products was not, and it probably did not take long to achieve control over the processes. Today, biotechnology has taken on a larger meaning by including any process whereby living organisms are used in industrial manufacture, and by adding the new field of genetic engineering, in which the organisms themselves are modified by **recombinant DNA technology** so that they 'perform better'. In this relationship we can see an increasing human influence over time, from simply breeding whole animals and plants through manipulation and selection of single-celled organisms, to the isolation and transfer of single strands of DNA from one organism to another.

Examples of modern biotechnology include the multi-billion-dollar attempts to mass produce single-celled protein (which failed); the commercial production of enzymes, antibiotics, growth hormones, insulin and monoclonal antibiotics; and the production of engineered bacteria suitable for use in sewage treatment, oil-spill amelioration and copper and uranium recovery from low-grade ores. Is this farming bacteria? Biotechnology promises a second 'green revolution' which may go some way toward redressing the problems of agriculture's chemical dependence created by the first Green Revolution. Some microbial 'pesticides' have already reached commercial development, recombinant DNA is being used to incorporate specific pest and disease resistance in crops and animals, and the insertion of foreign genes into plants for nitrogen fixation and environmental stress resistance are both possible in theory, if not yet in practice.

These promises are certainly not without risk. For example, the uncertainties of how a genetically engineered organism may behave in the environment outside the laboratory have caused a great deal of concern and have led to stringent but imperfect systems of voluntary control and legislation. The potential profits to multinational agribusinesses have created an investment boom in the last decade and may result in economic concentrations of this technology in a very few hands, to the possible detriment of low-income countries which need the benefits most. These and other concerns are addressed in the biotechnology chapter of *Agenda 21* (see Section 6.6).

Balancing the budgets

An equally important objective for future agriculture is to bring it to an ecologically stable state, which means that we must reduce its dependency on fossil fuels, artificial fertilisers and chemical pest control. In other words, we must balance the budgets for energy and nutrients. Several points have already been made about the potential of IPM and biotechnology, and it is important to note that there is still a role for modern chemicals in agriculture. We do not need to eliminate them, just use them differently and more wisely.

To advance agriculture toward sustainability, we really need a new relationship between science, technology, and traditional knowledge. For too long we have underrated the knowledge of traditional farmers, assumed they were ignorant, and disdainfully regarded their methods as backward and unproductive. The truth is that their farming methods have evolved over centuries and are often closely in tune with the environment. We have much to learn from the study of these systems. For example, intercropping is practised by indigenous people all over the world and it includes the following advantages over Western monocultures: better yields, reduced risk of total failure, a greater diversity of products, better use of labour through the year, and better control of weeds, pests and diseases. Intercropping takes advantage of soil moisture in different topographical positions, optimises shade tolerance, and reduces erosion because the soil is rarely exposed. Widespread adoption of a blend of traditional and scientific practices in small to medium permaculture systems could significantly improve agricultural stability and sustainability.

There are several routes toward replacing fossil fuels in modern agriculture. In China, **biogas** energy has become an important part of many commune farms, and in countries like Australia liquid fuels can be produced from crops or by-products by distillation to make alcohol, or by pressing vegetable oils for use in diesel engines. Both approaches have been shown to be practicable but they are marginally more expensive than fossil fuels. Collecting solar energy is more novel but may soon be a real possibility. In theory the roof of a typical farm shed has a sufficient surface area to provide enough power to run a tractor, even with existing battery and solar cell designs. Solar energy is already used for electric fencing and, although the manufacturing technology is complex, the finished product has the desirable properties of being largely maintenance-free and simple to operate.

Another way to reduce energy inputs to agriculture is to cultivate less frequently, and in recent years minimum tillage has become more common (Figure 2.8). Minimum tillage evolved because the most important factors driving change in Australian agriculture in the past 20 years have been the relative costs of labour, fuel and herbicides compared with the prices obtained for the farm produce. In 1973, when about 8 per cent of the work force was employed on farms, one tonne of wheat would buy 2600 litres of fuel or 18 litres of herbicide. By 1993 the farm work force had fallen to 4 per cent, and one tonne of wheat would buy only 300 litres of fuel but still 18 litres of herbicide. These economic factors have driven a revolution in minimum tillage and zero cultivation techniques, strongly promoted by herbicide manufacturers. This has not only given farmers cash and energy savings but

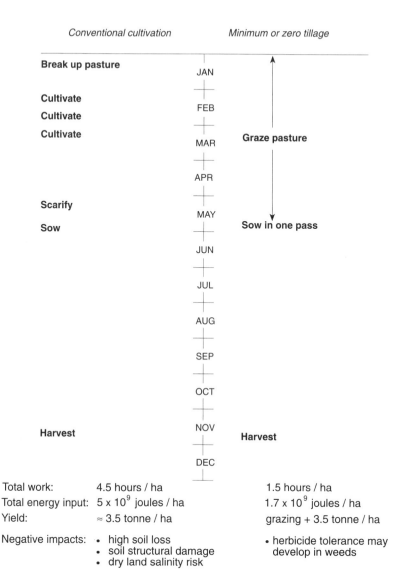

Conventional cultivation		Minimum or zero tillage
Break up pasture	JAN	
Cultivate	FEB	
Cultivate		
Cultivate	MAR	**Graze pasture**
	APR	
Scarify	MAY	
Sow		**Sow in one pass**
	JUN	
	JUL	
	AUG	
	SEP	
	OCT	
	NOV	
Harvest		**Harvest**
	DEC	

	Conventional	Minimum/zero tillage
Total work:	4.5 hours / ha	1.5 hours / ha
Total energy input:	5×10^9 joules / ha	1.7×10^9 joules / ha
Yield:	≈ 3.5 tonne / ha	grazing + 3.5 tonne / ha
Negative impacts:	• high soil loss • soil structural damage • dry land salinity risk	• herbicide tolerance may develop in weeds

Figure 2.8
Comparison between conventional cultivation and minimum or zero tillage of a typical Australian wheat crop. Conventional cultivation requires six to eight passes of a tractor and implements over the paddock for ground preparation.

has also led to improvements in soil condition and has often increased production.

In southern Australia, the area of direct-drilled cereal crops escalated from 47 000 ha in 1975 to 412 000 ha in 1980 and nearly 4 million ha in 1985. But this technique is not without problems. Early trials produced lower yields than conventional cultivation, infestations of root-feeding pests like grass grubs occurred, and herbicide-resistant weed species, especially annual rye grass, are now emerging. With good management, though, the advantages of direct drilling outweigh the disadvantages, and this is certainly one of the modern paths toward balanced energy and nutrient usage.[6]

Reducing soil loss and restoring land condition

In the next few decades we must also repair the effects of two, three or more centuries of land degradation evident in all countries, avoid creating more, and begin to reintegrate the present pattern of fragmented landscapes of conservation reserves, forests, agricultural land and urban land into coherent management units (Figure 2.9). A prerequisite to improving land condition is obviously to recognise that we have a problem and then to identify the steps we need to take to remedy it. Do we have this ability and knowledge? Do we have a suitable battery of technical remedies? The answers to these questions are cautiously affirmative, because we do not have complete knowledge and every person involved with any one problem will approach it within their own frame of reference.

Having recognised the problem and likely answers, the next task is to convince the land managers that they should put solutions in place. At this point the technology of catchment management, soil conservation or landscape rehabilitation is, in a sense, much less important than the sociology, politics, and economics of the whole land-use situation, a point which is discussed later in this section.

Improving access to clean water and sanitation

Just as we need to double food production, we need to more than double global access to clean water and sanitation facilities. In the early 1980s more than half the population of the low-income nations did not have access to safe water and 75 per cent had no better toilet facilities than a bucket or a short walk. There are two scales to these problems: that of the cities (see Chapter 4) and that of the rural villages.

At the village level, big engineering is rarely feasible. We should give serious thought to the construction of many small projects rather than more big ones. In China, for example, more than one-third of all hydroelectricity is generated from 87 000 village-sized works with an average installed capacity of 57 kW and a pressure head of only 10 metres. Village water-supply projects are also better handled with small distribution schemes utilising cheap plastic pipes, or with local wells and cisterns.

A reliable water supply is believed to be a prerequisite for improving living standards and health care. This was not always achieved, however, by placing a hand pump in a remote village. The pumps often broke down and the villagers returned to their old, polluted sources: UN teams have largely solved this problem with the development of a

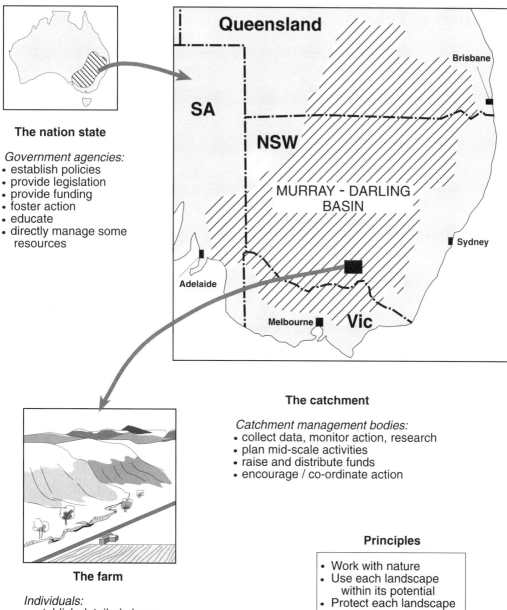

The nation state

Government agencies:
- establish policies
- provide legislation
- provide funding
- foster action
- educate
- directly manage some resources

The catchment

Catchment management bodies:
- collect data, monitor action, research
- plan mid-scale activities
- raise and distribute funds
- encourage / co-ordinate action

The farm

Individuals:
- establish detailed plans
- restore degraded lands
- reintegrate natural systems
- maintain / improve productivity
- reduce energy / fertiliser / chemical impacts
- co-operate with neighbours

Principles

- Work with nature
- Use each landscape within its potential
- Protect each landscape according to its needs
- Maintain physical and biological integrity
- Link compatible land uses
- Preserve special resources

Figure 2.9
An approach to the restoration of fragmented landscapes and sustainable land use; the Murray–Darling Basin as a case study.

sturdy, simple pump and a training program for village maintenance teams. More importantly, there are also cultural barriers to the adoption of better ways of life — health and wealth are thought by many people to go together and they find it difficult to accept that something as simple as a better water supply or changed toilet habits will improve health. At the village level, diarrhoea accompanied by malnutrition is the major killer, and this is one of the toughest diseases to control because it requires a constantly high standard of personal cleanliness which is simply impossible to achieve without the basics of clean water and sanitation. Cultural factors, including class and gender differences, and how well the people understand the ways diseases spread, must be taken into account when suggesting improvements in water supply or sanitation.

The biggest attraction of a new village water supply is often convenience. The shorter carrying distances can save as much as six hours per day, a telling point in creating a preference for any new supply. Time savings of this order are probably the most important benefit of the new water supply because they free the women for other activities and this alone may make a real difference to the peoples' lifestyle by, for example, allowing more time with children or in cultivating vegetable gardens.

The ten years from 1981 to 1990 were designated by the UN as the International Drinking Water Supply and Sanitation Decade, during which time the aim was to supply basic water and sanitation facilities to 1 to 2 billion people. About US$300 billion was spent and the objectives were achieved, but these advances did little more than maintain the status quo against population growth. We need several more such plans, and we need them now. To put the costs in perspective, US$80 million a day was spent to achieve the aims of the program and at the same time we spent (worldwide) US$250 million a day on tobacco and US$2000 million a day on armaments.

The wildcard of climate change

Chapter 5 deals at length with our understanding of greenhouse-induced climate change and shows that even the best computer models are not yet detailed enough to make reliable predictions about the likely direction of change at a particular locality or even in a region (Section 5.5). The one thing that most experts are agreed on, however, is that change will occur. It follows that all of the adjustments we must make in food and water supply will need to be made in the face of greenhouse uncertainty. Not that all of this is bad news, because the enhance greenhouse effect could improve some climates and may

enhance plant growth. Therefore, there will be greenhouse opportunities for us to exploit.

It is not just the enhanced greenhouse effect that we need to consider, though. Even in the last few decades, normal changes in climate
and extreme weather events have had a much bigger effect on food
and water supply than enhanced greenhouse conditions imposed on
an average year are likely to have. Some parts of the world are very
susceptible to extreme climatic events, and not necessarily because the
event is so big, but because other social, political or economic conditions are so critical that the effects are magnified. For example, a
drought in the Sahel region on the southern fringes of the Sahara
Desert, however minor, has a much greater local impact (including
desertification and possibly famine) than an event of the same magnitude in arid Australia because the Sahel has a comparatively undeveloped infrastructure and, on a regional or national scale, a much
smaller buffer of reserves.

The human dimension

Before any effective action can be taken on a large-scale problem of
the type we have been discussing, there are two critical levels or
thresholds of community recognition which must be reached. Firstly,
the people most immediately affected — farmers and consumers —
must see that it is causing them economic loss, inconvenience, or ill-
health. Secondly, the people must convince the politicians representing them that there is a problem that needs addressing and, frankly,
that there are votes in it.

When these thresholds are passed, some form of integrated remedial action can be implemented. This inevitably involves the money
and time of a whole range of people, from the farmers who till the land
through to governments. Intervention will usually disrupt individuals
in the affected community to varying degrees, so if remedial actions
are to be in the best interests of the people with the problem there
must be full co-operation and consultation at all stages. Nowhere is
this more obvious than when experts from high-income countries try
to impose their 'solutions' on communities in low-income countries
(see Sections 7.2 and 7.6).

The basic rationale for the existence of government soil conservation departments and the like is to research, test, demonstrate and
encourage the use of the best available land management practices.
The last of these tasks is extraordinarily difficult as, almost universally,
the scientifically proven techniques are not readily adopted by the
average farmer. When they are used, they are frequently much less

effective than the research programs showed they could be. There are several reasons for this:

- Costs may be too great. Farmers will pick up innovations that clearly make a monetary return, but even the most aware farmers will be reluctant to adopt a technique which will bring them no short-term return or, worse, actually leave them out of pocket. Farmers are no more altruistic than the rest of us.
- Community status may be a problem. The first innovator does not want to be seen to violate community norms and perhaps be labelled untidy or lazy. Extension officers and others need to work hard on their education programs to overcome this reluctance.
- Research officers and aid experts are not the peers of farmers, and both sides need to work hard at effective communication. The 'experts' often find it difficult to take local conditions, including local cultures, into account and need to work with local people in developing practical management plans (see Section 7.2).
- The level of education of the average farmer is likely to be less than that of the research or extension officer, and if the farmers do not appreciate or understand all the nuances of the method they may not be able to implement it successfully.
- New ideas and techniques have to be learnt, and even the best of farmers have to climb the learning curve before getting them right. In the case of a new cultivation technique, for example, the farmer may only get one try a year, but it might take five trials to achieve a standard where returns are shown and so the farmer could well be discouraged and give up the new method as a failure.

These barriers to the adoption of new ideas are relevant to all societies, and we ignore them to our cost.

The typical approach to a conservation/management problem has been to impose a 'top-down' answer, especially when overseas experts have been working in low-income countries. This rarely works, and one of the most important lessons we must learn in seeking answers to all the global crises is that, when it comes to action on the ground, the approach must be 'bottom-up' and it should be the role of governments to facilitate the application of solutions rather than to impose them (see Section 7.2).

Technical solutions are available for all of the problems mentioned in this chapter. They may not be perfect, but we do know where to start. There is an abundance of theoretical and practical knowledge about stock-carrying capacities, vegetation cover, cultivation techniques, the proper use of fertilisers, pesticides, and alternatives to them; and soil conservation methods suitable for all types of agricultural lands. We know how to treat rivers kindly, prevent pollution and clean it up, and how to select the best dam sites and construct sound water supply and sanitation systems.

We also know that most environmental problems cannot be isolated from one another and that they should really be addressed in an integrated way across the whole of the region in which they occur and by all of the people concerned. The ideal natural region for dealing with many such problems is the stream catchment, and one way ahead is through specific organisations working within a total catchment management (TCM) policy that is co-ordinated and funded by government. The biggest problem with catchments is often that their boundaries do not match political boundaries so that larger multi-state organisations may be needed. Precedents exist for the successful establishment of such organisations: the Murray–Darling Basin Commission is a sound example of how such a body can work (see Box 1.1).

SOME AUSTRALIAN RESPONSES 2.6

The establishment in 1988 of the Murray–Darling Basin Commission and its political master, the Murray–Darling Basin Ministerial Council, took a decade of political pressure and the coincidence of Labor governments in three of the four relevant states and the Commonwealth. The Commission and the Council have taken some very important steps forward in undertaking baseline studies, establishing management policy and facilitating practical steps in river and water quality improvement.

Other water management reforms are under way in all states of Australia. These include concepts like water and drainage property rights, **riparian zone** and wetlands management, and integrated management of all catchment activities which impinge on water quality and quantity. Supply authorities are also paying attention to managing consumer demand. With modern technology it is possible for farmers to cut consumption by 10–50 per cent, industries by 40–90 per cent, and cities by 30 per cent. A basic need for these reductions in demand is to set a price for water that reflects the real cost of production and supply.

Since 1990 Australia has also embarked on a Decade of **Landcare**.[7] This developed from discussions between the National Farmers Federation and the Australian Conservation Foundation and is a good example of two disparate groups coming together for the good of the environment. Within 18 months, 900 community groups were organised across Australia and by March 1994 more than 2000 registered groups were functioning in environments as diverse as urban bushland

and arid rangeland in central Australia. It is estimated that about 30 per cent of all farmers are now involved, despite the financial difficulties most of them face in an extended period of depressed markets for primary produce. A number of programs have been moderately funded by state and federal governments, and all have received very strong community support. The principles of TCM are fundamental to Landcare, and plan preparation and action has come from the bottom up. Landcare groups in different catchments face very disparate problems, but all exhibit a heartening enthusiasm, and more progress is being made in landscape restoration and in changing conventional values about the environment than has been achieved in years of government extension work.

Landcare involves education as well as action, and includes school groups who take an active part in monitoring programs designed to collect point-specific information about water quality in streams (Streamwatch), soil salinity (Saltwatch) and earthworm populations (Wormwatch). Perhaps the single most important achievement of all the activities under Landcare is not the millions of trees planted or the square kilometres of soil erosion controlled, but the tens of thousands of ordinary Australians who have volunteered to take action for the environment. In doing so they are gaining a new appreciation of their place in the biosphere. The economic and non-economic benefits of this volunteer activity are immeasurable, both to individuals and to the wider community.

During 1993, at a meeting held in Britain to plan action subsequent to the Earth Summit, and at the first Nairobi meeting to develop a Convention to Combat Drought and Desertification (see Section 6.5), considerable interest was shown in the operation of Australian Landcare groups. A number of delegates from low-income nations indicated that they thought the Landcare model might be a suitable approach to environmental problems in their countries, as it bases action on local communities.

2.7 CONCLUSION

All over the world people are becoming increasingly aware of their environmental problems. Australia's Landcare groups provide just one approach to these issues. There are many more, but they all share one common feature: the recognition that the people who are in the best position to deal with the problem are those who face the problem daily. When governments recognise this and do their best to encourage and fund action at grass roots level, we will begin to make sub-stantial progress toward making agriculture and water supply truly sustainable, and the world a better place for the next generation. When we finally move in this direction, we will no longer be talking just about agriculture or water supply, but also about forestry, catch-ments, conservation reserves, mining, manufacturing, education, eco-nomics, politics, our place in the world — in short, about everything. We will then be talking about the sustainability of the Earth as the habitat for humans: that must be the ultimate goal.

FURTHER READING

Barr, N. and Cary, J., *Greening a Brown Land: The Australian search for sustainable land use*, Macmillan (Melbourne, 1992). [A comprehensive history of agricultural land use and resulting land degradation in Australia.]

Blaikie, P., and Brookfield, H., *Land Degradation and Society*, Methuen (London, 1987). [An important alternative perspective on land degradation which considers the sociology of soil erosion under different political regimes.]

Dover, M.J. and Talbot, L.M., *To Feed the Earth: Agro-ecology for sustainable development*, World Resources Institute (Washington, 1987). [An overview of agricultural production techniques with an emphasis on the importance of traditional practices.]

Heathcote, R.L. and Mabbutt, J.A. (eds), *Land, Water and People: Geographical essays in Australian resource management*, Allen & Unwin (Sydney, 1988). [Essays on Australian water resource use, arid rangelands, Aboriginal lands and problems in urban development.]

Hobbs, R.J. and Saunders, D.A. (eds), *Reintegrating Fragmented Landscapes*, Springer-Verlag (New York, 1993). [Analysis of the exploitation of Western Australian wheat lands, their present condition, and approaches to reconstructing a stable and productive environment.]

Joss, P.J., Lynch, P.W. and Williams, D.B. (eds), *Rangelands: A resource under siege*, Cambridge University Press (Cambridge, UK, 1987). [Conference papers dealing with rangelands management in semi-arid environments all over the world, especially Australia.]

Lipton, M. and Longhurst, R., *New Seeds and Poor People*, Unwin Hyman (London, 1989). [The economics, politics, and relative success of the introduction of modern varieties of cereal crops to poorer countries during the Green Revolution.]

McTainsh, G. and Boughton, W.C. (eds), *Land Degradation Processes in Australia*, Longman Cheshire (Melbourne, 1993). [A geomorphic view of the processes of soil degradation, erosion, salinisation, and structural decline.]

Mollison, W., *Permaculture: A designer's manual,* Tagari Publications (Tyalgum, NSW, 1988). [A comprehensive descriptive handbook for the establishment of permaculture agricultural systems at several scales in all environments. Numerous examples are drawn from many parts of the world.]

NOTES

1 Graham, O.P. et al., *Land degradation survey, New South Wales 1987–1988,* Soil Conservation Service of NSW (Sydney, 1989).
2 Morgan, R.P.C. and Davidson, D.A., *Soil Erosion and Conservation,* Longman (London, 1986).
3 Williamson, D.R., 'Salinity: an old environmental problem', in *Year Book Australia 1990,* Australian Bureau of Statistics (Canberra, 1991).
4 Evanari, M., Shanon, L. and Tadmor, N., *The Negev: The challenge of a desert,* Harvard University Press (Cambridge, USA, 1971).
5 Kogan, M. (ed.), *Ecological Theory and Integrated Pest Management Practice,* Wiley (New York, 1986).
6 Cornish, P.S. and Pratley, J.E. (eds), *Tillage: New directions in Australian agriculture,* Inkata Press (Melbourne, 1987).
7 Beale, B. and Fray, P., *The Vanishing Continent: Australia's degraded environment,* Hodder & Stoughton (Sydney, 1990).

FORESTS

THE WORLD'S FORESTS   3.1

Forests are arguably the most important vegetation type on the face of the Earth today. They play a far greater role in the well-being of the planetary ecosystem than they are often given credit for, and we may soon find that forests will effectively be called upon to make a still more critical contribution to planetary stability. Yet on every side, from the equator to the arctic, forests are being depleted or will shortly be depleted through human agency at a rate that could well reduce many of them to impoverished remnants by the end of the next century.

... forests ... are the repository of a greater abundance and diversity of terrestrial life forms than the rest of the earth put together. Tropical forests are specially rich in species and in the evolutionary capacity to generate new species. As tropical forests are cleared wholesale, there will be an impoverishing impact on the very course of evolution itself.[1]

Such a view presents forests as reservoirs of **biodiversity**, as habitats for endangered plant and animal species, and as essential regulators of the environment. Other people see forests very differently. Forests provide homes, food and livelihoods for many of the world's indigenous peoples. They are places of wilderness and beauty in the eyes of others, havens of naturalness in a world increasingly altered by human action. They are land resources to be cleared to provide space and agricultural land for burgeoning populations, especially in low-income nations, or for large-scale commercial agriculture. Finally, they provide opportunities for the commercial exploitation of timber resources, the basis for a global industry with international trade worth A$150 billion annually.

Similarly, human attitudes to the forests have changed markedly over time. In many early societies forests were feared as alien places, the domain of the supernatural and refuges for dangerous animals such as wolves and bears. Perhaps arising out of such fears, other societies have made the forests themselves, or specific trees, landscape features, or animals in them, the object of worship. Medieval Christian communities saw things rather differently: there was a duty to God to clear the forest, to impose 'order' on the land and make it available for God's work in the form of farming or other obviously productive activity. In some frontier societies such as the USA, emerging from this tradition, clearing the forest had an almost sacred motivation alongside the secular objective of achieving economic progress. In consequence, the imagery of forests and backwoodsmen still runs deep in North American culture and pervades attitudes to economic progress and the natural environment. Similar attitudes have been evident throughout the European history of Australia.

Humans interpret, value and use forests in a large variety of ways, depending on their history, culture, scientific knowledge and economic interests. Some indication of the extent of the differences is given by attempts to put a monetary value on trees and forests, although this is a difficult exercise and some people would deny that it is even possible. One study calculated that an average tree is worth perhaps A$800 as timber for milling, rather less as woodchips to make paper. Yet the same tree might be worth around A$250 000 to society at large if we put a realistic value on its ecological contribution, for example, in supplying oxygen, absorbing carbon dioxide, and controlling erosion. With that sort of difference, it is surprising that we cut down any trees at all. One reason is that the A$800 is paid in cash to an individual or company, whereas the A$250 000 comes as benefits in kind dispersed among the whole community (see the discussion of commons in Section 6.1 for similar cases).

Forests thus have a series of extrinsic values — their worth to individuals, groups and human societies. They also have an intrinsic value — one that extends beyond what the forests offer to any individual or human community — which involves valuing forests for what they are rather than for what they offer us. Forests are an important source of conflict because of these widely varying interpretations: they are valued in different ways, leading to major disagreements over their appropriate use.

Forests are therefore an important and appropriate choice as a case study of a global environmental crisis. They are among the world's most important **biomes**. They are certainly some of the most threatened environments. They are sources of continuing conflict between differing human attitudes, perceptions, values and aspirations. Forests and the process of deforestation can be appropriately explored using the conceptual framework outlined in Chapter 1.

Forest types and characteristics

The world's forests and woodlands display an almost infinite variety, and any attempt to categorise them into types involves a degree of simplification. There have been many such classifications, using different criteria and carried out for different purposes: one of these, recognising six major forest types, is shown in Plate A and described in Box 3.1. It is important to realise that this map, like many similar ones, does not show the geography of existing forests; instead, it is a generalised illustration of the natural distribution of forest inferred from the climatic controls of temperature and precipitation. It understates the diversity of forests. It ignores important local or regional variations in forest types arising, for example, from differences in soil type and altitude. And it ignores the effects of human action: in particular, clearance of much of the mid-latitude forest, especially in Eurasia and North America, means that about half the world's remaining forest and woodland lies in the tropics and around one-third in high latitudes.

Types of forests, as depicted in Plate A

B O X

3.1

Tropical rainforest

Tropical rainforests lie in broad belts around the equator in South America, Africa and the South-east Asia/Western Pacific region; there are also outliers in Central America and Madagascar. The constantly warm, moist climate, with only small seasonal and diurnal ranges in conditions, means that there are no climatic limits on the growing season. The forest as a whole is evergreen, with leaves falling constantly rather than at particular seasons. Favourable climatic conditions mean a high biological productivity (the highest of any terrestrial biome) and a quick decay of leaf litter and generally rapid nutrient recycling, though the soils themselves are often impoverished. The dominant botanical characteristic is a very high level of species diversity, though this is less marked in Africa and at higher altitudes. The vertical structure of the vegetation is also typically complex, with the highest trees reaching 50 metres.

Seasonal tropical forest

Polewards from the tropical rainforests belts, the dry season becomes more marked and forests change character. They are generally lower (no more than 20–30 metres), less complex and less floristically diverse. There are several variants across the Americas and the Asia–Pacific region; in Africa they are less distinct but tend to be discontinuous, with stands of trees separated by scrub or grassland. In drier areas the vegetation becomes progressively more open. Because of the marked dry season, fire is a major ecological force.

Temperate deciduous forests

Large areas of mid-latitude Eurasia and North America were once dominated by deciduous forest: in Europe from the Atlantic to the Urals; in eastern Asia, across northern China, parts of Korea and the south-eastern part of the former USSR; and in North America between the Atlantic and the Mississippi. In all areas, these belts have been attractive for settlement and the forests have for centuries been the focus of clearance for agricultural land. The limited residual areas of forests have been heavily modified.

Temperate coniferous forest

Especially in North America, there are significant temperate areas of coniferous forest. A western belt stretches from lowland Alaska, through British Columbia and across much of Washington and Oregon. Towards the southern end of this range, species such as western hemlock and coastal redwood rise to heights of 80 metres or more. Across the continent, in the south-east, are large stands of pine species, typically growing on relatively infertile sandy or boggy ground.

Boreal forest

Almost coast-to-coast across the northern parts of Eurasia and North America lie huge expanses of forests dominated by mainly evergreen conifers. Their ability to withstand extreme winter conditions by minimising water loss through their needle-like leaves and to grow rapidly in the short summer season ensures their dominance. The characteristic species vary spatially, but an important feature is the low species diversity across extensive areas: often there are extensive stands of almost single-species forests. Such characteristics can make commercial exploitation relatively straightforward, but they also cause problems for regeneration after clearfelling or destructive fires.

Mixed forest

In addition to these five reasonably distinct classes, numerous other forest areas are either transitional between other types, often sharing characteristics of both, or are distinctive but insufficiently important on a world scale to classify separately. Of the former type are large areas of Europe and western Asia that grade into the boreal forest to the north and the temperate deciduous forest to the south. There is another belt in the north-eastern United States (sometimes called 'transition forest') and a further zone in eastern Asia. In the second group, in both hemispheres, there are relatively restricted areas of evergreen forests dominated by broadleaved species: this vegetation is characteristic of parts of New Zealand, central China and southern Japan. The sclerophyllous vegetation of south-eastern and south-western Australia and the vegetation of other regions with Mediterranean climates, such as South Africa and Chile, have affinities with this second group.

Plate A is particularly poor in representing the forests of the Southern Hemisphere. Australia has very few coniferous or deciduous trees, so that the main basis of the classification is not valid in this continent. Australia's vegetation has a very high proportion of **endemic** species, many of which can resist drought, fire, or both. Two genera dominate the tree **stratum**: there are 550 species of *Eucalyptus* and about 850 species of *Acacia*. The eucalypts include the most important commercial species and are almost exclusively Australian, with a very few species found in New Guinea and the islands to the west and north, including Timor and the Philippines. Various alternative bases for classifying Australian vegetation have been considered. The most widely used focuses on structural characteristics: forests and woodlands are defined by the presence of trees (woody plants greater than 5 metres tall), and differentiated from each other by the proportion of land surface covered by their foliage. Plates B and C use this type of classification to compare the distribution of Australian forests thought to have existed at the time of European colonisation with the pattern of the late 1980s.

How much forest is there?

We still do not know with certainty how much forest there is on the globe. Estimates have varied from under 30 million km² to over 60 million km², or from around 20 per cent to 45 per cent of the Earth's land surface. There are many reasons for this uncertainty, one being the differing definitions of forest.

Amongst the most authoritative sources on such matters is the **Food and Agriculture Organization** (FAO) of the United Nations. For the FAO, 'forest' and 'woodland' consist of areas with natural or planted stands of trees, or land from which trees have been removed, for example by **shifting cultivation**, but which will be reforested in the foreseeable future. 'Forest' is land where tree crowns cover more than 20 per cent of the land surface, while in 'woodland' the crowns cover 5–20 per cent. Although this definition is based on structural characteristics, like the Australian work which is the source of Plates B and C, both the definition of trees (for FAO, they are taller than 7 metres), and the proportions of the land surface covered differ. There are, of course, many much more complex classifications of forests and woodlands.

According to FAO estimates, there are around 40 million km² of forest and woodland, about 31 per cent of the globe's land surface. Perhaps 28 million km² are forest and the balance more open woodland, although the latter figure in particular is subject to error. The continental distributions are highly uneven (Table 3.1): the former USSR, North America (especially Canada) and South America (primarily Brazil) account for over two-thirds of the forest, while perhaps half the woodland is in Africa.

Another way of looking at the global distribution of forests and woodlands is to consider geographical variations in the proportion of the land surface that is timbered (Figure 3.1). Regions with above-average proportions are concentrated in low or high latitudes: parts of the equatorial zone through South America, Africa and the Asia–Pacific zone on the one hand; and parts of Scandinavia and to a lesser extent Canada and the former USSR on the other. Among the exceptions to this simple pattern, Japan, North Korea and South Korea stand out as being unusually well forested for mid-latitude nations. Conversely, much of Western Europe in similar latitudes, and especially the British Isles, has very limited forest cover, as do the arid and

Table 3.1 Distribution of the world's forest and woodland.

Region	Forest		Woodland	
	Area (million km²)	Percentage of world total	Area (million km²)	Percentage of world total
North America	6.30	22.5	0.00	0.0
Central America	0.60	2.1	0.02	0.2
South America	5.30	19.0	1.50	13.9
Africa	1.90	6.8	5.70	53.0
Europe	1.40	5.0	0.29	2.7
Former USSR	7.65	27.4	1.15	10.6
Asia	4.00	14.3	1.05	9.8
Pacific	0.80	2.9	1.05	9.8
World	28.00	100.0	~10.80	100.0

Source: After Mather, A.S., *Global Forest Resources*, Belhaven Press (London, 1990), 61; contains rounding errors.

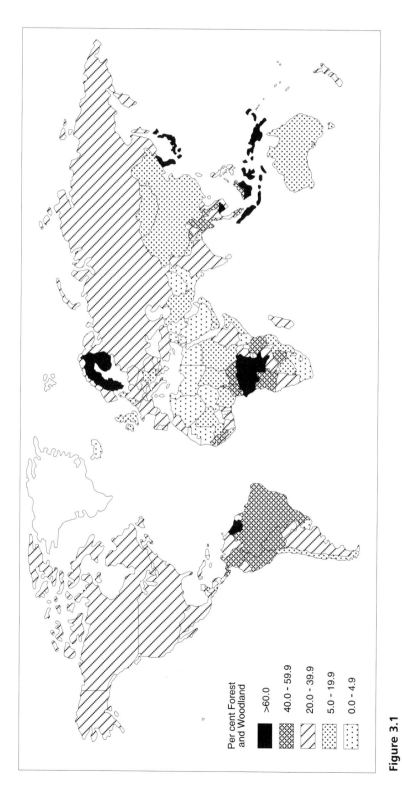

Figure 3.1

Forest and woodland as a percentage of land area, by country, 1989–91. (Source: Data from Hammond, A.L., *World Resources 1994–95: A guide to the global environment*, Oxford University Press (New York, 1994), 284–5.)

Per cent Forest and Woodland

>60.0

40.0 - 59.9

20.0 - 39.9

5.0 - 19.9

0.0 - 4.9

semi-arid subtropical regions of Africa and Asia. Such a geography reflects both environmental controls and human activity.

Much the same applies to Australia, which is among the Earth's less-timbered nations. Only about 5 per cent of the land surface is forested (although another 8 or 9 per cent is classified as woodland) and vast areas of the continent are virtually treeless. By contrast, much of the eastern seaboard is still heavily timbered; perhaps 16 per cent of Victoria and as much as 31 per cent of Tasmania is classified as forest.

Almost one-third of the Earth's surface is still forested, almost three times more than is cultivated. In what sense, then, can this be said to represent a global crisis? Firstly, the extent of the forests has declined substantially during human history and there is little sign of the loss slowing. Secondly, there is a clear geography of forest change and in some parts of the world forests are disappearing at very high rates. Finally, there are massive ecological and social consequences for those regions, and ultimately for the global environment and for humanity as a whole.

3.2 DIMENSIONS OF DEFORESTATION

Once again the literature is characterised by vagueness, ambiguity and contradiction: there are references to deforestation, forest degradation, depletion, and similar terms. Here we use the term 'deforestation' to refer to the complete loss of forest in an area; that is, the replacement of forest with another land use such as agriculture. This definition has the merits of being broadly in line with that used by the FAO and of reflecting a clear physical change in the forest and in land use, facilitating detection from satellite images.

Humans have a huge range of other effects on forests and woodlands beside complete clearance. These effects, when adverse, can be termed 'forest degradation'. They include a wide variety of changes in the physical, ecological and age characteristics of the forests and the plant and animal **communities** constituting them. Shifting cultivation, for example, involves the periodic clearance of small patches of forest (a process often known as 'slash and burn'), several years of cultivation, and then a long fallow period during which the forest regenerates to some extent. It is not, according to our definition, deforestation, but rather degradation — a change in the characteristics of the forest rather than its complete disappearance. The same is true of selective logging — the extraction of particular tree species or only those with desirable properties. In either case the forest can be dramatically altered, but the process is not regarded as deforestation.

One important implication is that many estimates of the rate of deforestation are underestimates of the extent of the human impact on
forests.

Forest losses in history and prehistory

The characteristics and location of forests have changed through geological time in response to climate change and other factors. For
example, over at least the last 10 million years in Australia there has
been a massive decline in the extent of rainforests because of increasing aridity. However, for millennia people have been having even
more dramatic impacts on the forests. Expanding regional populations,
the mastery of fire, the use of increasingly sophisticated tools such as
axes, and in some places a change from nomadic to sedentary lifestyles, all placed greater demands on the land. People learned how to
manage the forests and other vegetation types to meet their particular
needs, and human communities around the world came to have even
greater impacts on the 'natural' environment.

In Australia, a collapse in the relative importance of fire-sensitive
vegetation and a massive increase in the importance of fire-tolerant
species around 50 000 years ago is generally interpreted as being the
result of Aboriginal land-use practices, notably periodic burning (see
Section 2.2). There is also a long record of vegetation change in
Central and South America. One authority suggests that, over a period
of no less than 23 000 years, about 200 000 km² of Amazon rainforest
in Peru (almost the size of the state of Victoria) has been converted to
almost treeless plains. By their repeated use of fire to keep the plains
open for hunting game animals, notably llamas and alpacas, the various civilisations living in valleys in and around the Andes ensured that
the forest was given little chance to regenerate.

In North America, the native peoples occupied many of the rich
flood plains and terraces along the major river systems by about
10 000 BC; intensified cropping gradually converted the landscape
into a mosaic of permanent villages and croplands, regenerating
forests on abandoned croplands, and original deciduous forests on
higher ground. In the British Isles, the fringes of the upland moors,
such as the Pennines and Dartmoor, were being cleared by successive
burning during the Mesolithic period (8000–3500 BC). In continental
Europe, as elsewhere, many clearances were temporary and the forest
gradually recovered as people moved to new areas, but after about
3000 BC the numbers of people and livestock increased to the extent
that the forest became permanently degraded.

Deforestation, therefore, is not simply a modern phenomenon, but was well under way in the ancient world. Sometimes the consequences were relatively minor, sometimes profound. They were often beneficial to the societies occupying the lands, but in other cases they brought catastrophic environmental changes that undermined the ability of the land to sustain civilisations. During the classical eras of ancient Greece and Rome, from around 1000 BC, increasing population and urbanisation, more intensive agriculture, shipbuilding and metal smelting, and minor climate shifts brought immense changes to the vegetation. Both contemporary written accounts and archaeological and geomorphological evidence make it clear that the lands north and east of the Mediterranean were much more heavily timbered prior to this period than they are today, while in North Africa large areas that today are semi-arid supported sizeable populations.

Similarly, India has experienced sometimes devastating change over a long period. Around 8000 years ago about 70 per cent of the land was forested, but the proportion is now under 8 per cent; some of the former forested land is under grass or is cultivated, some is semi-arid steppe and some has degraded to near-desert. What is now the Thar Desert in Punjab, an arid area of 150 000 km^2, was dense jungle 2000 years ago. As late as the tenth century the forest seems to have been actively protected, but the arrival of Muslim control is thought to have increased predations on the forests because the new rulers did not recognise sacred trees and had no religious scruples about their destruction. There are parallels with developments in medieval Europe and Britain, a time of active expansion when both religious and secular communities colonised lands around the settled frontier. There was a deep belief in human command of the Earth and the need to extend that command: clearing forests and replacing them with agriculture was almost a religious duty. The forest and the wilderness it represented was indicative of the old pre-Christian order, and so to clear it was to do God's work.

Human impacts on the forests increased markedly in the early modern period, from around 1500 until World War II. World population grew rapidly, from 600 million in 1500 to 1600 million in 1900 (see Section 1.3). The consumption of food and raw materials rose substantially in Europe and later in the USA. In Europe, surviving forest remnants increasingly fell to the demands of agriculture, construction, shipbuilding and industry. There was also a process of internal colonisation into the more sparsely populated regions of the continent, especially eastward into the mixed deciduous and coniferous forests of central European Russia.

Perhaps most importantly, though, European civilisation reached out rapidly to dominate the world, eventually overseeing the creation of a global economy. Until the middle of the nineteenth century the forested lands were the key targets for European expansion, though after that time grasslands increasingly became the major focus. Even so, the human assault on the forests continued. Several estimates suggest that something like 2.4 million km^2 of forest and perhaps 1.5 million km^2 of woodland were cleared around the world between 1860 and 1978 alone: the total of around 4 million km^2 may represent half of the total loss in human history, which has variously but somewhat speculatively been put in the range 7–10 million km^2.

New peoples, crops, animals and social and economic systems were imposed on existing societies and environments in the process of global colonisation by Europeans. We can identify three consequences for the forests:

- European colonies were established in many hitherto sparsely settled parts of the world, taking with them European notions of the virtues of 'improvement' of the land, agriculture and freehold occupation. Tree growth was considered a key indicator of high soil fertility, so vast areas of forest were cleared for farming. While in many places the indigenous peoples had already made profound changes to the landscape, this new European influence meant that the geographical extent, degree and rate of change all increased. In the USA, for example, the native peoples had done some clearing but the European habit was to remove most forests and replace them with settled agriculture. One estimate suggests that by 1850 Europeans had cleared about 60 000 km^2 of forest in the USA; there was a massive increase to about 660 000 km^2 by 1910, a much greater rate of destruction than had ever occurred in Europe. Rapid clearance also occurred in other colonial lands such as Canada, South Africa, New Zealand and Australia.
- The introduction of European systems of economic exploitation led, in many places, to the replacement of the original forest by crops promising higher financial returns. This was particularly important in tropical and subtropical regions, and commonly involved the plantation system; for example, in growing sugar in the West Indies, coffee and sugar in the coastal forest of Brazil, cotton and tobacco in the southern USA and rubber in Malaya. As well as the global movements of people and societies, the economic expansion and increasing integration of a global economy involved the interchange of such crops on a world scale. Elsewhere, small-scale farmers were drawn into the international commercial market, replacing their earlier subsistence lifestyle or their reliance on local

markets: the massive expansion of rice growing and other cropping in Burma and India are good examples.

- As well as the ever-increasing demand for forest land to grow new crops, graze animals and settle people, there was a rising demand for the products of the forests themselves. Examples included hardwood timber, such as teak and mahogany, for construction and furniture; timber for shipbuilding and materials for naval stores such as masts, pitch and turpentine; timber for houses, fences and railway sleepers; and a huge demand for fuelwood.

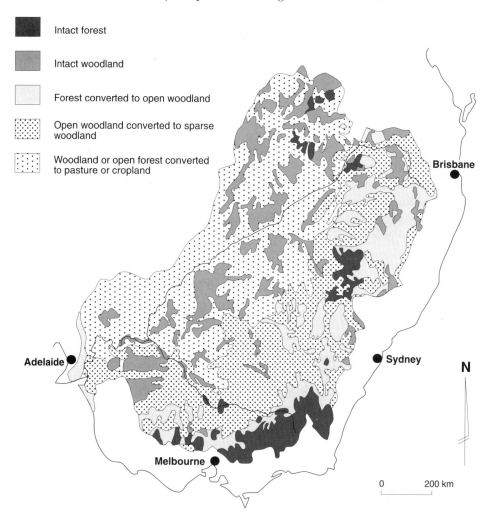

Intact forest

Intact woodland

Forest converted to open woodland

Open woodland converted to sparse woodland

Woodland or open forest converted to pasture or cropland

Figure 3.2
Tree loss in the Murray–Darling Basin. (Source: CSIRO *Land Care: science in action*, CSIRO (Melbourne, 1993), 33.)

Australia illustrates many of the consequences of these developments. Since the first European settlement in 1788 it has had close
international links, first with Britain, the colonial power, then increasingly with an emerging world economy. Its landscapes have been
transformed in playing a variety of economic and political roles: as a
gaol; as a home for large numbers of free migrants; as a location for
profitable investments; and above all as a source of raw materials.
While much of the land was largely devoid of trees when Europeans
arrived, huge areas of forests and woodlands have been eliminated or
severely degraded since then, especially in the east, south-east and
south-west (compare Plates B and C), either to make way for agriculture or to supply incessant demands for timber. Some of the greatest
changes have occurred across the Murray–Darling Basin (Figure 3.2).
One estimate is that between 15 and 18 billion trees have been
removed from the basin in less than two centuries.

By contrast with the situation in Australia, the Americas and elsewhere, colonialism and the rise of a world economy did not bring
massive immigration to the European-controlled territories of South
and South-east Asia. Yet from the middle of the nineteenth century it
did bring commercial cash cropping to large numbers of small-scale
farmers, deliberate attempts by the colonial authorities to improve
agriculture in some areas, and significant increases in indigenous
populations. All this meant a dramatic increase in the farmed area,
largely at the expense of the forests. Between 1880 and 1950 almost a
quarter of the total forest area was lost, as well as much woodland.
Across much of this area the rate of forest loss has accelerated since
1950 (Table 3.2).

Table 3.2 Land use in selected areas of South and South-east Asia, 1880–1980 (thousand km²).

Land use	1880	1950	1980
Forest	888	675	542
Interrupted woodland	592	520	486
Arable	757	1092	1253
Other	1594	1544	1550
Total	3831	3831	3831

Source: Richards, J.F., et al., *Changing Land Use in Pakistan, Northern India, Bangladesh, Burma, Malaysia, and Brunei, 1880–1980*, manuscript report to the US Department of Energy (1987), cited in Turner, B.L., et al. (eds), *The Earth as Transformed by Human Action: Global and regional changes in the biosphere over the past 300 years*, Cambridge University Press (Cambridge, UK, 1990), 188.

So the greatest human impact on the forests historically has been in temperate and semi-arid areas: across much of Europe, the Mediterranean Basin, the USA and parts of Australia, forests have been removed altogether or have been profoundly modified. Consequently, much of the largest remaining forest belts lie in the humid tropics and the boreal regions of the Northern Hemisphere. However, few if any of the world's forests are unaffected by millennia of human activity, so that, although the extent of the disturbance and the degree to which the forest has been allowed to recover vary enormously, ecologists are now very cautious about using terms such as 'virgin' forests (never having been altered by human action) or distinguishing between 'primary' and 'secondary' forest. It is perhaps more useful to distinguish 'old-growth' forest from 'regrowth' forest. The former is relatively undisturbed by recent human activity, and so contains trees of a wide range of ages from seedlings to the mature trees that are so important as fauna habitats. Regrowth forest, on the other hand, typically consists of vegetation which is more uniform in age and botanically less diverse. There are major concerns about the fate of old-growth forests because of their much greater ecological and aesthetic value.

Forest change in the modern world

Human impacts on the forests have become even greater since World War II. Examples of the pattern of deforestation in specific regions abound in the literature: Figure 3.3 illustrates the rapid disappearance of pristine forests on the island of Sumatra, for example. However, it has proved very difficult to quantify the global extent of deforestation, with estimates of the amount of forest being lost varying by a factor of three. Some of the apparent differences are explicable in terms of the definitions being used: the notion of deforestation as used here will produce very much lower figures than broader concepts such as degradation or disturbance. Another question is whether data refer to gross or net change — the amount of relatively unspoiled forest being lost, or that amount less an allowance for new forest, whether regenerated or replanted. There remain real uncertainties about the precise rate of deforestation even once such differences are accounted for, because of deficiencies in data collection. In the past most global figures have been aggregated from national data, some of which are based on careful survey but many of which are approximations, at best. The increased use of remote sensing is slowly improving the quality of information; for example, the French SPOT satellite, launched in 1986, provides stereoscopic images of the Earth's surface at a resolution of 20 metres, much better than the earlier Landsat system. Never-

1932

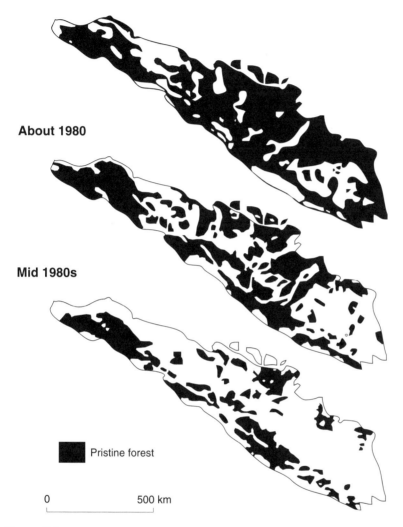

About 1980

Mid 1980s

Pristine forest

0   500 km

Figure 3.3
Pristine forests in Sumatra since the 1930s. (Source: Collins, N.M. et al.,
The Conservation Atlas of Tropical Forests: Asia and the Pacific, Macmillan
(London, 1991).)

theless, many problems remain, including the very high cost of
detailed assessments and full analysis of the information that has
become available, and — even with the best sensing technologies —
distinguishing permanent deforestation from temporary change. As
well, figures for deforestation as defined here neglect qualitative deterioration in the forests. Indeed, all the available global estimates

consider only the area of forest and there is little concern with other measures such as their ecological or commercial value.

Any numerical summary of global forest change must be used with extreme caution. FAO data suggest that the total area of forest and woodland fell by around 830 000 km² between 1975 and 1985; this figure is equivalent to around 2 per cent of the present world total and equal to the size of New South Wales. Substantial though it is, it is now apparent that this figure markedly understates even net deforestation; gross deforestation and total degradation are clearly very much greater. One merit of the FAO figures is that they give some indication of the geographical distribution of forest change. What stands out is the extreme unevenness of the pattern: while there are deforestation crises in some temperate regions, such as parts of Canada and Australia, on a global scale by far the greatest contemporary forest loss is occurring in the tropics.

This conclusion is reinforced by new FAO estimates released in 1993. They indicate that between 1980 and 1990 tropical forests shrank by an average of 154 000 km² (0.8 per cent) annually, more than twice the area of Tasmania; an even larger area of tropical forest was degraded each year. All but a tiny proportion of the loss affected previously relatively undisturbed forest. Almost half the deforestation was in Latin America and the Caribbean with the rest divided more or less equally between Africa and the Asia–Pacific region. The annual *rate* of loss was, however, substantially higher in the last region (1.2 per cent) than in Latin America and the Caribbean (0.8 per cent) or Africa (0.7 per cent).

The same study indicates that, while few tropical nations were un-affected, about half the global loss of tropical forest during the decade occurred in six countries — Brazil, Indonesia, Zaire, Mexico, Bolivia and Venezuela. The highest rates of decline among heavily forested tropical Asia–Pacific nations were in Thailand (2.9 per cent annually), the Philippines (2.9) and Malaysia (1.8). In Latin America, Costa Rica, El Salvador, Honduras and Paraguay all experienced rates of 2.0 per cent or greater.

The geography of deforestation changes over time as forests are depleted in one area and the attention of loggers, farmers and settlers turns to others. In South-east Asia the rate of deforestation increased markedly during the 1980s in Burma, Cambodia, Thailand and Vietnam, while in the 1990s there has been a rapid increase in Papua New Guinea and many of the island nations of the Pacific, such as the Solomon Islands. (Australia in August 1994 made a substantial grant of aid to South Pacific nations to assist them in curbing future forest loss.) Given the large areas involved, the high rates of loss and the number of nations affected, it is no wonder that tropical deforestation has come to be seen as one of the major global environmental crises of the 1980s and 1990s.

Reafforestation

Before exploring the causes and consequences of deforestation, it is important to make the point that forests are not in retreat everywhere. Across many countries of the temperate latitudes, and some elsewhere, there is a slow, sustained net increase in forest area. This arises for three main reasons: forest reversion as marginal agricultural land is abandoned; planned reafforestation to create commercial reserves of timber; and creation of conservation reserves, either through deliberate planting or by protecting areas to permit natural tree growth. The first process has been especially important in the USA, where as much as 240 000 km² may have reverted to forest between 1910 and 1980. The creation of plantations has been important in China, the former USSR, much of Western Europe and North America. The third process is sometimes difficult to distinguish from the other two, but in North Africa, for example, large areas of plantations have been established in attempts to overcome desertification (see Section 2.3). As a result of planned and spontaneous reafforestation, many nations in arid, semi-arid and temperate zones have experienced net increases in forest area over recent decades (Figure 3.4).

Reafforestation has also been important in Australia. Since the late nineteenth century, but especially over the last three decades, there has been large-scale commercial planting by private companies and public agencies. Plantations cover about 9000 km². Although they represent barely 2 per cent of Australia's forests, their commercial contribution is much greater than this, and rising rapidly. Overwhelmingly, though, they comprise exotic species, notably the conifer *Pinus radiata*. There are also many individuals and community groups, often supported by government, engaged in reversing the destruction of trees in rural Australia (see Section 2.6). Finally, there are examples of spontaneous forest regrowth on abandoned farm lands, such as in parts of the Pilliga Scrub and former dairying areas in far south-eastern New South Wales.

CONSEQUENCES OF DEFORESTATION 3.3

Why should we worry about large-scale deforestation? An important point is that, at least at a global scale, the concern is not primarily

Figure 3.4

Net change in area of forest and woodland by country, 1979–81 to 1989–91. (Source: Data from Hammond, A.L., *World Resources 1994–95: A guide to the global environment*, Oxford University Press (New York, 1994), 284–5).

Per cent change

>+10.0

+1.1 to +10.0

-1.0 to +1.0

-10.0 to -1.1

-20.0 to -10.1

<-20.0

about depletion of a commercial resource, as it was for many people with regard to minerals, energy and other resources in the 1970s. Indeed, the volume of wood in exploitable forests is still increasing, and there is not a world-wide shortage. Total annual extraction of wood amounts to about 0.65 m³ for every person on Earth and, although the total has been rising at between 2 and 3 per cent a year (somewhat faster than the increase in global population), it is still barely two-thirds of the estimated annual increment in growing timber in exploitable forests and woodlands. Of course, there are major spatial variations in the balance between wood growth and extraction, so that in some countries, such as Pakistan, wood is being consumed far more rapidly than it is growing. Nevertheless, an absolute shortage is not the key problem globally.

Loss of forest cover has numerous other consequences, most of which are seriously detrimental to both the natural and human worlds. Some of the major effects of deforestation are summarised in the following sections. The point is not that forest use has no benefits. Rather, it is going on too quickly, affects too large an area, is often in the wrong places, and is not being managed to minimise its impacts. As a result, the benefits to society are increasingly being outweighed by human and environmental costs. This imbalance is made worse by the fact that the costs are often paid by groups, societies and economies other than those that receive the benefits. The costs also tend to be diffused more widely than the benefits, which often accrue to individuals, companies or small groups (see Section 6.1).

Biophysical consequences of deforestation

Climate

Forest clearance is releasing substantial volumes of carbon, in the form of carbon dioxide, into the atmosphere as the vegetation is burnt or decays (see Chapter 5). This is not a new phenomenon: some studies suggest that between 1860 and 1980 forest clearance around the world contributed between 135 and 228 gigatonnes of carbon to the atmosphere. The annual discharge is now estimated to be about 1.6 gigatonnes, the great bulk of it coming from tropical regions. Figures like these suggest that destruction of the forests has been a significant contributor to global warming. Nevertheless, the net impact may be less than might appear. One reason is that regrowth on cleared forest areas takes up significant amounts of carbon. Another is that it appears over the last century that rates of tree growth in the great boreal forests of the Northern Hemisphere have increased sharply in response to (and partly counteracting) increased levels of atmospheric carbon dioxide.

There is still much that we do not know about the effects of deforestation on climate. There have been many attempts to explore this issue using computer simulations of the effect of deforestation in Amazonia, but the results have been rather varied and sometimes contradictory, partly because of the inadequacies of the climate models used (see Section 5.6). The current consensus arising from such work is that tropical deforestation decreases precipitation and evaporation but increases runoff and temperatures in the areas affected.

Observational and experimental work largely confirms these conclusions at the local scale. Forest clearance increases the incidence of solar radiation on the soil surface. This in turn increases maximum soil temperatures (by up to 10°C), reduces minimum temperatures, introduces considerable diurnal variations of relative humidity (contrasting with the relatively stable levels in tropical forests), reduces evaporation and increases wind speeds. All of these may have flow-on consequences, for example, for vegetation. These effects mean that isolated patches of tropical rainforest are generally not self-sustaining, unlike similar patches in more temperate regions. Drying and wind action around the edges mean that the forest gradually becomes degraded and foreign species invade it.

Of still more concern is the possibility of regional-scale effects. For example, clearance of forest in one area may interrupt the processes of moisture cycling to such an extent that forests or other lands elsewhere gradually become desiccated. Farmers in Burkina Faso and other areas of the Sahel, for example, certainly see a clear connection between loss of tree cover and desertification of surrounding croplands.[2] However, climate models have not yet shown that tropical deforestation causes regional and global impacts on the Earth's climate away from the immediate area of deforestation. But this may not reflect conditions in the real world: it may merely result from inadequacies of the models, especially a failure to take into account fully the effect of the release of carbon dioxide on climate (see Section 5.6).

Land degradation

Forests have a vital role as stores of water and stabilisers of soil. Disturbance of forests and changes in land use are among the most important causes of soil erosion and other forms of land degradation (Chapter 2). Even low-intensity selective logging affects the hydrological cycle. The forest canopy is opened, tracks cleared, roads constructed and the soil disturbed. The effects are to reduce rainfall infiltration into the soil, increase the quantity of runoff, increase water turbidity, and increase the speed with which water moves downriver. Estimates for the USA indicate that harvesting a previously un-disturbed forest may raise sediment yield 500-fold. While rates of soil erosion quickly decline after this post-clearance peak and stabilise over a period of years or decades, they remain at substantially higher levels than in undisturbed forest; 200 times the original level is pos-sible for cropland and 10 times for pasture (see Section 2.3).

Forest clearance consequently results in the rivers carrying much higher silt loads, which in turn leads to the extension of river deltas, the siltation of reservoirs and a greater incidence and increased sever-ity of flooding. The severity of such consequences depends on a range of factors, including the extent of the clearance, the nature of the replacement vegetation, the steepness of slopes and the intensity of precipitation. In areas such as the Amazon and Congo basins where there are low to moderate slopes, the volume of soil erosion is less than in areas of similar rainfall intensity in Central America where slopes are generally steeper. In the Ganges–Brahmaputra Basin, massive land clearance across northern India and the Himalayan foothills has in-creased the volume and speed of runoff and allowed sediment to build up in the river beds. River flood peaks have risen by as much as 2 metres between 1913 and 1978 in the Brahmaputra. Devastating floods in Bangladesh (much of which lies across the Ganges Delta) several times in the last decade seem to testify to the severity of the consequences, although many scholars believe that tectonic activity and other natural causes have amplified the effects of land-use changes.

Forest clearance changes the chemistry of the soil. For example, soils in areas of tropical rainforest typically have very low fertility: almost all nutrients in the rainforest environment are bound up in the vegetation rather than the soils, and are recycled rapidly by a complex array of mechanisms. Removing the forest destroys these mechanisms, and burning the trees concentrates much of the nutrient in the re-sidual ash. Along with any remaining organic matter, this ash becomes the major source of fertility immediately after clearing, but once that nutrient has been taken up by one or two years of crops or by pasture, or has been washed out by heavy rains, there is little to sustain further growth.

In addition, forest clearance can lead to important physical changes in the nature of the soil. While evidence from the Amazon region indicates that traditional shifting cultivation produces only limited changes, clearance using modern machinery causes considerable damage, particularly by compacting the soil. This may make it impos-sible to grow crops without some remedial cultivation such as plough-ing, which might itself lead to further erosion.

Vegetation

Forest clearance by definition involves changes in vegetation, but even where the cause of the initial clearance is removed, the forest may not recover its former characteristics, or it may do so only slowly. Many estimates suggest that cleared tropical rainforests take 150 to 500 years to recover to something like their former selves. The important points here are that (i) there is likely to be great variation from place to place in the nature, speed and extent of the recovery process, depending on conditions in the areas concerned, and (ii) mere regrowth of trees does not reproduce the original forest.

In temperate areas, forests may never recover. On the once heavily forested moorlands and downlands of Britain, agriculture is much less intensive than in previous times, but there is still sufficient grazing by livestock and rabbits to prevent tree growth. In Tasmania, cool temperate rainforest often does not regenerate once it has been cleared by accidental fire or other means, although it may be replaced by eucalypt forest. A number of mechanisms may be responsible, including grazing by livestock and wild animals; destruction of the seed bank from which forest plants could grow; and shifts of climate which have not of themselves been sufficient to remove relict forests, but which are adequate to prevent their recovery from natural or human-induced destruction.

In tropical areas tree regrowth may be much faster, but even here it is difficult to predict how well forests will regenerate. Firstly, the speed and extent of the recovery depends on the intensity with which the land had been used after clearance. While lightly used land tends to regrow forests vigorously, land used for intensive pasture over longer periods does not appear to regenerate. Secondly, even where there is substantial tree growth the characteristics of the vegetation often change markedly. The regrowth is not the same as the original old-growth forest: for a long period the volume of the biomass remains lower, it is commonly poorer and often somewhat different in species, trees are more uniform in age and animal habitats are less diverse. Thirdly, in areas like parts of the Amazon Basin where frequent burning is becoming more common, abandoned sites may not return to forest at all and the land may be irreversibly degraded.

Loss of biodiversity

Tropical rainforests are more biologically diverse and carry a greater biomass than any other terrestrial biome, though parts of the oceans may rival their diversity (see Section 6.2). They are the domain of at least half of all the planet's species, variously put at between 10 and

30 million — perhaps even 50 million — though only 1.4 million have been formally described. Other species-rich terrestrial environments exist, notably the heathlands of southern Africa and south-west Western Australia, but the diversity is greatest in the tropical rainforests, most notably amongst the insects and the flowering plants. There are many examples of this quoted in the literature. In ten one-hectare plots in Kalimantan there are over 700 tree species, as many as the total number of trees native to North America. From just one tree in Peru, 43 species of ant were collected, the number found in the whole of the United Kingdom. It used to be thought that such diversity derived from the geological, environmental and climatic stability of the tropical forests which supposedly allowed a long period for the evolution of species. It is now recognised that even the tropical forests are subject to more disturbance than formerly believed, and some ecologists attribute the biodiversity to a warm, humid, non-seasonal climate, which is apparently conducive to rapid evolution of species, especially among invertebrates and flowering plants.

Paralleling this diversity, the tropical rainforests appear to be witnessing extreme rates of species extinction. Both the geological and historical records are biased, incomplete and open to varying interpretations, but the evidence suggests that there have been five major mass extinction events in geological times, the largest being towards the end of the Permian, around 225 million years ago. At other times background extinction rates were probably quite low, but it seems clear that as humans appeared rates rose, often quite sharply. Thus, the arrival of people in Australia around 50 000 years ago was followed by the loss of nearly all very large mammals and giant snakes and reptiles (Section 2.2). Worldwide, at least 484 species of animals have become extinct since 1600, with the rate of loss rising sharply this century.

Two main processes have increased the rate of extinction. One is the over-killing (by hunting or the predations of introduced animals) of particular species, which may have highly localised distributions; examples include flightless birds such as the great auk and the dodo. The other mechanism is the destruction of habitats; by far the most important example has been deforestation, and especially the attack on the tropical forests. Species are particularly vulnerable to extinction in the tropical rainforests because many species have few individuals per unit area, so that mating and thus reproduction is more difficult; in many cases species are endemic to very small areas, so that destruction of the area means the loss of the species; and many species have a very narrow ecological specialisation (**niche**) and find it difficult to accommodate any disturbance.

Current estimates suggest that extinction rates in the near future are likely to be 2 to 5 per cent per decade in the tropical rainforests; if there are perhaps 20 million species in these forests, this would translate into annual losses of 40 000–100 000 species, the vast bulk of them unrecorded by science. It is important to remember, though, that such figures are based not on observation but on extrapolations from estimates of habitat loss coupled with assumptions derived from biogeography relating to numbers of species per unit area of habitat. Nevertheless, they do appear to be reasonably robust and are more realistic than assertions made a decade or so ago that up to 50 per cent of species would disappear by the end of the century. Even the revised estimates suggest that species are being lost at rates not seen since the dinosaurs died out 65 million years ago, and perhaps greater even than the mass extinctions of the Permian.

Apart from ethical and philosophical questions about humanity's right to preside over the mass destruction of species — the view that we are stewards of the planet with a mandate to conserve, not destroy — there are at least two reasons why we should be concerned about extinctions on such a scale. The first is the impoverishing impact on the future direction of evolution itself. Judging by the experience of previous mass-extinction phases, it could take millions of years before the diversity of species begins to recover to the levels of a few hundred years ago. The second is potentially of more immediate, utilitarian concern to us: it is the elimination of genetic resources which might contribute to human well-being. There are already many examples of such contributions, even though scientists have thoroughly investigated only perhaps one plant species in 100: one out of four medicines available on prescription originated in raw materials from tropical rainforest plants; a drug derived from the rosy periwinkle found in Madagascar's dry forests is five times more effective than its synthetic equivalent in treating certain childhood leukaemias; improved crop species have been developed; and industrial materials such as gums, resins, dyes and insecticides have been harvested or manufactured. As habitats and species disappear, so do products of current or potential value, genes which might improve livestock and crop varieties, and the natural abilities of the world's biological resources to respond to environmental change.

A former British Environment Secretary summed up both the importance of biodiversity and our lack of knowledge about it when he said that it is

> rather as if the owner of a priceless collection of pictures were not only to remain ignorant of what he possessed but also took a knife to a Renoir or a Rembrandt every other day.[3]

Consequences for people and cultures

Many tropical forests are inhabited by indigenous peoples who have survived, usually as hunters and gatherers rather than as farmers, for millennia with little or no contact with the outside world. The destruction of these forests is having catastrophic effects on the cultures and even the survival of these peoples. In some cases forest clearance leads to them being dispossessed of their traditional lands or forced into even smaller and more remote enclaves; new roads allow new settlers to intrude into their former tribal areas; and contact with outside 'civilisation' and widespread government policies of assimilation and resettlement lead to the erosion and often disappearance of traditional cultures. Less intentional consequences of the breaking down of isolation, such as the spread of disease, often also take a heavy toll.

One well-known example involves the Penan and other forest peoples of the Malaysian state of Sarawak. Between 1963 and 1985 about 28 000 km² of forest, or about 30 per cent of Sarawak's total, were logged, mainly to supply sawlogs for export. By the mid-1980s about 2700 km² of tropical rainforest were being cut every year, the state having become the focus of some of the largest logging operations in any tropical rainforest, and more than half the remaining forest area was licensed for future logging. After government attempts to bring the Penan and other forest peoples into the mainstream of development and encourage them to take up settled agriculture, only a tiny fraction of the 7000–9000 Penan (no more than 5 per cent) remain fully nomadic; most of the others still depend on the forest for at least some of their food and other resources. Until operations begin they are often unaware that their customary rights over land have been legally extinguished and the forest licensed for logging. Denied any other means of opposing the loggers who, supported by the State Government, were progressively destroying their homes and livelihoods, the Penan and other forest peoples set up blockades in twelve areas in 1987 to prevent them gaining access and removing logs. Some blockades were eventually broken up, often violently, by police and army action. Others have continued intermittently and have slowed logging operations in a few areas. As recently as 1993, new blockades were being erected.

The blockades initially appeared to do little to reduce the rate of deforestation or the problems faced by the Penan. Indeed, the rate of logging in Sarawak increased by more than 50 per cent in the second half of the 1980s, and at the new rates the whole of the state's forests outside national parks and reserves would have been logged at least once by the end of the 1990s. However, the blockades did serve to draw international and Malaysian Federal Government attention to the situation. Partly as a result, the Sarawak Government agreed in 1991 to comply with a report of the International Tropical Timber Organization which recommended progressive reduction in output from 18.9 million m^3 per year to what was claimed to be a sustainable level of 9.2 million m^3 per year by 2000, and undertaking more downstream processing to offset the job and revenue losses.

Nevertheless, in 1994 log output still amounted to almost 16 million m^3, about 70 per cent above the target. Worse still, the target assumed a dramatic improvement in forest management practices, without which sustainable yields would be markedly lower, yet there is little sign of serious attention to new methods. Instead of investing their profits in improved methods and in downstream processing in Sarawak, timber companies are preparing for the time when the forests are depleted by investing in logging rights in other tropical countries, for example in Papua New Guinea, taking their unsustainable methods with them. In these circumstances, Sarawak's indigenous peoples seem likely to lose most of their forests and the way of life that goes with them without obtaining significant benefits from the economic development supposed to follow.

3.4 CAUSES OF DEFORESTATION

Forest change is a complex process, with multiple causes and varying outcomes, of which deforestation — in the sense of complete, permanent loss of tree cover — is the most extreme. Changes in the natural environment form one group of causes of forest change. For example, it is thought that the boreal forests may be profoundly affected by greenhouse warming; we might expect these forests to migrate poleward as temperatures rise, but the rise may be so rapid that the forests will not be able to keep pace, so that they will suffer changes in species, degenerate into shrubland and decline in extent. On a smaller scale, vegetation has long been influenced by naturally occurring fires, especially in semi-arid areas such as Australia. More locally still, forests are affected by natural hazards such as landslides and cyclones.

Nevertheless, the greatest contemporary cause of forest change is undoubtedly human activity. Rapid increases in population numbers, changes in ways of living, developing technologies and similar factors have all dramatically increased our impact on the forests. Mather has grouped human uses of forest resources into three categories (Table 3.3): traditional use and 'minor' products; supplying industrial raw materials and fuel; and non-consumptive uses. About 3400 million m^3

Table 3.3 Use of forest resources.

Traditional uses and 'minor products'	Industrial uses	Non-consumptive uses
Fodder, grazing, shifting cultivation	Sawlogs	Soil conservation
Food, e.g. fruit, nuts, honey, game	Pulpwood	Water conservation
Medicines	Veneer logs	Nature conservation
Fibres	Fuelwood and charcoal	Amenity
Latex gums, resins	Minor industrial products	Recreation
Wood for utensils and furnishings	e.g. cork, turpentine	Partial maintenance of atmospheric
Fuelwood		composition and climate controls

Source: After Mather, A.S., *Global Forest Resources*, Belhaven (London, 1990), 124.

of roundwood is removed annually from the world's forests and wood-lands to meet these needs.[4] Around 60 per cent comes from hardwoods and 40 per cent from softwoods (conifers); the latter figure is declining slowly as more of the wood extraction shifts toward the tropics where hardwoods dominate. However, neither these figures nor Mather's table take account of one of the major 'uses' of the forest, both historically and in the modern world: its clearance to provide land for settlement and agriculture.

It is useful to consider human impacts on the forests under the four major dimensions identified in Section 1.4, which encompass our use of both the forests and the land on which they stand. Note, though, that while it is convenient to distinguish 'natural' and 'anthropogenic' influences on the forests, in reality the distinction is often blurred. For example, human actions often increase the incidence of fire and its impact on vegetation. In Borneo in 1982–83, drought associated with an intense **El Niño** event, combined with the effects of logging and shifting cultivation, created the conditions where numerous large fires damaged perhaps 35 000 km² in East Kalimantan and 10 000 km² in Sabah. Selectively logged lands suffered more than relatively undisturbed forest, apparently because logging debris provided additional dry fuel. With increasing human activity in and around forests, fire is likely to become a more common cause of deforestation, even in rainforest areas, a conclusion supported by further devastating outbreaks in East Kalimantan in the early 1990s.

Population

Rural settlement and small-scale agriculture

Population growth was one of the major factors that led communities to expand the settled area by clearing forests across large areas of

Europe, North America and elsewhere. In the modern world, continuing growth of cities in industrialised nations often means expansion into timbered areas or, more frequently, onto cropland which is then replaced by deforestation, with impacts that are locally extremely destructive. Globally, though, the bulk of the 90 million or so annual net increase in population is occurring in low-income nations. While there has been a massive drift of population to the cities in many of these countries (see Section 4.1), the number of people living in rural areas has also risen very sharply. Supporting these people requires either bringing more land into agricultural use or making more intensive use of what is already utilised, or a combination of the two. In many countries much of the 'new' land comes, of course, from forests; the rate of encroachment is likely to be highest in countries where population growth pressures are greatest and where the opportunities for increasing the productivity of land already in agricultural use are least. Such encroachments take two broad forms: the 'spontaneous' or 'unplanned' settlement of new land, often forest land; and 'planned' settlement where new land is opened up according to some predetermined scheme. It is estimated that three-quarters of land settlement worldwide is spontaneous rather than planned.

Spontaneous settlement results in a twofold attack on the forests: they are cleared at the fringes while gradually more intensive use is made of land within the forests themselves. In much of the low-income world the typical form of small-scale agriculture has been shifting cultivation. In forest areas the fallow periods allowed the partial recovery of tree cover, so that shifting cultivation and tropical forests coexisted for thousands of years. As long as there were only a few farmers per square kilometre, and as long as the cleared patches were left for at least a decade before being cropped again, the traditional system of shifting agriculture had only limited impacts on the forest. As population increases, though, the number of cultivators in any area rises, the length of rotations shortens, and the duration of the fallow periods decreases, eventually to nothing. The forest has less chance to recover and disappears at accelerating rates. In addition, small-scale sedentary cultivation is making inroads into the forests, often in association with roads built for logging, dam construction or other purposes. Plate D is a satellite image of an area of the Amazon Basin, showing forest clearance along roads in the 1970s and 1980s. The forest becomes a patchwork of agricultural land, degraded scrub and ever-diminishing patches of relatively undisturbed forest. These processes, evident in many tropical countries, appear to be the greatest immediate cause of deforestation in tropical regions: one estimate suggests that in the early 1980s it accounted for about 45 per cent of the decline of tropical forests, while another gives a figure of about 60 per cent in the late 1980s.

Planned settlement schemes are generally implemented by governments to alleviate population pressures in some regions by transferring people to less densely populated districts where there is scope for land clearance to accommodate agriculture. In contrast with spontaneous expansion into the forest, such schemes are deliberately planned, often on a large scale (in comparison with the often diffuse or sporadic nature of spontaneous settlement). They also commonly form a catalyst for further, unplanned resettlement.

There are many examples around the world. Indonesia's Transmigration Project, for example, has involved the assisted migration of around 3 million people from the densely populated and environmentally degraded islands of Java, Bali, Lombok and Madura to less-populated islands, especially to forested lands in Sumatra, Irian Jaya and Kalimantan. Partly funded by international agencies such as the **World Bank**, with an apparent but unstated goal of 'Javanising' the outer islands, the project has had numerous unsatisfactory consequences. Many of the settlers lacked appropriate agricultural knowledge. Much of the land to which they were moved was unsuited to farming, poorly prepared, or inappropriately managed. More importantly for our purposes, large areas of forest were cleared or badly damaged, and one estimate suggests that 33 000 km² of rainforest is still at risk. Indigenous forest dwellers have been displaced from their traditional territories, many of which were allocated to newcomers: some 2800 km² of such land has been lost in Irian Jaya, for example, and many of the displaced people have taken refuge in neighbouring Papua New Guinea. Under recent revisions, the project's budget has been cut, no new areas are to be cleared, and investment is to concentrate on improving existing sites.

Fuelwood

As well as requiring land to live on and to farm, growing populations place many other burdens on forests. One of the most important arises from the need for fuel for cooking and heating. In low-income countries, perhaps 2000 million people, close to 40 per cent of the world's total, rely on fuelwood or charcoal, each person on average using between one and two tonnes of wood every year. As well, such fuels often provide the energy source for small industries such as brewing, baking and brick-making. In many parts of Africa, wood and charcoal account for as much as 90 per cent of total energy use. Consequently, in low-income nations as a whole, about 80 per cent of total roundwood cut is used for fuelwood and charcoal (Figure 3.5): in many African countries the figure is over 90 per cent. By contrast, in high-income nations only about 16 per cent of roundwood goes to these uses. Nevertheless, just over half the roundwood cut globally since 1980 has been used as fuel or for making charcoal.[5]

In many areas of the low-income world, heavy reliance on fuelwood represents an ecological and social disaster of major dimensions, or will do so soon. This time the main pressure is not primarily on the tropical rainforests, but on drier seasonal forests and woodlands, notably in the Andean region of Latin America, much of the Indian subcontinent (particularly Nepal), and especially in Africa. Across wide belts of these regions, fuelwood use is well above replacement rates. Around many major cities, especially those of Africa's Sahel such as Niamey (in Niger) and Ouagadougou (in Burkina Faso), there are zones, sometimes 100 km in radius, that have been virtually denuded of trees. In rural areas, fuel requirements can sometimes be met by gathering dead wood or through other benign practices, but as population densities rise and the amount of forest land cleared for agriculture grows, fuel demand eventually exceeds the sustainable supply available from timber growth and requirements can only be met by destroying the forest. In either case the environmental consequences are clear, often encompassing severe land degradation and desertification (see Section 2.3), although it is important to note that in some areas, such as parts of Mali, drought is the major cause of desertification. But there are also significant human costs: the price of

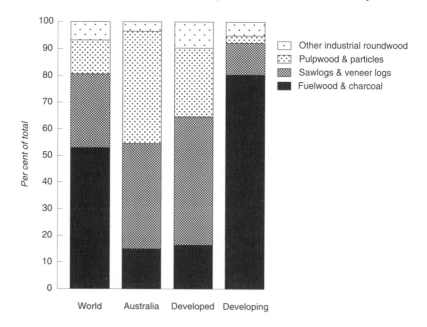

Figure 3.5
Roundwood use, 1991. (Source: Data from *FAO Yearbook: Forest products 1991*, Food and Agriculture Organization (Rome, 1993).)

fuel rises sharply, often taking one-third of family incomes or, where it is simply collected by the users, requiring up to three-quarters of the working year to obtain.

Economy

Whereas in the previous section we were concerned primarily with the individual's search for a livelihood, often at subsistence levels, here we consider commercial activity carried out for profit. We saw earlier how the history of European colonialism involved a few nations extending political and economic control over new territories, primarily in order to obtain control of sources of raw materials for their factories and supplies of food for factory workers, and to secure potential markets for the manufactured goods produced by those factories.[6] Such a system had profound consequences for the forests. Colonialism as a political system is largely dead, but it was one of the formative influences on the modern international economic system. The system, based on capitalist production and exchange for profit, involves a complex mesh of financial, raw material supply, production and marketing links. Few parts of the world remain untouched by this system (Section 7.4). Five factors are especially important in understanding forest change: commercial pastoralism, logging, international trade, industrial production, and poverty and debt.

Commercial pastoralism

While small-scale agriculture is the largest overall contributor to the loss of tropical forests, in some parts of the world the main pressure is coming from large-scale pastoralism. This is true in Central America, where the amount of human-created pasture more than doubled between 1950 and 1975, almost entirely at the expense of the forests. Generally, clearance is carried out by relatively small numbers of *hacienda* owners, a contrast with the small-scale agriculture we have already considered. Their aim is to rear cattle on a large scale in order to produce beef for domestic consumption and, in some cases, to supply North American markets for hamburger meat and pet food.

In Brazil, too, cattle ranching has become a major land use in many parts of the Amazon Basin, often involving very large corporate investors. The rush into this type of activity was encouraged in Brazil by the availability, until the 1980s, of generous government incentives. In other cases the increase of land values was an important reason, especially as a shelter against Brazil's perennially high rates of inflation; often the agronomic value of the land was so limited that production was carried out at a loss or could only be sustained for a few years, but increases in land values still made pastoralism worthwhile for the proprietors concerned.

Logging

Logging for industrial purposes accounts for rather less than half the wood removed from world forests, around 1600 million m^3 annually, although the proportion varies from 20 per cent in the low-income world to about 84 per cent in high-income nations as a whole (Figure 3.5). While most nations have some commercial logging, the USA, the former USSR and Canada account for more than half the industrial timber produced (Table 3.4). Not altogether surprisingly for a land-based industry, the five largest producers in the late 1980s (before the break-up of the USSR) were the five geographically largest countries, though the rank order differed. Australia is the sixth largest country in area, but ranked only fourteenth (and much lower if fuelwood is also considered), reflecting the small fraction of its land area covered by forest or woodland.

The proportion of industrial timber obtained from coniferous forests is falling slowly and is now just below 70 per cent. This fall is associated with declining production or relatively slow output growth in some of the major Northern Hemisphere producers such as the former USSR, Sweden and Finland (Table 3.4). By contrast, commercial logging has increased dramatically in many tropical nations since the 1960s. Whereas in temperate regions logging is commonly at rates below natural or plantation regrowth, in many tropical nations it has occurred at very high and unsustainable rates. In the Philippines, Thailand, Indonesia and several West African countries, for example, industrial timber production grew quickly, then fell sharply. In the 1980s, the greatest volumes of tropical industrial timber came from Brazil, Malaysia and Indonesia, in the latter two at rates which are clearly unsustainable for more than a very few years.

A similar pattern is occurring elsewhere as more tropical countries look to exploit their resources and loggers search for replacement resources: the production of countries such as Congo, Paraguay and Panama was much more than doubled in the decade to the late 1980s, although from low base levels, while in many of the smaller nations of the Asia–Pacific region, such as Papua New Guinea, Fiji and the Solomon Islands, there are accelerating rates of logging. In most cases exploitation is occurring at rates which are wholly unsustainable and there will inevitably be disastrous consequences for local ecologies and economies. In Papua New Guinea, for example, the annual sustainable

Table 3.4 Major producers of industrial roundwood, annual average 1989–91.

Rank	Nation	Production (million m³)	% of world total	% change since 1979–81
1	USA	417.9	24.9	26
2	USSR (former)	294.3	17.7	6
3	Canada	172.2	10.4	15
4	China	92.9	5.6	20
5	Brazil	76.0	4.6	29
6	Germany	54.8	3.3	48
7	Sweden	49.3	3.0	6
8	Malaysia	41.2	2.5	37
9	Finland	38.3	2.3	−7
10	France	34.5	2.1	22
11	Japan	29.3	1.8	−11
12	Indonesia	26.8	1.6	−6
13	India	24.4	1.5	24
14	Australia	16.7	1.0	11
15	Poland	16.3	1.0	−12
	World	1661.1	100.0	15

Source: After Hammond, A.L. (ed.), *World Resources, 1994–95: A guide to the global environment*, Oxford University Press (New York, 1994), 310–1.

yield of sawlogs was estimated in 1994 to be just over 3 million m³, while the annual permitted cut is nearly three times greater at 8.5 million m³, and actual removals (including illegal logging) are even larger.

The purpose of commercial logging — the final use of the wood — has changed quite markedly over the last 40 years. Globally, there has been relatively modest growth in the production of sawlogs (used for construction, solid wood furniture and so on), but a much more rapid increase in the production of manufactured wood products. In general, the greater the processing — that is, the higher the 'value added' — the higher the growth rate: increases have been greatest for high-quality paper, rather less for wood-based panels (plywood, composite boards) and less still for pulpwood, though in all categories the rate of increase was above that for sawlogs until the 1980s.

These sorts of trends have had important implications for resource availability because, in general, requirements for sawlogs are much more restrictive than those for, say, pulping, as wood processing can handle a much wider range of ages, species and conditions of timber. It also means that it is possible to utilise a much higher proportion of the wood available in any particular forest during logging operations. While this in turn implies a move away from selective logging towards clearfelling, the differential pattern of growth in demand for the different forest products probably means some, at least relative, decline in the pressure on the least disturbed forests, with more emphasis on plantations and regrowth areas.

By contrast with the marked changes during the 1960s and 1970s, the pattern of final industrial usage of timber has stabilised since the early 1980s, even though the overall volume cut has continued to increase. Globally, somewhat less than 30 per cent of all roundwood is cut for sawlogs or veneer logs, and about one-eighth for pulpwood (for paper-making). In low-income nations, where fuelwood use dominates, the figures are very much lower, whereas in high-income nations sawlogs represent almost half of all roundwood cut and pulpwood about one-quarter. Unusually, pulpwood is the biggest single use in Australia (Figure 3.5), and this sector is dominated by woodchipping, largely for export to Japan.

International trade

International trade is important both as a contributor to deforestation and in the economies of many of the countries involved, even though globally over 90 per cent of wood is used within the country in which it is harvested. The proportion entering international trade is greatest for the highest value-added products (over 20 per cent in the case of paper), low for sawlogs, and virtually zero for firewood. Furthermore, the bias towards higher-value products is becoming more marked.

The pattern of international trade is quite complex, but several features stand out. Firstly, many high-income countries are both importers and exporters, tending to import raw materials and less-processed commodities while exporting higher-value products. Secondly, and largely because of this, a high proportion (still well over 80 per cent, but falling) of the value of exports is accounted for by low-income nations. Thirdly, around half of all trade occurs within North America, or within Western Europe, or between northern and Western Europe. Finally, in value terms, the largest importer of forest products is the USA, but this trade is almost offset by exports, so that Japan is by far the world's largest net importer.

Japan's involvement in the forest products industry and trade is a key influence on the fate of the forests around the Pacific Rim. Japan is one of the world's more heavily forested countries, yet wood production has declined in recent years as it has moved to protect more of its forests and to base its forest-products industry more firmly on imports of raw materials and semi-processed goods. It has become a major importer of primary products — sawlogs, veneer logs and woodchips — and increasingly of semi-processed goods such as wood pulp, veneers and plywood. Its major sources are the USA, the former USSR and Canada for coniferous products, and South-east Asia, especially Malaysia, for hardwood timbers. These, along with similar flows into neighbouring China and South Korea, form the world's largest movements of sawlogs and veneer logs (Figure 3.6).

Approximately half of all internationally traded tropical timbers go to Japan; both the volume involved and the proportion of the world total have increased sharply in recent decades. The source of Japanese

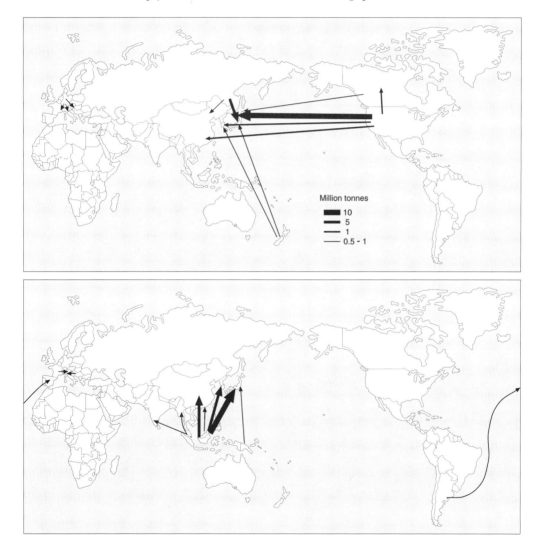

Figure 3.6
International trade in coniferous sawlogs (top) and non-coniferous sawlogs and veneer logs (bottom), 1991. (Source: Data from *FAO Yearbook: Forest products 1991*, Food and Agriculture Organization (Rome, 1993).)

supply is also heavily concentrated spatially: over 80 per cent of tropical hardwood sawlogs come from the Malaysian states of Sarawak and Sabah on the island of Borneo, with Papua New Guinea the only other major supplier. Indonesia, Malaysia (mainly West Malaysia) and the Philippines are the main sources of sawn timber; veneers come primarily from Malaysia; and rapidly growing imports of plywood are supplied mainly by Indonesia. For several decades Japan has also been a major importer of hardwood chips for paper-making, primarily from Australia (eucalypts) and Malaysia (mangroves and rubber trees).

Japan's role in the international forest products industry as an importer and, to a lesser extent, grower of raw materials, and as a manufacturer, consumer and exporter of finished products, has been changing. It is putting ever more emphasis on the later stages of processing and changing the balance of imports from raw materials towards semi-processed goods: pulp rather than woodchips, and plywood rather than sawlogs, for example. There are many reasons for this. Japan found itself increasingly uncompetitive in the initial processing stages as its plants became outdated and it became more cost-effective to encourage investment in new plant in low-income countries, a pattern that also helped Japan distance itself from rising concerns about pollution. The trend has also been encouraged by bans on exports of sawlogs from a number of countries (for example, Indonesia and Thailand) increasingly concerned about dwindling supplies and the need to maximise economic returns. This is part of the context for several proposals in recent years to develop export-oriented pulp mills in Australia (the ill-fated Wesley Vale scheme in northern Tasmania, for example) and for industrialisation strategies in a number of low-income nations.

Industrial production

Many low-income tropical nations are attempting to maximise the returns from their diminishing forest resources by establishing processing industries, to provide products for export or to meet what is often rapidly growing domestic demand for manufactured goods. Such developments mean continuing pressure on the forests, but they do offer the possibility of greater local financial returns and more employment. Moreover, they generally necessitate more sustainable forest management practices: the considerable investment involved can often only be justified if the continuity of raw material supply is guaranteed.

In some countries, industrialisation strategies not directly using the forest resources themselves are having substantial consequences for relatively undisturbed forests. For example, various mining, processing and hydroelectric power generation schemes have been developed in Brazilian Amazonia. There are at least four consequences. Firstly, and often least significantly in the long term, many projects are on a very large scale and thus destroy large areas of forest — cleared for mining, spoil heaps and buildings, or drowned under water impoundments. Secondly, some of the processing schemes are significant polluters, sometimes with substantial local and regional consequences for the forests; there are parallels in the acid rain phenomenon of industrialised nations (see Box 4.1). Thirdly, some processing projects are using large amounts of charcoal: for example, large-scale pig-iron production in the Grande Carajas Project in Brazil's eastern Para State requires logging 2500 km^2 of forest each year. The biggest single consequence for the forests, however, often comes from construction of new transport routes into previously inaccessible areas, which opens up the forest to small-scale settlers.

Poverty and debt

Especially in low-income tropical nations, deforestation has been accentuated by poverty and debt created largely by exploitative economic relations at local, national and international scales, often closely linked, as we have already seen, with overpopulation. Three examples illustrate some of the problems.

Firstly, many nations sought to industrialise along 'Western' lines. While some achieved at least a measure of success, it was often at the expense of the poor. Governments commonly sought to maintain low prices for agricultural products, especially food, so that industrial workers could survive on relatively low wages. Manufacturing was thus a profitable and attractive investment proposition, but farmers remained very poor. In Brazil, for example, this poverty was an important factor encouraging farmers to move to new lands in the Amazon Basin and to engage in the land speculation that was a significant contributor to deforestation.

Elsewhere, governments promoted the development of export cropping. This is often the preserve of large-scale commercial farms and production is highly mechanised, so that existing large farms replaced a lot of the workers with machinery, while new ones often took over land previously occupied by small-scale farmers. Either way, large numbers of people were displaced from the land. While some of them moved to the cities, many went in search of new land in the forest.

Thirdly, many low-income nations accrued very large foreign debts from the mid-1970s through to the early 1980s, particularly as banks in high-income nations sought profitable investment outlets for the huge capital accumulations earned by the oil-exporting nations following major energy price rises. Many low-income nations borrowed heavily, either to maintain living standards in the face of economic recession or to invest in economic development. They expected to be able to repay loans from enhanced income streams, but in many cases the borrowings quickly went out of control and reached very high levels that could not easily be repaid, especially when export commodity prices fell (see also Section 7.4). Throughout Latin America, many nations came close to defaulting on their debts in the early 1980s.

While many low-income countries have overcome the worst of the debt problem, others, notably in Africa, remain in severe difficulties. This has huge consequences for both people and the environment. For example, one means of dealing with the debt is to 'deflate' the domestic economy; that is, to sharply reduce the level of economic activity and domestic consumption, in part to reduce the volume of imports and so leave export revenue to help pay off the debt. The consequence is a reduction in the number of paid jobs, a sharp increase in unemployment, and real wage cuts for those who retain their jobs; some of the displaced workers inevitably seek alternative livelihoods by settling in the forests. Similarly, increased pressure to raise national income and export revenue means greater emphasis on things like export-oriented cropping, with the consequences already noted, or more fully exploiting the resources of the forests, for example through higher rates of logging. An even more explicit example of the impact on forests comes from Cameroon in West Africa: in late 1993 the government reached an agreement whereby France would cancel part of the Cameroon national debt in return for a substantial increase in the proportion of the country's forests available for logging and a decrease in the number of logging licences available to non-French firms. Such examples demonstrate that there is a close link between the international economy, debt, poverty and environmental degradation. Section 7.4 revisits these interrelated topics.

Technology

Technologies are critical foundations for the way we live and for our standard of living (Section 1.4). They are also central to the way we interact with the natural environment and our impacts on it. In the case of forest change, as in many other fields of human activity, new technologies tend to appear in successive waves, each opening up new opportunities and having new ranges of outcomes.

It is convenient to separate our discussion into considerations of supply and demand issues, although the two are often opposite sides of the same coin. On the supply side, there have been major changes in the technologies of timber cutting, transport and processing throughout history. Early in human history, stone and then metal axes were the major implements, though fire was often the main tool in clearing trees. Even in the late nineteenth century trees were still being cut using hand axes and cross-cut saws, and the logs were still being removed by human effort or animal power; in some countries where there is a labour surplus, human physical effort is still a vital means of log removal. Nevertheless, the striking feature of the last century has been the rapid mechanisation of the industry: tramways, railways, motor trucks, crawler tractors and power winches for transport; bulldozers to create access roads; and chainsaws for felling. Increasingly, the whole process of logging, trimming and transport can be handled by single large machines. The consequence of this technology has been a rapid increase in our capacity to clear forests and to cause 'collateral damage', whether through compaction of soil or damage to standing trees by heavy machinery. As one example, a study of part of West Malaysia found that while only eighteen trees per hectare were being harvested (3.3 per cent of trees present), half the trees were removed (for example, for access) or killed during logging.

A different range of technological innovations has affected demand for timber. There have been important changes in sawmills, including a switch from steam to electric power; development of more efficient saws, planers and surfacers; and introduction of more automated handling. Collectively, these have been associated with an increase in typical mill size and have sharply reduced the labour requirements and overall costs, but they have also often resulted in less efficient use of the timber resource, with more waste from a given log. Some of the most striking changes, however, have been in the manufacture of paper. Until the nineteenth century, paper was made from a great variety of materials, but perfection of technologies for using wood pulp dramatically reduced the cost and increased demand for paper; this has been one major reason for the sharp increase in forest loss in recent decades. Initially, the overwhelming proportion of paper was made from coniferous feedstock, but in recent decades there has been a marked shift towards using hardwoods. Increasingly, paper recycling will reduce the demand for hardwood pulp, though coniferous feedstock will still be required because its long fibres are necessary in most paper grades to ensure strength.

These trends have had major consequences for Australian forests. Considerable research was undertaken in Australia in the 1920s and 1930s to develop methods of making paper from native hardwoods. Success led to the construction of paper mills in Tasmania and

Victoria, and to a sharp increase in timber removals from the forests of those states, providing a clear example of how purposeful creation of technology allowed exploitation of a natural resource, indeed created a resource that could be commercially exploited for the first time. Further dramatic increases came around 1970 when Japan began to import large quantities of hardwood chips from Australia for paper-making. Similar technological developments have allowed Japan to source woodchips from very mixed tropical forests, for example in Papua New Guinea. In both cases the consequence was a switch from selective logging, where only limited numbers of favoured species, ages and conditions were exploited, to integrated logging, generally involving clearfelling and the use of a much higher proportion of the timber in a particular area. This trend is also reinforced by the substantial increase in the use of manufactured or composite boards to replace solid wood, as these boards can be made from otherwise unmerchantable timber.

Politics and political systems

Governments are major actors in all aspects of human affairs, includ-ing our interaction with the environment. Of course, their actions do not simply emerge from thin air, but are the outcome of a political process. There are many ways of looking at that process, but at a very simple level it reflects a variety of influences: culture, ideology, inter-ests of governing groups and those they represent, and pressures from inside and outside the country.

Amongst the ideological influences, the most pervasive has long been a belief in the merits of 'Western'-style development, particularly the so-called free market. This has often led governments to foster the maximum use of what they see as under-used commercial resources, often irrespective of either longer-term sustainability of the resource or the ecological value of the forests concerned. Such attitudes under-lie the current very high rates of logging in Sarawak, for example, but have also long been a powerful influence in all Australian states.

These attitudes are commonly reinforced by a range of pressures on governments, often economic, demographic and political. Thus, for example, pressures of rapidly rising populations have led many gov-ernments to implement resettlement schemes, moving people to more sparsely populated forests; beside the examples already cited, Brazilian Amazonia has often been seen as 'a land without people for a people without land' — which of course ignores the large numbers of indig-enous peoples and customary users of the forest.

Governments govern for a variety of interest groups, sometimes narrowly defined, sometimes much broader. While the rhetoric may be about 'governing in the national interest', particular actions may in fact be determined by the interests of specific groups. In the case of the forests, the interests of indigenous peoples and customary users are rarely high on the list of priorities influencing government actions. In many ex-colonial nations there is commonly legal expropriation of land held customarily by native peoples, with logging, mining or agricultural concessions awarded or sold to other parties. Other influential interest groups usually include industry organisations and conservation groups.

There are many other political dimensions, but these three provide a reasonable framework for considering many of them. One of particular importance, especially in industrialised nations, is the emergence of new attitudes, new ideologies and specific-interest groups favouring the protection of forests for values other than the potential commercial returns they offer. As with so much else discussed here, these emerging dimensions are socially constructed: they arise from deliberate human decisions, something which offers some hope for the future.

The political debate over Australia's forests: a Queensland example

Clashes of ideologies, dispossession of indigenous peoples, and policy conflicts between levels of government, geographical areas and socio-economic groups have been perennial themes in debates over forest use and management in Australia. Queensland illustrates them well, particularly the prolonged and vigorous debate during the 1980s about the future of the tropical rainforests in the north-east of the state, culminating in the designation of 750 000 ha as being of **World Heritage** status in late 1988 (Figure 3.7).

Developmentalism and a utilitarian view of the state's resources have long dominated Queensland politics, although the way these ideologies were expressed changed over time, leading to changing patterns of conflict between alternative approaches to forest use.[7] Such ideologies had their origins in the pioneering frontier attitudes laid down in the early days of European settlement. During the second half of the nineteenth century the rainforest lands were valued mainly for their agricultural potential and the high-quality timbers they could provide. Attitudes gradually changed, and during the first half of the twentieth century a conflict emerged between continued forest clearance for various forms of settlement and land use, rarely backed

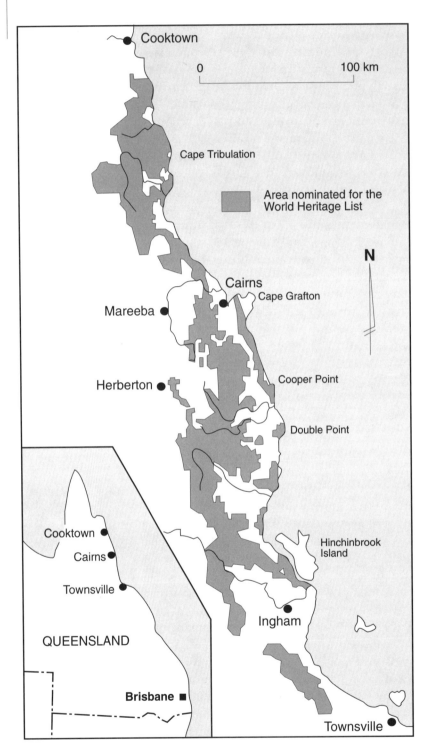

0   100 km

Cooktown

Cape Tribulation

Area nominated for the
World Heritage List

N

Cairns
Cape Grafton

Mareeba

Herberton

Cooper Point

Double Point

Hinchinbrook
Island

Cooktown

Cairns

Townsville

Ingham

QUEENSLAND

Brisbane ■

Townsville

Figure 3.7
The Wet Tropics of
Queensland World
Heritage Area.
(Source: After
Mercer, D.,
*A Question of
Balance: Natural
resources conflict
issues in Australia*,
Federation Press
(Sydney, 1991), 112.)

by any scientific or economic analysis, and maintenance of the forest cover for production forestry. After about 1960, pressures to clear rainforests for settlement and other land uses (tobacco growing and dairying on the Atherton Tablelands, for example) gradually subsided, but commercial forestry later became increasingly challenged by an emerging campaign to preserve what was left of the rainforests, a challenge which eventually led to the World Heritage listing.

Developmentalism, perhaps the dominant theme in Queensland politics and life (as in several other states), was increasingly challenged, and in this case defeated, by a largely urban-based conservation movement. But there were other dimensions to the conflict, in particular the conflict between state and federal governments. Land use is generally a state responsibility in Australia and the Queensland National Party government, in power from 1957 to 1989, pursued a strong campaign in pursuit of its developmentalist goals, exploiting anti-federalist rhetoric and sentiments.

World Heritage nominations must be made by national governments. So after attempts to reach compromise with Queensland over management of its north-east rainforests failed, the Commonwealth determined to take this course as the route most likely to ensure their protection: successful nomination would allow the Commonwealth to override the normal powers of the states by virtue of its superior constitutional powers relating to international obligations. The nomination was eventually approved and the Commonwealth's powers survived a High Court challenge from the Queensland Government. The 'Wet Tropics of Queensland' region, extending over almost 9000 km^2, was added to the World Heritage list by UNESCO's World Heritage Committee meeting in Brasilia in December 1988.

The details of this case study are unique, but many of the issues run through numerous debates, some resolved but many continuing, about the management and use of Australia's forests. Those debates typically focus on the perennial conflict between developmentalism and exploitation on the one hand and preservation on the other, often simplistically expressed as 'jobs versus the environment'. But commonly a variety of other issues are threaded through such conflicts: for example, competition for increasingly scarce high-quality timber resources between different commercial users of the forests; differences between political parties; conflicts between state and federal governments; disagreements over the ecological value of particular forests and their ability to regenerate after logging; increasingly strenuous criticism of the quality of forest management being exercised by state authorities; the low return to the public purse from commercial forest exploitation; and, in a few cases, land claims from Aboriginal Australians. This is an excellent example of the complexity of the human dimensions of most environmental debates.

Tasmania's forests

Debates over the use and conservation of forests have been especially prominent, and particularly vigorous, in Tasmania. This reflects the relatively large proportion of the state which is, or has been, tree-covered; Tasmania's narrow economic base with its reliance upon a limited range of resource-based activities; its consequent economic vulnerability; and a strong culture of developmentalism that pervades Tasmanian politics and society.

Forestry and forest products industries have long played a central role in Tasmania. The basis for this was established in the decades around the beginning of the twentieth century when the State Government evolved a system of offering potential investors exclusive rights, generally at very low cost, over large tracts of publicly owned forests; this was seen as an appropriate way of attracting investment, encouraging industrial development, and creating employment. At first this concession system was used to attract sawmilling companies, but the development of new technology in the 1930s to enable paper to be made from eucalypts led to the establishment of several paper mills and a rapid increase in the exploitation of the forests. Further massive increases came in the early 1970s with the establishment of the woodchip trade with Japan, a trade in which Tasmania has the largest share of any Australia state.

In the 1990s the forest products industry plays a larger role in Tasmania's economy than in any other state. Nevertheless, while the volume of timber extracted from the forests has continued to increase, the industry's economic contribution, and especially the number of jobs created, has been in decline. This is partly because a large and increasing share of timber goes to end uses, such as woodchip exports and local paper-making, where job creation is inherently low, and partly because rapid structural change within all branches of the forest products industries has seen the replacement of labour-intensive facilities with generally larger, capital-intensive operations.

Tasmania has been left with an unfortunate paradox: on the one hand, increasing timber extractions at well above sustainable levels in the name of economic development and individual profit, and consequently rising environmental costs of logging (especially in old-growth forests), yet on the other hand declining employment levels and other economic benefits. It is thus not surprising that the forests have been the focus of numerous conflicts.

Indeed, Tasmania has been the scene of some of Australia's most important environmental battles. Two of the most important have been those surrounding plans to flood the Serpentine Valley and so drown Lake Pedder in the early 1970s and to dam the Franklin River in the early 1980s, in each case to allow the generation of additional hydroelectric power. The former scheme eventually proceeded while the latter was ultimately prevented by the Federal Government. Its right to do so had survived a Tasmanian Government challenge in the High Court, that right deriving from the area being included on the World Heritage List ('The Western Tasmania Wilderness National Parks') and the resultant international treaty obligations that allowed the Federal Government to override the normal State Government control over such matters. The importance of these events lies, firstly, in the environmental consequences of the two outcomes; secondly, in confirming the Commonwealth's constitutional powers in such matters (which it may or may not choose to exercise); thirdly, in dramatically increasing the public's awareness of the issues involved and the environmental costs of natural resource exploitation in Tasmania (an awareness that extended far beyond the specific cases being fought at the time); and finally, in underlining the importance of mobilising that support at national and, indeed, international level — as was done in the Franklin case — in campaigns to overcome the normally dominant developmentalism of states like Tasmania.

Despite the conservation movement's success in the Franklin case, there has been a succession of environmental battles since then, many of them surrounding the fate of Tasmania's forests. In most cases the same underlying issues have emerged, although while the State Government's resource exploitation approach has changed relatively little, the Commonwealth has shown itself reluctant to intervene decisively in the way it did over the Franklin Dam. There have been some successes for environmentalists, most notably the extension of the existing World Heritage Area in 1989 to protect significant old-growth forest areas (forming the 'Tasmanian Wilderness World Heritage Area'), and the abandonment by the potential investors of a proposed export pulp mill at Wesley Vale in the face of extensive local and national protests and possible Commonwealth intervention. Yet Tasmania's forests remain under severe threat: licences for woodchip exports have been renewed and new ones granted by the Commonwealth; forestry operations have moved into new areas, including old-growth forests of high conservation value; and large areas of forest, especially in the north-east and the north-west, remain unprotected from further exploitation. Conflict over Tasmania's forests seems destined to continue until the last unprotected old-growth stands have been logged.

3.5 CONCLUSION

Humans are having huge impacts on the forests. Destruction and profound modification of forests continue with little sign of slowing, at least at a global level. Yet humanity is making some progress in coming to terms with the future of the forests: there is growing recognition of the finite nature of the forests; of the multiplicity of ways of interpreting and evaluating them; of the importance of seeking to attain intergenerational equity of access to whatever the forests offer; and of the fact that they have intrinsic value, a worth that goes beyond what they offer humanity. While people have been managing and even protecting forests for centuries, growing awareness and increasing understanding surely provide the basis for achieving less damaging, more sustainable human interaction with the forests.

This is not the place for a lengthy treatise on forest management. It is, however, useful to conclude by outlining a framework that links the innumerable management strategies that are being used or contemplated (Table 3.5). This framework recognises that there are multiple objectives in forest management, that particular types of management strategies can be used to achieve specific objectives, and that the 'action spaces' for specific strategies can vary in geographical scale or political jurisdiction from the local to the global (with many spanning two or three levels). It is all too easy to develop a list of possible strategies to manage forests and to ameliorate human impacts on them, without providing much sense of how the various strategies fit together; Table 3.5 is an attempt to overcome this problem.

A clear message of this framework is that action is required at all geographical or political scales, a point developed in more general terms in Section 7.2. At the local scale, one possibility is to try to reduce the destructiveness of shifting cultivation under conditions of rapid population increase. Numerous experiments have been carried out to employ 'low-input' soil management techniques that minimise the need for purchased inputs such as fertiliser and maximise the recycling of nutrients, thus alleviating many of the problems of fertility loss arising from 'slash and burn' agriculture as population densities increase. If successful, this should reduce the need for continual clearance of more forest, but techniques need to be applied to deal with specific combinations of soil characteristics, climate and social structure. One project in the Amazonian region of Peru was outstandingly successful in that every hectare cultivated using these methods eliminated the need to clear five to ten hectares of forest every year.

Table 3.5 An illustrative typology of strategies for forest management.

Issue/objective	Geographical scale / level of political jurisdiction				
	Local	Regional	National	International	Global
Preserve natural areas		Create reserves and parks	Create reserves and parks; seek World Heritage status; end subsidies or incentives for logging	Debt swaps; bans on imports of tropical timber; cross-border reserves	Include on UNESCO's World Heritage list
Maintain environmental services	Improve forestry practices; encourage forest regeneration	Create reserves and parks; reafforestation programs	Create reserves and parks; reafforestation programs; value natural resources appropriately	Debt swaps	UNCED conventions
Protect indigenous peoples	Community action (e.g., Penan blockades)	Create reserves	Create reserves; reform land tenure; introduce land rights legislation	Debt swaps	Human rights conventions
Provide domestic fuel	Plant fast-growing species for fuel		Provide alternative fuels at affordable prices	Assist with appropriate energy technology	
Land for shifting agriculture	Improve efficiency of shifting agriculture		Reform land tenure		
Provide commercial timber resources		Reafforestation programs	Reafforestation programs		International Tropical Timber Organization; Tropical Forestry Action Plan
Promote economic development	Local self-help development schemes	Improve management of forest resources	Downstream processing of timber; develop alternative resources; ban exports of unprocessed timber; value natural timber resources appropriately	Expand and reform development assistance programs	International Tropical Timber Organization; Tropical Forestry Action Plan; assistance through Global Environment Facility

A different range of strategies can be employed at regional or national scales. For example, wilderness protection and reafforestation schemes are usually conceived at these levels. The Australian Government's success in ensuring the protection of forests of high conservation value in Queensland, New South Wales and Tasmania by securing designation as World Heritage Areas, sometimes in the face of opposition from state administrations, is in the former category. In the latter category, the Federal Government recognised the ecological (and electoral?) benefits of tree planting with its commitment in the 1989 *Environment Statement* to ensure the planting of 1000 million trees by the end of the century, later revised to a commitment to oversee the establishment, through planting and natural seeding, of 1000 million trees, a recognition of the fact that it was unlikely that the country could actually plant the 230 000 trees every day required by the first announcement. Despite this high-profile gesture, the Federal Government has done little during the early 1990s to discourage further clearance of forests and woodlands. Indeed, it has continued to renew and even extend licences for the export of woodchips. These apparently conflicting actions well illustrate the difficulties democratic governments often face in balancing the competing claims of different interest groups.

At the international and global levels — as used here, the first implies bilateral relations or links between a small number of nations, whereas the second relates to the worldwide community at large or a major part of it — a new series of issues and strategies emerges. One widely discussed approach at the bilateral level is the debt swap (see Section 7.4). The burgeoning national debts of many low-income nations have required them to increase the exploitation of whatever resources they possess and have often caused them to embark on ecologically unsustainable development paths, often merely to pay the interest bill. The debt swap came to prominence in the late 1980s as a means whereby debtor nations agreed to protect areas of forest in return for part of the debt being written off.

Some of the potentially most powerful policy options, however, involve political and economic action at the global level. These are reviewed in Section 6.5 and Chapter 7. For the moment, it is appropriate to conclude that securing the future of the forests requires a huge range of actions planned and carried out across all geographical scales and political levels. They must recognise the diversity of human viewpoints and objectives, seeking wherever possible to achieve those objectives via less destructive routes. Most importantly, they must build on a clear understanding of the origins of ecological change. Contributing to this understanding is the primary purpose of this chapter and this book.

FURTHER READING

Adam, P., *Australian Rain Forests*, Clarendon Press (Oxford, 1992).
[A comprehensive discussion of the ecology of Australian rainforests.]

Aiken, S.R. and Leigh, C.H., *Vanishing Rain Forests: The ecological transition in Malaysia*, Clarendon Press (Oxford, 1992). [An excellent discussion of the ecology of Malaysian forests, the history of human impacts on them, and contemporary management issues; it includes a useful discussion of recent conflicts in Sarawak and Sabah.]

Australian Heritage Commission, *The Rainforest Legacy: Australian National Rainforest Study*, Australian Government Publishing Service (Canberra, 1987). [A three-volume publication which includes a wide range of technical material on the ecology of Australian rainforests and surveys of recent management issues.]

Cleary, M. and Eaton, P., *Borneo: Change and development*, Oxford University Press (Singapore, 1992). [Useful in setting contemporary problems of forest use and deforestation into the wider geographical context.]

Coveney, J., *Australia's Conservation Reserves*, Cambridge University Press (Cambridge, UK, 1993). [A helpful introduction to a wider range of conservation issues and types of reserves in Australia.]

Grainger, A. *Controlling Tropical Deforestation*, Earthscan (London, 1993). [A wide-ranging survey of the causes and effects of tropical deforestation.]

Mather, A.S., *Global Forest Resources*, Belhaven Press (London, 1990). [A detailed examination of human exploitation of the world's forests.]

Mather, A.S., *Afforestation: Policies, planning and progress*, Belhaven Press (London, 1993). [Includes chapters on afforestation in a wide range of the world's nations, including Australia.]

Mercer, D., *A Question of Balance: Natural resource conflict issues in Australia*, Federation Press (Sydney, 1991). [An excellent, detailed investigation of conflicts over use of natural resources in Australia; two of the six major chapters relate to forests.]

Park, C.C., *Tropical Rainforests*, Routledge (London, 1992). [A concise summary of the characteristics of tropical rainforests, the causes and consequences of tropical deforestation, and possible solutions; an excellent starting point for further reading on these topics.]

Turner, B.L. et al., *The Earth as Transformed by Human Action: Global and regional changes in the biosphere over the past 300 years*, Cambridge University Press (Cambridge, UK, 1990). [This huge compilation of material on a wide range of environmental changes includes an excellent chapter on forests.]

Whitmore, T.C., *An Introduction to Tropical Rain Forests*, Clarendon Press (Oxford, 1990). [Focuses on the ecology of tropical rainforests, with detailed consideration of features such as flora and fauna, nutrient cycling, biodiversity and human impacts.]

Williams, M., *Americans and Their Forests: An historical geography*, Cambridge University Press (Cambridge, UK, 1989). [The definitive text on the history of human exploitation of forests in the USA; hugely detailed, but an excellent example of the historical geographer's craft.]

World Conservation Monitoring Centre, *Global Biodiversity: Status of the Earth's living resources*, Chapman and Hall (London, 1992). [A major survey of biodiversity with a detailed treatment of biodiversity in many of the world's major environments, including forests.]

NOTES

1   Myers, N., 'The future of forests', in Friday, L. and Laskey, R. (eds), *The Fragile Environment*, Cambridge University Press (Cambridge, UK, 1989), 23.

2   Harrison, P., *The Third Revolution: Population, environment and a sustainable world*, Penguin (Harmondsworth, UK, 1992), Chapter 10.

3   Annual Lecture to the Environment Research Council by the Rt Hon. Chris Patten MP, UK Secretary for the Environment, 20 November 1990.

4   Roundwood is wood in its natural state as felled or otherwise harvested. The figure of 3400 million m^3 includes measures or estimates of all commercial and subsistence extraction of timber; it excludes forests burned or allowed to rot in situ; for example, in making way for agriculture.

5   The volume of fuelwood used globally has risen year by year since 1980, but as a proportion of total roundwood cut it has fluctuated between 50 and 53 per cent. The proportion has been highest when high-income nations have been suffering recession (so that their use of industrial roundwood is depressed) and lowest when they have been experiencing boom (and their industrial roundwood use is buoyant).

6   There were other motivations, more or less closely intertwined, including a search for additional labour, or for homes for surplus workers, or a desire to propagate Christianity. Most of these motivations were closely linked with spreading modern capitalism to new territories.

7   This material draws primarily on Frawley, K.J., 'Queensland rainforest management: frontier attitudes and public policy', *Journal of Rural Studies* **7(3)** (1991), 219–39.

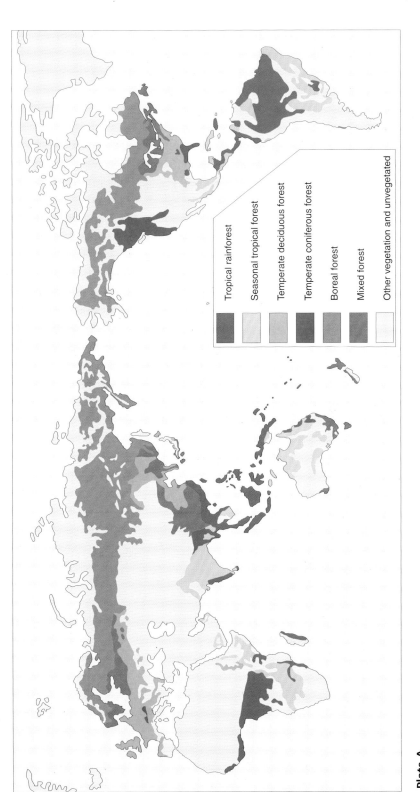

Plate A

Global distribution of forests. The forest types shown are described in Box 3.1.
(Source: Adapted from *The Times Atlas of the World* (Comprehensive edition),
Times Books (London, 1980), Plate 5.)

Legend:

- Tropical rainforest
- Seasonal tropical forest
- Temperate deciduous forest
- Temperate coniferous forest
- Boreal forest
- Mixed forest
- Other vegetation and unvegetated

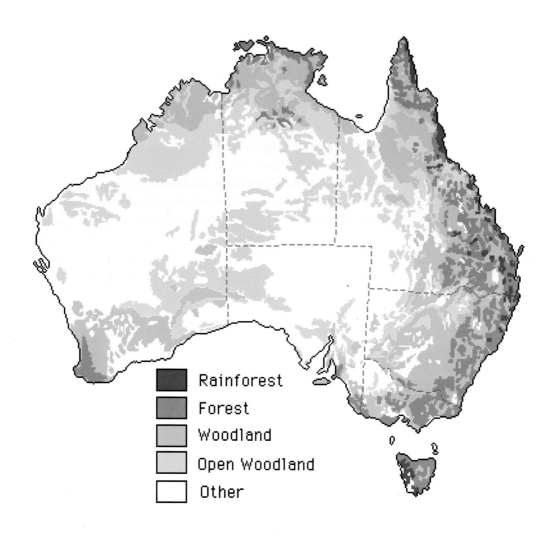

Rainforest
Forest
Woodland
Open Woodland
Other

Plate B
Forests and woodlands in Australia, c. 1788. (Source: Adapted from AUSMAP, *Natural Vegetation: Australia's vegetation in the 1780s*, Australian Surveying and Land Information Group (Canberra, 1989).)

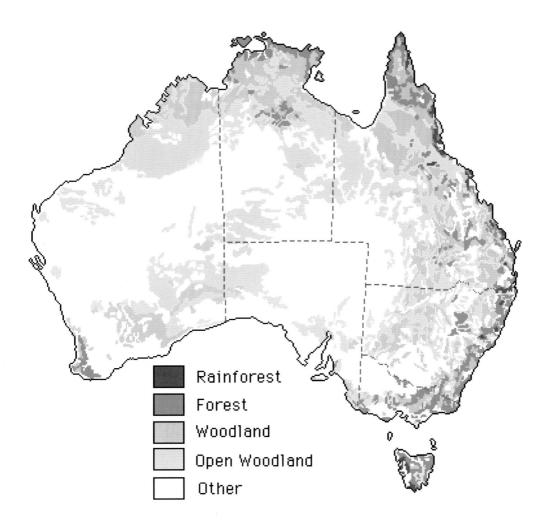

Rainforest
Forest
Woodland
Open Woodland
Other

Plate C
Forests and woodlands in Australia, c. 1988. (Source: Adapted from AUSMAP,
Present Vegetation: Australia's vegetation in the 1980s, Australian Surveying
and Land Information Group (Canberra, 1989).)

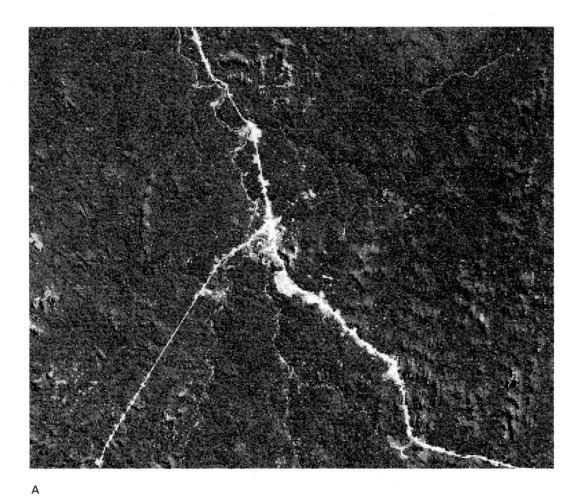

A

Plate D
Tropical deforestation in the Amazon. Satellite images of land cover in an area of Rondônia, Brazil in A) 1975 and B) 1986 (opposite). Notice the importance of transport routes in opening up the rainforest (which shows as red-purple in these false-colour images) for rapid conversion to pasture and cropland. The images each cover an area approximately 50 x 60 km, i.e. about 3000 km^2. Reproduced by kind permission of CSIRO Office of Space Science and Applications from their International Space Year publication Graetz, D., Fisher, R. and Wilson, M., *Looking Back: The changing face of the Australian continent, 1972–1992*, COSSA (Canberra, 1992).

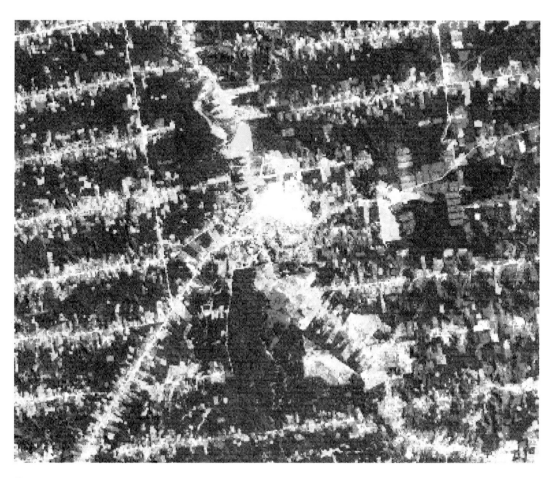

B

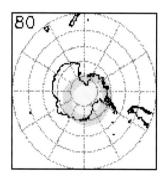 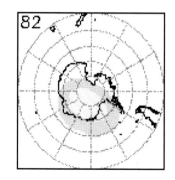 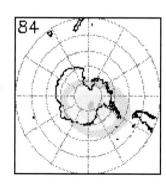

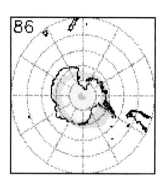 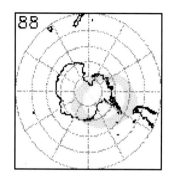 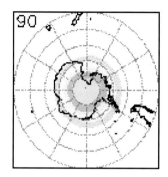

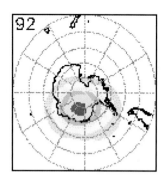

<150 150–   170–   190–   210– >250
      170   190   210   250

Dobson Units

Plate E
The development of the ozone hole over the Antarctic from 1980 to 1992. The data for this plate were collected by the Nimbus-7 Total Ozone Mapping Spectrometer (TOMS); they were archived and made available by the Goddard Distributed Active Archive Center (DAAC).

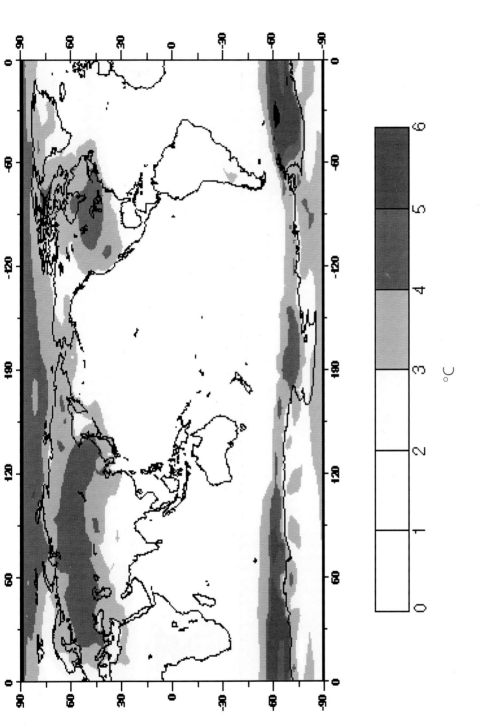

Plate F
Change in the annual mean air temperature due to a doubling of CO_2 as simulated by the Bureau of Meteorology Research Centre's GCM.

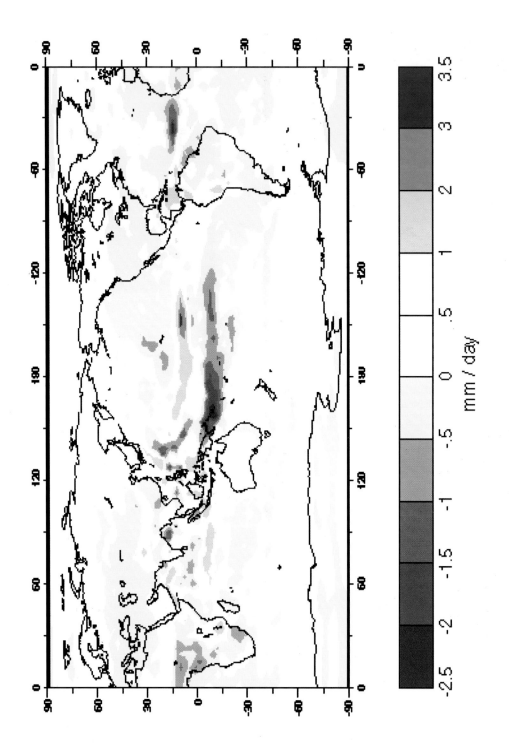

Plate G

Change in the annual total precipitation due to a doubling of CO_2 as simulated by the Bureau of Meteorology Research Centre's GCM.

URBAN ENVIRONMENTS

4

ITIES PLAY SUCH an important role in twentieth-century society that there have been very many books written on a wide range of urban issues. This chapter focuses primarily on the urban biophysical environment and includes discussions of biophysical processes, their impacts on cities, and the impact of cities on them. Its central theme is that the interaction of biophysical and human systems, as outlined in Chapter 1, must be understood if we are to understand the impacts of urbanisation locally or on a global scale. The urban system is used as the organising framework for discussing the role of cities as agents of environmental change, and of the impacts of urban growth on the environment. This chapter does not, however, claim to deal at length with a wide range of other urban problems of a more obviously social and economic nature.

Emphasis is placed on the local scale of the city, because it is at that scale that most urban effects are felt; it is also the scale at which many solutions must come through resident actions, government policy, or the efforts of city planning authorities. Yet despite their seeming insignificance in areal extent — only around 0.3 per cent of the Earth's surface area is devoted to urban land uses — and the predominance of local effects, cities also have an enormous influence at regional and global scales. For example, while **photochemical smog** affects the local urban population's health and reduces visibility, damage to vegetation from related high concentrations of tropospheric ozone is a regional problem, as is the destruction of forests and lakes from acid rain (see Box 4.1); and burning fossil fuels as a domestic and industrial energy source, largely to provide energy to urban areas, contributes to the enhanced greenhouse effect and thus to global warming (see Chapter 5). Urban land use affects local and regional flows of energy and water as urban areas develop their own hydrology and climate; the combined influence of all cities across the globe may alter global hydrology and climate. Cities also modify flows of nutrients and food

supplies, thus affecting regional and global ecosystems and economies. In terms of water supply, disease and ill-health from inadequate
supplies of high-quality fresh water are a threat to a large portion of
the global population, including large numbers in cities, while contamination of rivers and groundwater ultimately affects the oceans.
Finally, while the urban land area is certainly small, the urban population is large and continuing to increase, so these 'local' impacts will
determine the health and livelihood of the three billion people who
will live in cities by the turn of the century.

4.1 URBAN GROWTH AND URBANISATION

Changes that accompany the growth of a city from a small settlement
to a thriving metropolis represent one of the most profound human
impacts on the Earth's biophysical systems. Urban growth brings about
major alterations to topography, drainage systems, climate, economies
and social systems. In fact, the city is the ultimate example of an
anthropogenic landscape evolving on a human time-scale through the
dynamic interaction of the human and biophysical systems described
in Chapter 1. As we approach the twenty-first century, cities are growing larger and becoming more numerous, and an increasing proportion of the global population is living in them (Figure 4.1). By 2000 an
urban environment will be the local environment for about 50 per
cent of the world's population. Australia is one of the most urbanised
nations in the world, and the environmental and economic pressures
and benefits that arise from our cities are typical of the situation in
other high-income nations.

Global Trends

The annual average growth rate of the urban population was 2.8 per
cent from 1960 to 1990, higher than the overall global population
growth rate of 2 per cent (Figure 4.1).[1] The urban growth rate is far
from uniform, however, with large differences between high-income
and low-income nations. Most urban population growth currently
occurs in low-income countries, including the poorest nations, while
high-income industrialised nations are experiencing a slight decline in
the rate of increase. Figure 4.1 also shows that the high-income nations
had become highly urbanised by the 1950s, whereas the low-income
nations were still undergoing rapid urbanisation in the 1990s even
though they already contained the majority of the world's urban population. But this broad division still does not reveal much about the

(A)

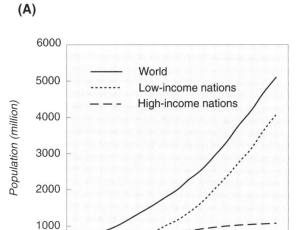

(B)

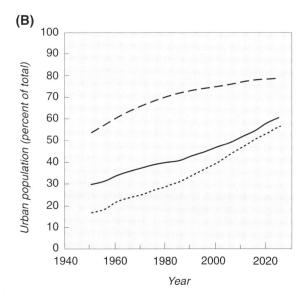

Figure 4.1
Population growth, 1950–2025: (a) urban population; (b) urban population
as a percentage of total population. Note: Figures are actual for 1950–1985
and projected after 1985. (Based on data from Oke, T.R., *Urban Climatology
and its Applications with Special Regard to Tropical Areas*, WMO No. 652,
World Meteorological Organization (Geneva, 1986), 63–86; and United
Nations, *Prospects of World Urbanization, 1988* (Population Studies 112),
United Nations (New York, 1989).)

geographical distribution of urban growth. In the period 1980–85 for example, eighteen of the twenty-three nations with the highest rates of urbanisation were in Africa, the remaining five being in Asia.[2]

Not only is the global population becoming more urbanised, but the number of cities, especially the larger megacities, is increasing. Between 1950 and 1980 the number of settlements with over 100 000 inhabitants more than doubled, and by 1990 there were 276 cities with populations exceeding one million. Increasingly, these larger cities are in low-income nations (Table 4.1).

Concerns arising from these trends go beyond direct impacts of large urban populations on the biophysical environment: there is a great risk that poverty and disease will increase with the growth in the number and size of cities. Much of the urban growth in low-income nations results from rural–urban migration, but there is little concurrent growth in urban employment or wealth to meet the needs of the growing urban population. As a result, cities are unable to provide basic services such as water supply, sanitation, housing and transport necessary for the health and well-being of the people.

Despite this, studies of individual cities show that there is often better provision of basic services in cities than in rural areas. In low-income countries, the largest number of people living in poverty are rural rather than urban dwellers; the latter may thus be 'better off' than the former, despite very real urban problems. Some writers go as far as to argue that urbanisation helps create rural poverty because rural–urban migration leads to a continual erosion of rural services. The term 'poverty' must, however, be used with caution: in particular,

Table 4.1 1992 population of megacities (millions), and estimated population in 2000.

		1992	*2000*			*1992*	*2000*
1	Tokyo, Japan	25.8	28.0	**11** Rio de Janeiro, Brazil		11.3	12.2
2	Sao Paulo, Brazil	19.2	22.6	**12** Calcutta, India		11.1	12.7
3	New York City, USA	16.2	16.6	**13** Jakarta, Indonesia		10.0	13.4
4	Mexico City, Mexico	15.3	16.2	**14** Tianjin, China		9.8	12.5
5	Shanghai, China	14.1	17.4	**15** Manila, Philippines		9.6	12.6
6	Bombay, India	13.3	18.1	**16** Cairo, Egypt		9.0	10.8
7	Los Angeles, USA	11.9	13.2	**17** New Delhi, India		8.8	11.7
8	Buenos Aires, Brazil	11.8	12.8	**18** Lagos, Nigeria		8.7	13.5
9	Seoul, South Korea	11.6	13.0	**19** Karachi, Pakistan		8.6	11.9
10	Beijing, China	11.4	14.4	**20** Bangkok, Thailand		7.6	9.9
				21 Dacca, Bangladesh		7.4	11.5

Source: Population Division of the UN Secretariat, cited in *Time*, 11 January 1993.

income is not always an adequate indicator of quality of life (Box 1.2). While urban areas may provide better access to food supplies, health care, social services and education, increasing degradation of water and air in urban areas will continue to increase health risks in poorer cities.

FRAMEWORK FOR ANALYSING IMPACTS 4.2

The urban system

People, economies, and environments, both within the geographical limits of the city and beyond, are influenced by the city. The far-reaching impacts of cities on human and biophysical systems can be better conceptualised by using the 'urban system' as a framework (Figure 4.2). The urban system is quite unlike natural ecosystems, as it has few negative feedback mechanisms to enable it to stay in equilibrium. Furthermore, its growth is not limited by available resources because technology and trade enable these to be imported over long distances.

Links between human and biophysical systems are nowhere more clearly demonstrated than in urban systems. Cities are sometimes planned from scratch, but they usually grow from small settlements in a relatively unplanned way. Planned or unplanned, their location and growth are in response to demands from the human system (the left-hand side of Figure 4.2). The basic reason for growth may be economic, political or military, but it will be most likely for a complex mixture of reasons. Whatever the driving force for growth, the settlement's initial structure, layout, and location often will have been heavily influenced by the physical landscape, and those initial characteristics usually continue to have a strong influence for centuries to come. An evolving city has buildings (including materials, design and construction) and a layout (the location of various land uses and transport routes) that reflect the joint influences of culture, technology and the biophysical environment: thus, the dynamic and evolving entity known as the city is positioned in the centre of Figure 4.2.

The five basic biophysical spheres outlined in Chapter 1 (lithosphere, biosphere, atmosphere, hydrosphere and cryosphere) are all changed by city growth; in fact, a new urban biophysical environment is created. This environment directly affects the human population through their health; their access to food, water and air; and the generation of wealth through economic activities. Technology is used to alter the environment and optimise its impact on the population (or sections of

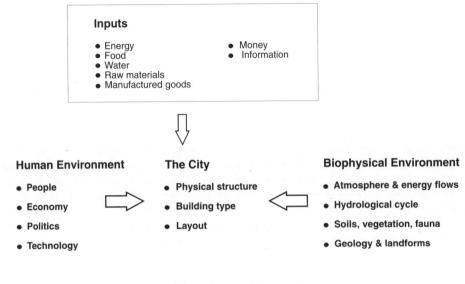

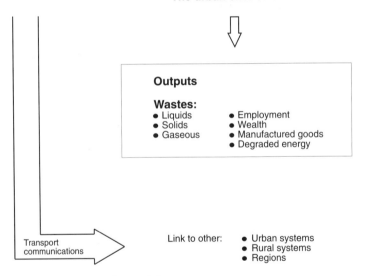

Figure 4.2
The urban system.

it), while economics and politics dictate the level of technology applied. City structure (including the transport system and land-use zones) and local human and biophysical systems comprise the total urban environment.

Resources required by the city appear in Figure 4.2 as inputs to the urban environment. Urban inhabitants must have food, water, air and shelter, while the growth and day-to-day operations of the city infrastructure and economic base require raw materials, labour and fi-nance. The demand for these inputs may be met from the immediate urban environment or they may be transported from afar. Finance, for example, moves along international routes and global economic fac-tors exert enormous influence on individual nations and regions.

On the other hand, manufactured goods, wealth and waste products created within the city are examples of outputs from the urban envi-ronment. These may be exported to other regions (true outputs) or be re-used within the city as new (recycled) inputs. These inputs and outputs, together with the urban environment, constitute the urban system, and this is linked to urban and rural systems elsewhere through transport and communications networks and through biophysical cycles and processes.

Inheritance of location

Concerns over environmental impacts have not figured prominently in the history of the development of human settlements and the subsequent growth of some into cities. In fact, if environmental impact assessments had been required over the last 1000 years or so, many of the world's cities would never have been built on their present sites.

Many cities, because of their inherited physical location, either suffer from environmental hazards or are themselves hazards to the environment. A disproportionately large number of cities are on coasts and river estuaries, for example, as these provide a transport node for imports and exports. About 20 per cent of the world's population — 1 billion people — live in coastal cities, despite the fact that coastal locations often have a very limited ability to disperse pollutants and the coast itself is often a fragile, vulnerable environment (see Section 6.2). Other cities are located close to rivers because they provide a water supply, a pathway for waste disposal, and a transport route; but such sites also mean that cities are vulnerable to damage from flooding. Jakarta, Bangkok and Bombay, for example, are all located in low-lying swampy areas and all have severe flooding problems. Bangkok is only one metre above sea level and is easily flooded, a situation exacerbated by subsidence resulting from groundwater extraction (Section 4.4). The related problems of poor drainage and impervious soils hamper waste disposal and restrict further urban development. Many of these problems mentioned will worsen in the future with global warming and rising sea levels (see Section 5.5). Finally, in terms of air pollution, Sydney, Melbourne, Los Angeles and Mexico City are all located in topographical settings that limit dispersion of atmospheric pollutants. (Section 4.5).

There are almost as many reasons for city locations as there are cities. The point is that important aspects of the physical environment of a city are inherited from the environment that existed prior to urban development. City growth involves ongoing evolution of the urban environment from that base.

City structure

City structure involves the form, or morphology, of the city and is influenced both by the physical layout of the city and by the types of buildings. The physical layout includes, among other things, the location of different land-use zones (industrial, commercial and residential, for example) and the nature and location of the transport system and its components. All of these influence the city's spatial form, a form unique to each city. But at the same time no city's form is static, as each evolves in response to changing circumstances, including resource availability, economic climate, technology and scientific knowledge, and public awareness and opinion. This evolution may be in response to environmental pressures as well as to economic opportunities.

The city plan

History is just one of many factors that influence the contemporary layout of a city, a fact well illustrated by cities in tropical Africa. African cities that have existed from precolonial times, like those in many ex-colonial regions, have a dual structure: a traditional core is separated from the more modern, outlying urban area, perhaps by a physical barrier such as a wall. The land-use and building layout in the inner, traditional core contrast with those of the outer areas settled in post-colonial times and characterised by 'Western'-style buildings. Many such cities now also have large areas that are post-colonial but definitely not 'Western', often at least partly in the form of so-called 'squatter settlements'.

Pressures from well beyond the individual city, including those stemming from international relationships in the global economy, affect all large cities. In African cities, for example, the establishment of industries is often of paramount importance, but all too often little attention is paid to appropriate siting. Urban planning practices common in high-income nations may be a luxury that poorer cities cannot afford.

Types of buildings

The characteristics of the built environment reflect a combination of cultural, physical and technological influences: these characteristics include construction materials, building heights, and the density, arrangement, and spacing of buildings. Very importantly, the built environment interacts with the urban biophysical environment in complex ways. For example, traditional buildings in tropical cities are often adapted to the climate, being designed to maximise airflow and minimise solar heating. But with colonisation the preferred building style often became more 'modern', usually with little consideration for the local climate. These modern buildings rely on artificial forms of heating and cooling, consuming large amounts of energy, rather than relying on passive means such as sunshine and natural ventilation. These changes therefore have important implications for energy consumption in urban areas. As another example, at the turn of this century the central business districts (CBDs) of high-income cities had few high-rise buildings, whereas the tall, closely spaced buildings that characterise the CBDs of many contemporary cities have been said to create urban canyons. The **microclimate** within these canyons is quite different from that of the earlier CBD, with less sunshine penetrating to the footpaths and gustier winds (Section 4.4).

THE URBAN SYSTEM: INPUTS AND OUTPUTS `4.3`

We often think of the impact of cities in terms of cultural and economic factors or in terms of the biophysical environment, but much of the impact results from the consumption and degradation of resources. Money, energy, food, raw materials for industry, construction materials and land are just some of the inputs required to maintain the urban system. Fresh air and clean water are also essential. Activities occurring within the urban environment generate outputs: waste products from homes, industries and transport are disposed of into the air, water and soil, or transported to dumps. Employment, education, wealth, manufactured goods, services, technological developments and cultural amenities are other outputs, usually thought of as being beneficial not only to people living in the city but also to those far beyond its boundaries. Very importantly, urban systems concentrate the consumption of resources and production of wastes into relatively small areas. An understanding of these inputs and outputs is fundamental to an understanding of the urban environment.

138 | Energy

As in all biophysical systems, energy is fundamental to the urban system and its functioning. Energy is required for manufacturing and transport and for domestic heating, cooking and lighting. The most common fuels used as energy sources are oil, coal, gas and biomass (wood, crop wastes or dung). All these fuels except biomass are effectively **non-renewable**. In poor countries about 60 per cent of the urban domestic fuel requirements are met by biomass, while oil is the most common commercial fuel. Deforestation and land degradation are common problems in regions surrounding cities where biomass is a major fuel source (Section 3.4). In many middle-income industrialised nations (particularly in Eastern Europe) as well as in China, coal is still a predominant energy source in the manufacturing and industrial sectors and for domestic heating.

In many cities, electricity is an important 'second generation' energy source; that is, it must be generated either from burning fossil fuels or by harnessing solar, hydroelectric or wind power. Indeed, about 50 per cent of the world's consumption of coal alone, and 30 per cent of the total fossil fuel consumption, is used to generate electricity. Cities are associated with an intensification in energy use and an increase in consumption of 'modern' fuels such as electricity, petrol and diesel oil. A recent study in Tanzania, for example, found that a 1 per cent increase in urbanisation led to a 12 per cent increase in electricity use and a 14 per cent increase in the consumption of petroleum fuels and charcoal.[3]

Food

During the early development of most cities, food requirements were met by market gardens surrounding and even within the settlement; in many Asian cities such gardens are still important sources of food. But as cities grow they build over any 'vacant' space within their boundaries and encroach onto surrounding farmland, reducing the number of market gardens and increasing the need to import food. Australian cities provide some excellent examples: Sydney, Melbourne and Adelaide are all surrounded by land with reasonable soils that were once intensively farmed to meet urban demand. With the encroachment of these cities onto their agricultural hinterlands, food requirements were increasingly met by importing food from other regions. For example, the irrigation of land in parts of the Murray–Darling Basin enabled the establishment of market gardens, orchards and vineyards which now supply produce to much of urban Australia.

The need to import food has several important impacts. Firstly, the areas in which food production and export activities are located are strongly influenced by the employment and wealth generated by food production activities. Secondly, intensive energy use has replaced labour in modern agriculture to enhance crop yields and reduce the limits to growth and productivity imposed by climate and soils, as well as to transport the food to urban consumers.

Increasing imports of food from modern agricultural areas thus increases the energy requirements generated by the urban system. Thirdly, the production and processing of food for urban markets creates wastes, pollution and land degradation, often in distant regions. The irrigation of land along the Murray River in Australia, for example, has led to severe soil degradation through rising saline water tables. So demand for food by urban Australia has contributed in part to this land degradation.

It is still possible to produce considerable quantities of food within urban areas. In many cities, gardens are established on vacant lots and fulfil an important social role. Moreover, they represent a level of self-sufficiency in poorer neighbourhoods and cities while improving the local climate and hydrology (Sections 4.4 and 4.5). The development of gardens on vacant blocks was a common and very productive practice in the UK during World War II and the period of post-war food shortages. There was renewed interest in such allotments during the period of inflation and escalating food costs in the 1970s, although the influence of alternative lifestyles and the permaculture movement may have been an important as economic factors in recent decades.

Clean water and air

Clean air and water are vital inputs to cities, yet ironically the atmosphere and waterways are major **sinks** for wastes generated by those same cities. Human health inevitably suffers without adequate clean air and water, and their provision is one of the most crucial problems facing urban areas, especially those in the low-income nations (see Section 4.5).

Construction materials

The 'fabric' that makes up a city — roads, buildings, drains, railways and so on — requires materials for its construction, including timber, bitumen, concrete and metal products as well as sand, gravel, clay and rock. Most of these tend to be bulky and expensive to transport, so cities seek local supplies wherever possible. Extractive industries then compete with agriculture and urban development for land outside the city core, usually on the urban–rural fringe — sand and gravel quarries are located in districts surrounding Sydney, for example, from Kiama in the south to Peats Ridge (near Gosford) in the north (Figure 4.3). In the 1990s there were also plans to extract sand from the ocean floor off Sydney, although environmental considerations were, in 1994, making it very difficult for the company concerned to gain permission from the government.

The extraction of raw materials and manufacture of asphalt, glass, cement, concrete and other building products have environmental costs. In addition to the land degradation associated with sand and gravel mining, manufacturing products such as glass consumes energy and emits hazardous wastes into the air and waterways. Cement factories, for example, emit airborne pollutants, including dust from both the raw materials and the cement, carbon dioxide (CO_2), and sulphur dioxide (SO_2). Both SO_2 and CO_2 have major impacts on the global atmosphere (see Chapter 5).

Timber is a common building material. It is also used extensively in general construction work (for example, plywood for concrete formwork) and is often discarded following the completion of construction. Most cities exhausted their local timber supplies long ago through its use in construction, for fuel and as an export. Urban demands have thus contributed to deforestation (Chapter 3).

Land

Growing cities consume land and air space. They either spread outwards or build vertically: Australian capital cities, particularly Sydney, are excellent examples of urban sprawl (Figure 4.4), while Hong Kong and Singapore are two examples of upward growth. The demand for space places considerable pressure on land values at the urban fringe. The provision of other inputs for the city also requires space (for example, food processing and extractive and manufacturing industries) and intensifies the demand for vacant land. The potential return from urban development of peripheral land typically exceeds its current return (often from cropping and market gardening), yet for the developer such land is still cheaper than that within the city. Often this price differential results in preferential location of space-hungry development in these fringe areas: assembly-line industrial plants, warehouses, plant nurseries, golf courses, and cemeteries have all been located on what was productive agricultural land.

Of course, the growing demand for more housing in cities like Melbourne and Sydney leads to new housing estates on the urban

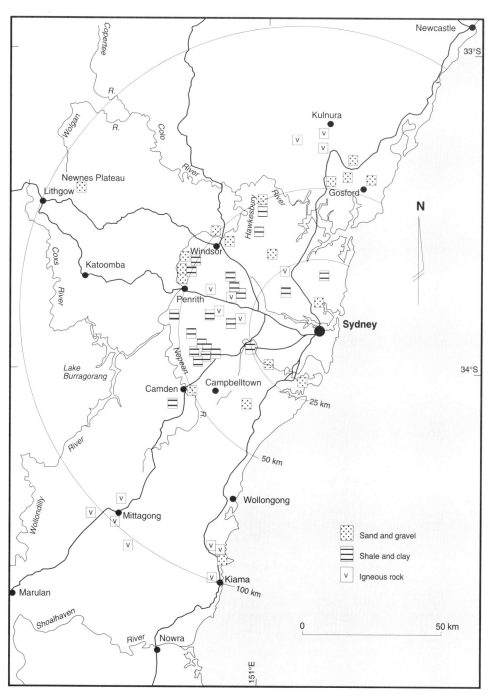

Figure 4.3
Location of quarries in the Sydney Region. (Source: Murphy, P. et al., *The Effect of Sand Mining in the Hawkesbury Valley*, Macquarie University, Diploma in Environmental Studies Report (Sydney, 1975).)

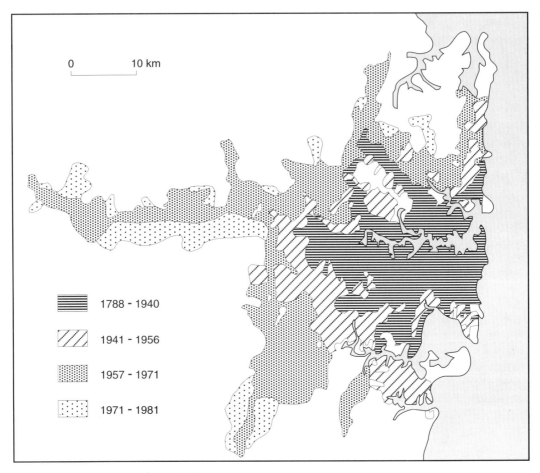

Figure 4.4
Sydney's expansion: 1788–1981. (Source: Adapted from Aplin, G.J., 'The rise of suburban Sydney', in Kelly, M. (ed.) *Sydney: City of suburbs*, New South Wales University Press (Sydney, 1987), 194).

fringe as well. In Vancouver, Canada, soaring real estate costs within the city have resulted in large-scale subdivision of prime agricultural lands in the fertile hinterland to supply more affordable housing. Peripheral housing estates are often interspersed with industry. In turn, this urban sprawl creates the need for even more land for transport and services (see Section 4.6).

A lack of affordable residential sites and housing in cities in low-income nations has led to many new housing areas developing informally. Most poorer migrants to the cities are, in fact, housed in 'illegal' settlements. These are all too often located on hazardous sites: for example, on steep hillslopes where landslides occur, on flood plains, or adjacent to industries emitting toxic wastes. Clearly such settlements constitute an enormous risk in terms of the health and safety of the population. Although it would be tempting to suggest that these settlements arise because of limited space, it is now becoming clear that, in many of these cities, there is sufficient space to house the newcomers. The problem is not so much a lack of space, then, as a question of economics and politics. These locations are the only ones the rural–urban migrants can afford. Governments often choose to ignore the so-called squatter settlements, so no sanitation or other infrastructure is provided, with the consequence that there is a lack of hygiene, clean water, drainage systems and other infrastructural support. The health and safety of the people living in these settlements are clearly affected. It is not all bad news, though. Many of these settlements achieve a great deal through self-help programs, while governments are increasingly recognising that it is better to assist in their 'regularisation' than to fight them.

Waste products

Consumption and transformation of inputs by the city create waste products (Figure 4.5). Disposal of city wastes affects not only the local environment but also the surrounding region, and often the neighbouring states or nations; the disposal of wastes in some circumstances even has global impacts, as with acid rain (Box 4.1), ozone depletion (Section 5.2), and ocean pollution (Section 6.2).

Figure 4.5
Waste products in the urban environment: note automobile and industrial air pollution, waste water discharge and landfill disposal of solid waste.

B O X

4.1

Acid rain — an example of long-range transport

The dying forests in Europe and North America point to the damage now known to result from acid deposition and ground-level ozone pollution. Both these forms of pollution are examples of long-range transport and illustrate the point that atmospheric pollutants are not contained within national boundaries — the atmosphere is a shared resource.

Acid rain results from the **oxidation** of atmospheric sulphur dioxide (SO_2) into sulphuric acid aerosols or sulphates. The oxidation of nitrogen oxides (NO_x) also leads to acidic aerosols and nitrate particles. The chemical reactions can occur in the gas and liquid phases, or on the surfaces of solids. These acid aerosols are deposited at the Earth's surface, either in precipitation (wet deposition) or in dry form (dry deposition).

Acid rain refers to a wet deposition episode in which the chemistry of the rainwater is altered from its natural **pH** of between 4.5 and 5.6; rainwater with a pH less than 5.0 is regarded as 'acid'.

Both SO_2 and NO_x are emitted into the atmosphere from anthropogenic activities (e.g., fossil fuel combustion, smelting and refining processes) and natural sources. A recent study cited SO_2 emissions in the USA of 21 Tg (teragrams) per year; about 4 per cent of these emissions were from natural sources. Oxidation and deposition can occur close to the source, but they may also occur many thousands of kilometres from this primary source. In particular, tall chimneys which have been used to reduce pollution in the immediate environs inject SO_2 and NO_x high into the atmosphere where they are transported by **synoptic** winds. Sulphate and SO_2 residence times depend on atmospheric humidity and effective emission height. Dry atmospheres or a large emission height lead to long residence times and enhance the potential for long-range transport.

The sources for acid rain are found in the heavy industrial regions of the USA and Europe, while the greatest impacts of acid rain have been experienced in the lakes, forests and tundra of Scandinavia, Western Europe and Northern Canada. A recent report found that wildlife and vegetation in parts of the UK have also been damaged by acid rain resulting from SO_2 emissions from coal-burning power stations within the UK and overseas. The loss of forest products in Europe resulting directly from air pollution was estimated at 82.3 million m³ per year in 1990. These losses represent around US$23 million in lost earnings.

Long-range pollutant transport is not an urban problem *per se*, but this is an illustration of the way urban outputs can affect areas far

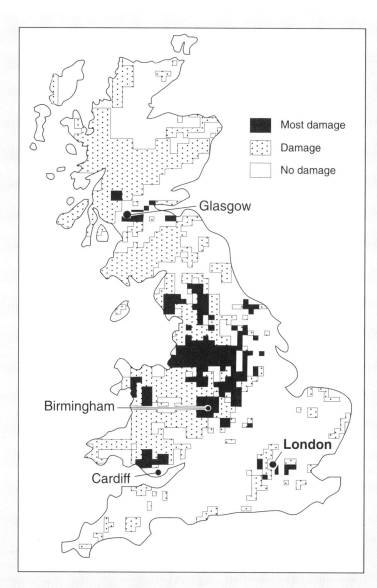

Most damage

Damage

No damage

Glasgow

Birmingham

Cardiff

London

Sites of acid rain
damage in Britain
(adapted from
*The Financial
Times*, 11 March
1994). Note the
concentration of
badly affected
areas in the
industrial districts
of the Midlands,
South Wales and
near Glasgow.

removed from the city. Thus far, these pollution effects appear to be
regional, rather than global. For example, there has been little evidence of acid rain transport across hemispheres to Australasia.

Sources

Olson, R.K., Binkley, D., and Bohm, M. (eds), 'The response of western forests to air
   pollution', *Ecological Studies: Analysis and Synthesis*, **97** (1992).
Critical Loads of Acidity in the UK, Department of the Environment, Air Quality
   Division; cited in *The Financial Times*, 11 March 1994.
Hammond, A.L. (ed.), *World Resources 1992–1993: A guide to the global environ-
   ment*, Oxford University Press (New York, 1992), 199.

Aside from minimising waste production in the first place, solid waste disposal can really only happen in three ways: dumping in landfills or offshore, burning, and recycling or conversion for re-use. While all methods are used in high-income countries, most household garbage, and some from industry, is dumped in landfill sites. Suitable new sites are now rare in or near most cities: according to a 1989 study, Melbourne was expected to have used all landfill sites in its region by 1994, Brisbane and Canberra to have done so by 1997, Sydney by 1999, and the other Australian capital cities by the first two or three years of the twenty-first century.[4] Once full, landfill sites are often developed for housing, recreation or industry. Many problems have arisen, however, particularly from the infiltration of toxic **leachates** into the underlying soil from unlined landfills, leading to contamination of groundwater and surface waters.

Low-income nations do not have the same type of waste problem. Their cities generate less household garbage, but also have fewer services to dispose of waste. Health problems arise when refuse is left to rot on the streets. However, unique forms of recycling have evolved. In Cairo, the economy of the Zabaline population (around 30 000) is based on the collection of garbage from about 20 per cent of Cairo's wealthy inhabitants. The rights for such collection have been bought from a freelance garbage-collection company, and the Zabaline collect, sort and recycle garbage for sale or re-use. Foodstuffs are fed to pigs which are fattened and sold, while glass, plastic and metal products are extracted and sold to industries and craftspeople.[5] Another example of an innovative approach, but on a more official level, is from Curitiba in Brazil, where recycling centres have been established in those parts of the city without sanitation services: garbage brought in by the local population for recycling is traded for fresh fruit and vegetables.[6]

Indeed, cities in low-income countries are generally more efficient recyclers of waste than cities in high-income nations. Unfortunately, the reasons for this are linked more to the poverty of the urban population than to a zeal for conservation. The comparison does, however, serve as a reminder that part of the solution to urban waste disposal is a reduction in volume. Much of the waste from cities in high-income nations is in fact recyclable, particularly metals, paper, glass and products derived from petroleum. People living in these cities are beginning to realise the importance of recycling, but this attitude change is generally ahead of the economic capacity of industry to recycle and the political will of governments to act to increase the cost-effectiveness of recycling.

The hazardous wastes generated by both households and industry are of more immediate concern. The US Environmental Protection

Agency defines hazardous waste as 'waste that is toxic, reactive, ignitable, corrosive, or infectious'. In low-income nations, most hazardous wastes are dumped in nearby waterways or landfill sites with little treatment. But this type of disposal is also all too common in high-income nations. There are numerous examples of heavily contaminated land, as well as extremely high levels of heavy metals in bays and rivers, in and near industrial cities. These contaminants often move into the food chain where they are subject to **biological magnification** in fish and livestock, which are consumed by people. There are serious health implications with this, as well as with direct breathing or ingestion of airborne and waterborne toxic pollutants (Section 4.5).

In closing this discussion of wastes, it is important to note that the disposal sites (referred to as sinks) for these wastes include waterways (rivers, lakes, dams and oceans) as well as the atmosphere and the land. The ability of these sinks to absorb wastes is determined by the nature of each city's particular biophysical environment as well as by the nature and quantity of wastes. There is thus a real link between the urban biophysical environment and the ability of the city to deal with its waste products.

CITIES AND THE BIOPHYSICAL ENVIRONMENT 4.4

Section 1.3 discussed the importance of the cycling of energy and water through the atmosphere, hydrosphere and biosphere. Modification of these flows by urban development will affect the functioning of the biophysical system. The focus of this section is on the way energy and water flows are altered by cities — one of the most important impacts of cities on the biophysical environment. While the urban biosphere and lithosphere are also influenced by the presence of the city, those influences are not included in this discussion.

Energy flows and climate

Cities have two forms of energy cycling: the natural flow of solar radiation (Box 4.2) which is modified by human activity as it enters the urban atmosphere and is absorbed at the urban surface; and the anthropogenic 'artificial' energy generated by the combustion of fossil fuels (although energy in fossil fuels is really just stored solar energy, its cycling occurs over such long periods by human standards that we consider it to be anthropogenic in origin). In a city, the two forms of energy — natural but human modified, and anthropogenic — combine to determine the amount of heating in the environment and, ultimately, the 'new' climate within the city.

Radiation

Radiation is a form of energy that can be transferred through a vacuum. Every object above absolute zero (–273°C) emits radiation. This emitted radiation behaves like travelling waves, which means that it has a particular wavelength and frequency. The energy of the radiation depends on its frequency: high-frequency, short-wavelength radiation carries a much greater amount of energy. The wavelength, frequency, and hence energy content of the radiation depends on the temperature of the emitting body. Hot objects emit short-wavelength, high-frequency, high-energy radiation; cooler objects emit longer-wavelength radiation which has less energy.

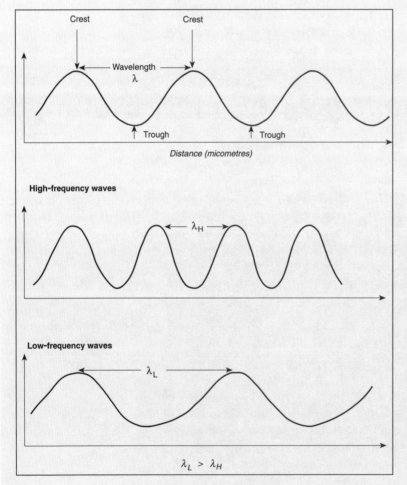

We think of electromagnetic radiation as being emitted as waves, and therefore radiation has a particular frequency and wavelength. The wavelength is defined as the distance between two crests (or two troughs) in the series of waves. It is usually given the Greek symbol λ (lambda) and is measured in metres. The frequency (f — the number of waves) is inversely proportional to the wavelength: $f = 1/\lambda$.

Radiation from the Sun (solar radiation) is the Earth's primary source of energy. Because the Sun is extremely hot (around 6000°C), it emits short-wavelength radiation. Ultraviolet radiation is an example of the short-wavelength high-energy radiation emitted by the Sun. The peak emissions in terms of energy are in a band of wavelengths from 4 to 7 μm (micrometres, or millionths of a metre) — this is the waveband that human eyes are adapted to and represents visible light. The earth also emits radiation, but it is much cooler than the Sun (about 15°C) and so the radiation it emits has longer wavelengths and less energy. This radiation is termed thermal infra-red radiation, sometimes called longwave radiation.

All objects are also able to reflect radiation impinging upon them. Most surfaces on Earth reflect very little thermal infra-red radiation (except for substances such as aluminium), but most substances do reflect solar radiation. The amount of radiation absorbed by a surface, therefore, depends on the difference between the amount received (solar and thermal infra-red) and the amount 'lost' by either reflection (of solar radiation) or emission (thermal infra-red radiation). The net all-wave radiation, or just net radiation, refers to this gain or loss of all-wavelength radiation for a surface.

Solar radiation

The atmosphere above a city contains dust, **aerosols**, and a cocktail of gases emitted from industries and automobiles. Solar radiation passing through this air is absorbed and scattered by these pollutants, reducing the amount that reaches the city beneath. At the same time, the polluted atmosphere above the city is warmed by its absorption of solar radiation. Observations from many different cities show that solar radiation reaching the surface can be reduced by as much as 25 per cent,[7] although the actual reduction depends on the time of day and the time of the year when the observations are taken, the kind of industries located in and near the city, and the number, type and density of vehicles. In general, cities with heavy industries or coal-burning power plants (for example, Shanghai) have the largest reductions in solar radiation, reaching 25–30 per cent. Less industrial cities, such as Sydney and Los Angeles, where photochemical smog is common, are found to have reductions of around 5–10 per cent.

Characteristics of cities also influence the amount of solar radiation absorbed at the urban surface. Despite the highly reflective nature of urban structures (for example, buildings sheathed with plate glass), cities have a lower **albedo** and absorb more solar radiation than does pasture or short grass. For the city as a whole, a large portion of solar radiation is absorbed by the city surface and only about 10–15 per cent is reflected back into space.[8] The relatively low albedo for the urban surface arises not just because of the presence of dark surfaces like asphalt, but also because of multiple reflections and hence radiation trapping within urban canyons. The solar radiation environment at street level is extremely variable — pedestrians may find themselves in shade at one instant and then exposed to very intense light at the next as sunlight is reflected off glass structures onto the ground.

Thermal infra-red radiation

Thermal infra-red radiation is important in determining near-surface urban air temperatures, particularly in the absence of solar radiation (Box 4.2). Downtown urban areas often contain tall, closely packed buildings which obscure the sky and emit much more thermal infra-red radiation than a flat landscape with no buildings. Some of this radiation is emitted downwards, resulting in greater warming in the built-up parts of the city. This is called the sky view effect, and the greater the density of buildings, the more important it will be. Polluted, warm urban air (arising from the urban heat island effect discussed later in this section) is also better able to emit thermal infra-red radiation than is clean, rural air. The net effect is that cities receive less solar radiation than rural areas but slightly more thermal infra-red radiation.

Anthropogenic energy

Anthropogenic energy is heat generated from internal combustion engines, air conditioners, domestic heating, machinery and many other sources. Compared to solar radiation this component is small, except in cities located in cold continental climates (for example, Montréal in Canada). As Table 4.2 shows, in those cities the absorbed solar and infra-red radiation (termed the net all-wave radiation; see Box 4.2) is very small, and so the anthropogenic term becomes dominant.

Airflow

Cities have another major impact on energy flows, and hence climate, through their affect on the strength and direction of the wind. The effect of cities on wind depends very much on the spatial scale under consideration. At the smallest scale, the pedestrian is concerned with wind flowing around buildings or clusters of buildings. Such a situa-

Table 4.2 Comparison of urban anthropogenic and net radiation energy fluxes at various latitudes.

Urban area (latitude)	Year of study	Ratio of anthropogenic heat flux to net radiation
Fairbanks (64°N)	1967–75	0.33
West Berlin (52°N)	1967	0.37
Vancouver (49°N)	1970	0.33
Budapest (47°N)	1970	1.0
Montréal (45°N)	1961	1.9
Manhattan (40°N)	1967	1.71
Los Angeles (34°N)	1965–70	0.19
Hong Kong (22°N)	1971	0.19
Singapore (1°N)	1972	0.33

Source: Oke, T.R., *Boundary Layer Climates* (2nd edn), Routledge (London, 1987)

tion is very complicated because it depends on the relative orientation of the buildings to the wind: what follows is only a very simple overview. If the wind is blowing parallel to buildings, for example, down a city street, then the wind is accelerated and a pedestrian would be in a 'jet' of fast-flowing air. If the wind is blowing perpendicularly to the building rows, then sheltering at the street level can occur. At intersections and building corners the wind becomes very turbulent, and poor siting of tall buildings, particularly in the CBD, can lead to dangerously turbulent winds that lift dust and litter and reduce visibility.

In an atmospheric layer extending to about a kilometre above the city, light winds (speeds less than 3 m/s or 11 km/h) are accelerated because of the thermal circulation that develops between the warm city and the cooler rural land surrounding it. In the simplest case, where there is no complicating topographic or coastal effect, air warms up faster in cities than in the surrounding countryside and rises, resulting in an inflow of air which converges near the city centre, rises, and enhances the rural–urban circulation. This may help to ventilate the city, while tall buildings in the CBD may also deflect faster-flowing upper air down to the city surface, also assisting with ventilation. On the other hand, the friction exerted by the 'rough' urban surface slows the airflow when winds are stronger (greater than 3 m/s). This may enhance pollutant trapping, or even alter the paths of storms as they move across the urban area. Under both light and strong winds, then, the city modifies wind speed and direction.

The wind field in an urban area also has an important role in determining the urban climate, especially the microclimate that is relevant to the inhabitants. From the perspective of a pedestrian, protection from wind at street level will cause higher air temperatures but also possibly higher concentrations of pollutants. In tropical climates ventilation is an important means of reducing thermal stress, while in cold climates sheltering conserves heat.

Urban climate

Cities modify the regional climate (temperatures, humidity and rainfall) through the basic mechanisms of altered radiation, heating effects and wind, creating specifically urban climates. This urban climate is felt at street level by the inhabitants, but also extends upward above the city for about a kilometre and downwind of the city for many kilometres. Some studies suggest that these urban effects may have an influence on the climate of continents, and perhaps even the globe.

Radiation absorbed at the ground heats the ground itself, depending on its thermal properties; evaporates water held on the ground (but this does not then lead to warming); or heats the air layers closest to the ground. Urban construction materials have quite different thermal properties from natural surfaces, and they heat up, retain heat and cool down at different rates to soil, rock or vegetation. There is also less vegetation in cities, so the evaporation component is smaller and there is more energy for heating. In general, the combination of sheltering by buildings, thermal properties and less vegetation means that this heating term is potentially large in cities. Cooling at night is also retarded because of the sky view effect described earlier.

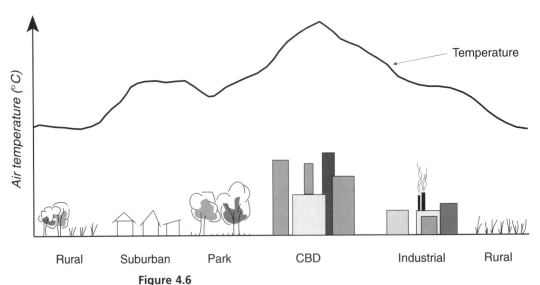

Figure 4.6
The hypothetical urban heat island (Source: adapted from Oke, T.R., *Boundary Layer Climates* (2nd edn), Routledge (London, 1987)).

It is not surprising, then, that one of the most widely documented aspects of urban climates is the increase in daily minimum and mean temperatures that accompanies urban development. Higher air temperatures have been observed in settlements ranging from villages to the largest cities, in geographical locations from the high latitudes (Fairbanks, Alaska) to the tropics (including cities in Mexico, India and Malaysia). This 'urban heat island' effect refers to the observation that, at night, cities are warmer than the surrounding rural landscape. A hypothetical example of the urban heat island is shown in Figure 4.6, which is a 'cross-section' of temperatures across a city. The strength of an urban heat island is measured by the difference between air temperatures at a rural site and those in an urban area. (Strictly speaking, the rural temperatures should be unaffected by the nearby city, a condition seldom met.) As the figure shows, the strength of the urban heat island is far from uniform across the city. Large parks and other vegetated areas are cool pockets, industrial sites and suburban residential areas are relatively warm, and the peak strength of the urban heat island typically occurs near the CBD. The effect is strongest on cloudless, calm evenings.

Cities may also modify rainfall by their influence on the two key causes of raindrop formation and rainfall. Firstly, air containing water vapour must be *cooled*, usually by being lifted through the atmosphere in thermals (vertical air currents arising from surface heating) or in air currents generated by flow over abrupt surface features such as mountains and, perhaps, cities. Secondly, water vapour needs to *condense* into cloud droplets, which must then grow to form rain droplets heavy enough to fall. The presence in the atmosphere of condensation nuclei — dust, sea salt, industrial pollutants or other small particles — will assist this growth of droplets. Cities clearly have the potential to enhance both of these mechanisms. Proving the existence of a rainfall increase near cities has been very difficult, although there is sufficient evidence of urban-enhanced rainfall to conclude that such an effect exists.[9]

Finally, humidity can also be altered. By day, cities tend to be less humid than their surroundings because of the extra heating and the reduction in moisture sources. At night, and possibly in the winter, this effect may be reversed.

Building design and city layout to minimise energy consumption

Cities in high-income nations are large consumers of anthropogenic energy, partly because city dwellers have not been encouraged to maximise their use of natural energy sources. The impacts of this dependence are both local and far-reaching. The enhanced greenhouse effect (Chapter 5) largely results from the burning of fossil fuels, and the most crucial response to the effect lies in reducing fossil fuel consumption. Much modern architecture relies on active systems such as air-conditioners or electric heating to control the microclimate, but these are too expensive for poorer nations. Most heating there comes from wood fires, which leads to both indoor and outdoor pollution problems as well as contributing to land degradation (see Section 3.4).

Building design and city structure can be manipulated to minimise energy use; in fact, many traditional building designs and urban layouts are well-suited to their local climate. For example, buildings in tropical cities are constructed in ways that minimise the penetration of solar radiation and maximise ventilation. In hot, dry areas, traditional building materials such as stone, adobe and brick are used because of their large **thermal mass**: walls constructed of these materials take a great deal of time to heat, thus keeping house interiors cool during the day. In more humid climates, lighter building materials are used to encourage ventilation. The scramble for modernisation and development has, unfortunately, seen an increasing desire to replace these well-adapted, indigenous styles with energy-intensive buildings.

The impact of cities on water: urban hydrology

The water cycle was introduced in Section 1.3 and Figure 1.4. For any area, we can define a water balance, which basically states that any input of water to an area must be balanced by the outputs. The urban water balance is:

Rainfall + piped-in water + groundwater	=	evaporation + runoff (piped and streamflow) + storage
Inputs		**Outputs**

The urban water cycle, like the energy cycle, has a human-modified natural component and an anthropogenic component. The natural water cycle is modified by urban growth: rainfall may be enhanced and the altered urban surface leads to increased runoff by reducing infiltration into the soil (affecting the storage term in the equation) and reducing groundwater recharge. The anthropogenic part of the cycle includes the piped inputs and outputs (part of the runoff term). The piped input frequently comes from a catchment other than that occupied by the city, and in high-income nations invariably involves a complex network of pipes and channels. The output is ultimately discharged, perhaps through a network of pipes and channels, into a river (possibly in a completely different catchment) or directly into the ocean.

In a natural landscape a catchment is the source area of water for the river system and is easily defined by topography, but urban catchments are not defined by topography alone and are changed dramatically from their natural or pre-urban state. Prior to urbanisation the surface would have been a combination of different vegetation types, rock, and soil. Urbanisation increases the proportion of impervious surfaces, and the resulting urban catchment is largely composed of roadways, vacant blocks of land (possibly disturbed), native and introduced vegetation, buildings and parking lots. Water channels are also altered: natural streams are straightened, dredged and possibly lined with impervious concrete, and new waterways are constructed, including stormwater drains, sewerage pipes and flood retention basins. A great deal of vegetation is removed during urban construction, exposing soil and rock to water erosion and increasing the sediment load in urban streams. The hydrology of an urban catchment is thus altered dramatically. An insight into the impact of the city on the water cycle can be gained by considering each of the components of the urban water balance, except rainfall.

Piped-in water supply

Cities are large consumers of water: to meet the demand and ensure a continuous supply, water is usually collected in reservoirs and piped to the consumers. This importation of water has a large impact on the water balance of the supply catchment and on downstream river levels. The regular water supply provided to cities reinforces the high levels of water consumption because the link between rainfall and water availability is no longer readily apparent to the user: water is available in a seemingly infinite supply, literally at the turn of a tap.

A study in Sydney[10] found that piped-in water represented 22 per cent of the total inputs to the annual water balance, while a similar study in suburban Vancouver (Canada)[11] found the piped-in contribution to be 33 per cent. In the latter case, the piped-in component was 1.5 times the rainfall received during summer; about 33 per cent of this was used for cooking, washing and drinking and the remaining 67 per cent was used on gardens and lawns.

Evaporation

Cities are usually thought of as being 'waterproof'; that is, they are made up of many impervious surfaces that allow water to rapidly run into stormwater drains rather than soak into the soil. When this is combined with fewer trees and shrubs, it would appear that less water would be evaporated or transpired from urban areas than from rural areas. However, the anthropogenic (piped-in) component of the water balance means that much urban vegetation, especially lawns and gardens in urban regions of high-income nations, is irrigated. This is an additional water input that can result in vegetated areas evaporating or transpiring more water into the atmosphere than surrounding rural areas. Such enhanced evaporation rates may lead to a cooler and more humid microclimate.

Furthermore, after rain much of the water that would normally infiltrate and recharge the soil moisture supply is instead evaporated from impervious surfaces such as footpaths and streets. This means that even more water may well enter the atmosphere through evaporation than is the case for a rural environment. Urban evaporation may thus be larger or smaller than it is in the surrounding countryside, depending on the extent to which artificial water supplies are available, whether vegetated areas are irrigated, the nature of precipitation events, and the proportions of different surfaces present.

Runoff

Runoff refers to the flow of water over the land surface, in artificial channels and drains, and in natural streams. Increased runoff is a precursor to flooding: in many cities flooding (often associated with soil erosion, especially landslides) is one of the major natural hazards. Flooding hazards arise because of alterations to the water balance due to urban development, together with the fact that many housing estates, planned and unplanned, are located on flood plains. Indeed, whole cities are sited on large flood plains because of the historical importance of rivers as trading routes (Section 4.2).

Urbanisation has two major impacts on runoff. Firstly, there is a transition from a pervious to a largely impervious catchment. Secondly, existing stream channels are changed and an artificial drainage system is established to move water along predetermined pathways. These changes in the urban catchment lead to an increase in the height of the flood wave, the rate at which it moves downstream, and the size of the flood discharge. This means that heavy downpours will produce a much greater discharge in natural streams and artificial channels in the urban area; they are often unable to contain this discharge, so flooding occurs. Channel modification also exacerbates the flooding problem for people living downstream, because the delay between peak rainfall and peak flood is considerably reduced in urbanised catchments. The increased discharge can also lead to erosion of the beds and banks of channels and streams, as well as of areas where vegetation has been removed during building construction. This adds sediment to urban streams, stormwater drains, estuaries and harbours, and degrades water quality.

Infiltration

The infiltration of water in the ground is often reduced during and following urban development for two reasons. The first is that rain falling on impervious surfaces is preferentially channelled into runoff through either human-modified natural channels or stormwater drains. The second is that the pervious surfaces in urban areas (chiefly parks and gardens) can also be highly compacted. Building and road construction also cause soil disturbance and compaction, which often leads to a reduced infiltration capacity.

Groundwater

Reduced infiltration and increased runoff result in lower groundwater recharge rates. In dry periods this reduction in groundwater flow leads to lower flows in streams, while increased runoff yields higher streamflows during rain periods. Urban streams thus tend to have higher peak flows and lower dry weather flows, resulting in altered rates of erosion and sedimentation in stream channels. Some cities have recharge basins which accumulate runoff and provide a buffer to minimise downstream flood levels while allowing the infiltration of retained water.

Another major impact of urbanisation on groundwater levels occurs where the groundwater is used as a water supply. Abstracting groundwater by pumping lowers groundwater levels, and land subsidence often eventually results. Bangkok and Jakarta are just two examples of the many cities with this problem. Both rely on groundwater to meet their water demands, and the **water table** has been lowered drastically in both cities, resulting in subsidence and cracked pavements, roads, and pipes. The intrusion of seawater into the groundwater supply in coastal areas is another serious risk when large volumes of water are extracted.

4.5 AIR AND WATER QUALITY

A breath of fresh air

Clean air, containing gases essential for life, is an important input to the urban system. But the atmosphere is also a sink for many other gases and fine solids emitted from the Earth's surface. While not all of these substances are anthropogenic in origin, it is the emissions from human activities that pose the greatest threat to the global environment on the time-scale of a human lifetime. Furthermore, the concentration of people, industry, vehicles and consumption in cities means that polluting activities and hence atmospheric wastes are most concentrated in urban areas. Ambient air quality monitoring has shown that atmospheric pollutant concentrations consistently exceed safe levels in many cities, even in high-income nations such as Australia (Box 4.3). This section discusses the major sources and types of urban anthropogenic atmospheric pollution, mechanisms for dispersal in the atmosphere, and major impacts. Chapter 5 deals with impacts on the atmosphere at the global scale, particularly in terms of global warming, in much greater detail.

Sulphur dioxide

Together with suspended particulate matter, sulphur dioxide (SO_2) is often used as a general indicator of atmospheric pollution. It irritates the respiratory system, so asthmatics and people with breathing difficulties are vulnerable to illness when concentrations are high. It is also the main constituent of acid rain and its deposition on foliage is particularly damaging. Acidification of soil, rivers and lakes through acid rain has affected many ecosystems in the Northern Hemisphere (Box 4.1).

SO_2 emissions result primarily from the combustion of fossil fuels containing sulphur: coal is the most common source, along with some metal-smelting industries and diesel engines. Given that more than 50 per cent of the world's coal consumption is for electricity generation, and that urbanisation is linked to increased electricity consumption, there is an obvious link between emissions and urban growth. Atmospheric concentrations of SO_2 were highest in the high-income countries in the 1960s and 1970s, illustrating the high use of coal for industrial processing and electricity generation at that stage. Once the link between SO_2 emissions and acid rain was realised in the 1980s, however, technology was introduced to enable cleaner and more efficient burning of coal and generation of electricity. As a result, the regions with the highest concentrations now tend to be the middle-to-low income nations (Figure 4.7). An estimated one billion people breathe air with concentrations exceeding health guidelines. China and Eastern Europe have some of the worst problems: in 1982, Prague experienced 24-hour concentrations that exceeded 3 mg/m³ — over 20 times the recommended maximum level, and similar to levels experienced during the fatal London smog of 1952. The problem is not as great in Australian cities, because Australian coal generally has a low sulphur content and most Australian coal-fired power stations are located on the coalfields beyond the major cities.

Suspended particulate matter

Suspended particulate matter (SPM) includes smoke, soot, dust and liquid droplets emitted from industrial processes, fuel combustion, agricultural practices and a number of natural sources. SPM is a major threat to air quality and human health in the cities of low-income

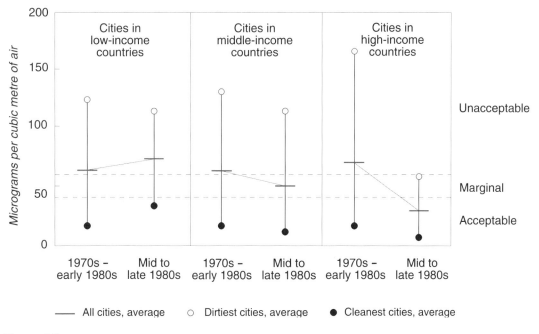

Figure 4.7
Urban air pollution and trends: concentrations of sulphur dioxide across country income groups (Source: adapted from World Bank, *Development and the Environment: World development report, 1992*, Oxford University Press (New York, 1992)).

BOX

4.3

Air pollution in Australian cities

In 1985 the Australian Environment Council published a report titled *Air Emission Inventories for the Australian Capital Cities*. This report presented data for the following pollutants: lead (Pb), carbon monoxide (CO), oxides of nitrogen (NO_x), sulphur dioxide (SO_2) and hydrocarbons (HC). It provided a detailed breakdown of the emissions from the following sources for each capital city:

- Motor vehicles: cars and equivalent, trucks, buses and motorcycles;
- Other mobile: aircraft, railways, marine vehicles and off-road vehicles;
- Waste combustion: municipal, commercial/industrial, domestic and other;
- Fuel combustion: power generation, industrial and domestic;
- Petroleum and solvents: petroleum refineries, petrochemical plants, bulk storage, distribution, surface coatings and other solvents; and
- Miscellaneous: gas leakage, utility engines, fires and other industrial.

The tables below are based on the data in this report.

The first table shows the percentage contribution to the pollutant emissions by each of the above sources. The overwhelming feature of this table is that motor vehicles are a major source of air pollutants. More than 40 per cent of the emissions of NO_x, CO, HC and Pb (the last is not included in the table) in Australia's capital cities come from motor vehicles. After motor vehicles, fuel combustion contributes 46 per cent of SO_2 emissions and accounts for 18 per cent of NO_x and 7 per cent of CO emissions. Petroleum and solvents generate around one-third of SO_2 and HC emissions.

The results for individual cities in the second table show that, except for SO_2 and HC, Sydney's contribution to each of the pollutant emissions is greater than the other capitals, and in each case except SO_2 is about 27 per cent. Sydney's Pb emissions are also substantially higher than those of other cities. Melbourne and Sydney show large emissions of HC, CO and NO_x. Except for SO_2, Perth, Adelaide and Brisbane share 'third place', with Canberra, Hobart and Darwin having fairly small emissions of each pollutant. However, there are surprising exceptions to this generalisation in the cases of Brisbane and Perth: Brisbane has relatively high emissions of Pb, NO_x and SO_2 while Brisbane and Perth lead the nation in SO_2 emissions. Darwin also has relatively high SO_2 emissions. The reason becomes clear when sources are examined: in Brisbane and Darwin the main sources of SO_2 are power generation and petroleum refineries, while the latter is the main source in Perth.

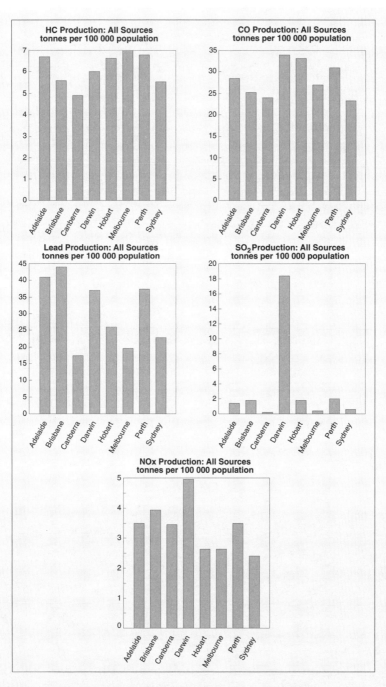

Per capita emissions of the major atmospheric pollutants in each Australian
capital city, mid-1980s. (Source: adapted from Australian Environment
Council, *Air Emission Inventories for the Australian Capital Cities*, AGPS
(Canberra, 1985).)

These results are as expected; the larger cities generally have the largest emission of pollutants. However, the bar charts show the emission rates of each of these pollutants per 100 000 people living in each city: some surprising results emerge. Darwin had a high per capita rate for all pollutants, especially SO_2, NO_x and CO, while Sydney had fairly low per capita rates, often lower than Brisbane, Adelaide and Perth. Canberra had the lowest per capita rate for all pollutants except NO_x.

In summary, motor vehicle use is certainly the most important source of air pollutants in Australia's capital cities. Cities which generate their own power within the physical city boundaries add to their emissions of SO_2 and CO, but the corresponding contributions from cities with power sources some distance away are not included in these data. As described in Chapter 4, the latter group of cities has 'exported' its pollution from this source. CO is the largest of these pollutants in terms of the overall volume emitted. This again points to the overwhelming dominance of the motor vehicle in Australia's urban air quality problems.

Pollutants produced by various sources, all Australian cities (% of all emissions).

	Pollutant			
Source	SO_2	NO_x	CO	HC
Motor vehicles	7.4	68.7	85.2	44.4
Other mobile sources	2.2	4.6	2.8	2.2
Waste combustion	0.3	0.2	1.5	1.5
Fuel combustion	45.6	18.1	7.4	10.3
Petroleum/solvents	30.4	3.3	0.1	35.4
Miscellaneous	14.1	5.0	3.1	6.2

Pollutants produced in Australian capital cities, all sources (% of all emissions).

	Pollutant				
City	SO_2	NO_x	CO	HC	Pb
Adelaide	13.3	12.5	11.2	11.6	15.2
Brisbane	22.4	16.5	11.9	11.0	19.0
Canberra	0.5	3.4	2.7	2.3	1.8
Darwin	13.6	1.2	0.9	0.7	0.9
Hobart	3.5	1.7	2.4	2.1	1.7
Melbourne	7.7	24.8	28.4	30.9	18.9
Perth	21.4	12.7	12.7	11.8	15.9
Sydney	17.6	27.1	29.7	29.7	26.5

nations (Figure 4.8). The Chinese cities of Beijing and Xian had the highest annual mean concentration of SPM in the period 1987–90, more than five times higher than most cities in high-income nations. A reliance on poor-quality coal was largely to blame, but another major source of SPM is biomass burning, already noted as a major energy source in poorer countries. About 1.3 billion people throughout the world are believed to be living in cities where levels of SPM exceed **World Health Organization** (WHO) standards. Illnesses associated with high concentrations are mostly respiratory; an estimated 300 000 to 700 000 premature deaths could be prevented in developing countries if particulate concentrations were reduced to WHO's safe levels.

Ozone, nitrogen oxides and hydrocarbons

Ozone (O_3), oxides of nitrogen (NO_x) and **hydrocarbons** are all involved in complex chemical reactions which, in the presence of sunlight, produce photochemical smog. Oxides of nitrogen, which are by-products of high-temperature fuel combustion, react with hydrocarbons to produce many chemicals, including large amounts of ozone,

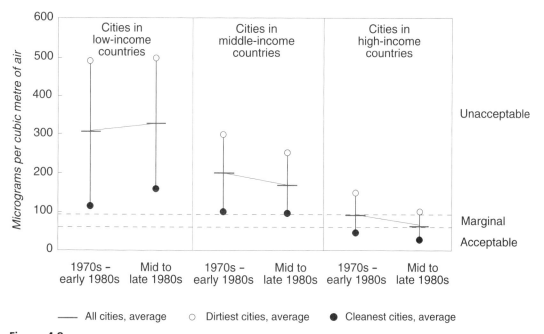

Figure 4.8
Urban air pollution levels and trends: concentrations of suspended particulate matter across country income groups (Source: adapted from World Bank, *Development and the Environment: World development report, 1992*, Oxford University Press (New York, 1992).)

an indicator of photochemical smog. It is important to note that these high levels of ozone occur in the lowest kilometre of the atmosphere (the lower **troposphere**) and are unrelated to the depletion of ozone in the **stratosphere** discussed in Section 5.2. Ozone damages lung tissue, so asthmatics are particularly vulnerable to high concentrations. Coughing, chest discomfort and stinging eyes are among the common symptoms of exposure. Ozone is also toxic to plants: by damaging cells within the leaves it interferes with photosynthesis and nutrient supply, reducing growth.

The major source of nitric oxide (NO) and nitrogen dioxide (NO_2), and thus of photochemical smog, is motor vehicles, with a small contribution from petrochemical and other manufacturing plants. Photochemical smog limits the air quality in North American, European, Japanese and Australian cities where hydrocarbons, NO_x and sunlight are all readily available. In fact, ozone is probably found in high concentrations in low-income nations too, but is considered less important than SPM, lead and SO_2 pollution. As vehicle ownership in these cities rises, so too will the occurrence of photochemical smog, especially in tropical cities where sunlight is plentiful and temperatures are high.

Carbon monoxide

Carbon monoxide (CO) interferes with the transport of oxygen in the blood, leading to drowsiness, headaches, and slow reactions: it is fatal in high concentrations. It is produced by the incomplete combustion of carbon-containing fuels: motor vehicles account for nearly all CO emissions, so reductions can be achieved by either reducing vehicle traffic or using engine-based emission controls. These measures have reduced CO emissions throughout high-income countries.

Lead

Lead (Pb) contributes to health problems in cities of both low and high-income nations. It has many sources, including fuel additives, metal smelting and battery manufacturing; it is also found in old house paints and water distribution pipes. Exhaust gases from cars using leaded petrol, however, are believed to be the most common source of airborne lead in cities, based on the incidence of high blood-lead levels in people living near roads with high traffic volumes. Humans absorb some lead through direct inhalation of exhaust gases, but probably derive a greater amount from inhalation and ingestion of lead-contaminated dust, vegetation, soil and water. Lead accumulates in the body and, while it adversely affects the health of adults, children are particularly vulnerable: slower neurological development in children exposed to lead and the resultant reduction in mental capacity and agility is of greatest concern. Studies in Bangkok estimate a reduction of four IQ points by the age of seven in those children exposed to high airborne lead concentrations.[12]

Lead contamination is a severe problem in the global urban environment: in one out of three cities the lead content of the air exceeds the WHO recommended maximum levels. Cities in low-income countries, such as Mexico City, are among the most seriously affected. Until very recently, up to 95 per cent of petrol used in Mexico City contained lead, and 29 per cent of all children there were found to have unacceptably high blood-lead levels. Urban inhabitants in poor countries are possibly also more exposed because of greater traffic congestion, inefficient and older cars, and more time spent outdoors.

Results from studies in the USA show that a 50 per cent reduction in leaded petrol use between 1976 and 1980 coincided with a 37 per cent reduction in blood-lead levels.[13] This put pressure on other countries to follow suit, and other higher-income nations have introduced unleaded petrol; some, including New Zealand and more recently Australia, have made leaded petrol more expensive than unleaded petrol to encourage drivers to switch to the latter. Unfortunately, Australia's relatively old car and truck fleet offsets some of the benefits, as some older cars cannot run on unleaded fuel. Some of the rapidly industrialising nations (Malaysia, Mexico and Thailand, for example) have also recently introduced measures such as unleaded petrol to curb airborne lead concentrations.

Studies in Sydney have found high blood-lead levels in children living in neighbourhoods with a high exposure to vehicle emissions, prompting calls for even lower lead levels, acted on in early 1993. Lead levels in Australia are set by the individual states: Victoria has a maximum of 0.25 grams/litre, while NSW urban areas have maximum levels of 0.2 grams/litre. In line with cities in other high-income nations, a reduction to 0.15 grams/litre has been suggested, and in mid-1994 Shell introduced 'half-lead' petrol (0.125 grams/litre in Victoria and 0.15 grams/litre in NSW) for older vehicles that cannot run on unleaded fuel.

General impacts of reduced air quality

The impacts of reduced air quality are most obvious at the local scale where the health of the urban population is affected. Respiratory illness is a common health problem, particularly in poorer cities, but warnings to asthma sufferers to remain indoors on days with high ozone concentrations are not infrequent in high-income nations. Globally, higher rates of illness mean increased health-care costs, increased premature death rates, reduced productivity and a diminished quality of life. Children may fail to reach their full potential because of the reduced mental capacity resulting from airborne lead, or because of childhood diseases which have impaired their sight or hearing. These affect not only the education levels achieved by individuals but also the future productivity and economic well-being of nations.

Both the atmospheric and biological environments are affected. SPM and photochemical smog alter the urban climate by reducing the input of solar radiation, increasing atmospheric warming and enhancing thermal infra-red radiation. Reduced visibility caused by large concentrations of SPM or photochemical smog may adversely affect road safety and income from tourism. Urban vegetation is easily damaged by exposure to high concentrations of ozone and SO_2 and even urban waterways, lakes and coastal areas are at risk from contamination as atmospheric pollutants settle.

Improving urban air quality

Levels of air pollution in the urban atmosphere depend essentially on the amounts emitted at the source and the amounts removed. Direct fallout removes pollutants either through wet deposition in rainfall or dry deposition, with major effects occurring at ground level. Pollutants are also moved horizontally by regional winds and eventually diluted. A reduction in air pollution thus requires either a reduction in emissions or an increase in the ability of the atmosphere to dilute the emitted pollution; that is, an increased ventilation capacity.

The amount of pollution emitted at the source depends on many factors, and this complexity severely limits the ability to improve air quality through source controls. Factors include the nature of the industry, the state of technology used, the type and amount of transport used and the locations of the sources. The types of pollutants emitted also depend strongly on the economic state of both the city and the nation, the technology available in the domestic and industrial spheres, and even the climate of the city. For example, Beijing has high SO_2 levels because coal is a primary heating source used extensively throughout its cold winters, and the technology needed to cleanly burn the local sulphur-rich coal has not yet been made available. Nations undergoing rapid industrialisation, including South Korea, Taiwan, Mexico and Brazil, all have serious air pollution problems: Seoul, for example, has been found by WHO to have the fourth-highest SO_2 concentrations among the world's cities, and Mexico City is renowned for its dangerously high lead levels.

Some solutions to air pollution can be found in exploiting favourable weather conditions, provided a detailed knowledge of the following factors is available:

- regional meteorology, which determines overall wind speed and direction;
- topography — for example, a valley or mountain will develop local winds;
- local wind systems, including sea breezes and urban circulation systems; and
- the arrangement of nearby buildings — city buildings create complex wind patterns and can lead to sheltering, just as if the pollutants were released in a valley.

An ability to influence land-use zoning, city layout and building design is also needed, as well as powerful, enforceable government regulations, compliance by industry, and the resources necessary to conduct continuous air quality and meteorological monitoring. Even so, this can only ever be a partial solution because many cities have weather patterns that predispose them to limited air quality.

Reductions in atmospheric pollution can also be achieved by curbing emissions, and the following options may also be part of the overall solution:

- switching to low-sulphur coals, oil or gas;
- using less coal in electricity generation by using alternative fuels or improving the efficiency of electricity generation and use;
- reducing motor vehicle use and congestion;
- modifying automobile engines and introducing emission controls;
- introducing regulatory controls on the timing and amount of emissions; and
- introducing various financial incentives or tradeable emissions.

Fresh water

Water is a remarkable substance: its molecular characteristics make it a good solvent, while it is thermally conservative and so an efficient coolant. Flowing water provides a transport route, irrigation sustains much of the global agricultural sector (Section 2.4), and our waterways have an important amenity value through recreation and tourism. Then there are the industrial uses: as a solvent, for cooling, for transporting wastes and as a raw material for incorporation in products. (It takes 150 000 litres of water to produce 1 tonne of steel, 250 000 litres to make 1 tonne of paper, and 2 million litres to make

1 tonne of plastic.) We quickly see that water is crucial to our very existence and, on a different level, to our current lifestyles; in high-income countries we use far more for domestic purposes than we need to (Section 2.1). It is little wonder that industrialised countries are such large consumers of water.

Water quantity and quality

Access to clean water for consumption by the world's urban population is crucial for human health. Clean water is thus an essential input for any city, but the output of degraded waste water (sewage, industrial effluent and runoff) has a negative effect on this provision. While this is not an exclusively urban problem (see Section 2.4 for a more general discussion of water quality issues), the concentration of people and consumption in urban areas also concentrates the demand for fresh water inputs and the generation of waste. At least 170 million people in the world's urban areas do not have access to safe drinking water. The main water-related issues in urban areas are having a sufficient quantity of water for domestic and industrial use, achieving an adequate quality of water for consumption, and removing, treating, or safely disposing of waste water. These issues are closely linked — the supply of fresh water involves issues of both quality and quantity. Sources of water and sinks for waste water are often not separated; for example, families will use the same water supply for drinking and washing. Improving the availability and quantity of water can also mean an improvement in quality by avoiding this type of multiple use.

Of the water extracted globally for industrial use, 86 per cent is returned as waste water to rivers, lakes and oceans. In other words, most industrial water is not actually consumed but is used for cooling (around 90 per cent) or as a pathway for waste disposal. Similarly, 60 per cent of the total withdrawn for domestic purposes is returned as waste water. Households in high-income nations consume most of their water during washing, not cooking and drinking. In short, waste water need not be wasted: recycling reduces both the impacts of excess runoff and those of high levels of consumption. On a regional scale, much of the water in many rivers, particularly in Europe, flows in and out of a number of cities on its way to the sea.

The contamination of groundwater supplies, which can proceed unnoticed for many years, is also of major concern, particularly as groundwater is especially difficult to cleanse. Groundwater contamination arises from toxic chemicals leaching from landfill sites (Section 4.3), leaking fuel tanks and other storage tanks, faulty or overloaded septic tanks, and seawater intrusion resulting from excessive groundwater withdrawals in coastal areas. Replacing septic tanks with piped sewerage systems reduces the chance of groundwater contamination, but surface waters will become similarly polluted unless sewage treatment works are constructed.

Sources and effects of reduced water quality

The major sources and impacts of water pollution and reduced water quality in lakes and rivers are summarised in Table 4.3.

Sediment is a frequent cause of lowered water quality, altering the chemical composition of stream water and changing the functioning of aquatic ecosystems within the waterway. Sediments enter urban waterways either from erosion in the urban catchment during heavy rains or from erosion of the channel itself during high-velocity flows (Section 4.4), while deposition in the channel alters its shape and reduces the volume of water that can be carried, thus increasing the potential for overbank flooding. The amount of sediment in urban waterways depends on the stage of urban development in the catchment. During the construction phase, vegetation is removed, soils are often disturbed and rainfall easily scours and removes soil particles, leading to accelerated erosion and instream sedimentation. After the initial development, erosion of the catchment surfaces will be lessened because of extensive paving and landscaping and the growth of gardens and lawns: sediment loads from the urban catchment may thus be reduced. At this stage of urbanisation, channel erosion will be the

Table 4.3 Major sources and impacts of water pollution.

Pollutants	Source	Impacts
Organic wastes	• Urban and agricultural runoff • Industrial effluent • Untreated or partially treated sewage	• Depleted oxygen in streams: fish and aquatic plant life die • Increased turbidity
Inorganic wastes	• Industrial effluent • Urban and rural sediments	• Heavy metals (e.g. cadmium, mercury, lead) and other toxins become concentrated in the food-chain: cause death or serious illness
Pathogens	• Untreated sewage	• Spread of diseases such as typhoid, diarrhoea and cholera
Heat	• Power stations and industrial cooling systems	• Impacts on in-stream biota: locally raises production and may deplete oxygen

greatest source of sediment in urban waterways. These phases need not occur consecutively as, in any city, large sediment loads will be associated with construction-phase urban development at the urban–rural fringe or redevelopment of existing suburbs. Of course, the specific effects of construction on sediment yield depend on local factors such as terrain, climate, soil type and construction methods.

Overall, contamination of drinking water most often results from untreated human wastes. Sewage treatment and improved water quality have increased in the high-income nations, resulting in far fewer waterborne diseases. Sewered cities have a system of pipes that transport raw sewage to a plant where some degree of treatment is performed. However, when there is a lot of runoff the sewerage system often backs up and the contents spill into stormwater drains, a significant and frequent source of pollution in sewered cities. Such a problem, together with other forms of pollution caused by excessive runoff, can be reduced by the use of retention (retarding) basins that absorb peak flows and thus protect streams from high flows and high pollutant loadings.

Sewage is treated in two stages: primary (the physical screening of wastes) and secondary (removal of contaminants by biological means). Neither stage removes all pollutants, nutrients or human pathogens — their elimination requires even further treatment. Not surprisingly, such advanced treatment plants cost more to build and maintain in the short term, so their installation is often postponed by politicians for as long as possible.

Despite considerable efforts to improve the supply of clean water, it is generally believed that water quality is deteriorating in the low-income countries, especially in cities. A UN study gives the example of sub-Saharan Africa where, despite a doubling in the population served by sanitation facilities, the number of urban dwellers without access to safe water increased by 29 per cent over the period 1981–90.[14] More than 95 per cent of urban sewage in low-income nations is discharged into surface waters without treatment: many cities lack a network of sewer pipes let alone treatment facilities, as illustrated by the examples in Table 4.4.

4.6 CHALLENGES AND SOLUTIONS

This final section integrates the major environmental issues arising from the global increase in urbanisation, identifies the major challenges to be faced by cities in the future, and presents some of the solutions that can maximise the benefits of urban living and minimise

Table 4.4 Examples of sanitation and water-supply facilities in low-income nations.

City and population	Sanitation	Water supply
Bangkok 7.6 million	• 2% of population connected to sewers • human wastes disposed of via septic tanks • all waste water directed into stormwater drains or canals	• 33% of population have no access to public water and it must be purchased from vendor • groundwater contamination widespread
Jakarta 10 million	• no central sewage system • 68% of population are served by septic tanks • much of population use drainage canals for bathing, laundry and toilet	• < 33% have direct access to piped water • 30% depend on water vendors • 33% use wells or river water
Dar es Salaam 2 million	• 89% of households used pit latrines which overflow in rainy season • only 13% of dirty water and sewage is disposed of regularly	• survey of 6000 found 47% with no piped water supply • average water consumption is 23.6 litres/day

Source: Adapted from Hardoy, J.E., Mitlin, D. and Satherwaite, D. *Environmental Problems in Third World Cities*, Earthscan (London, 1992).

the costs. Although many of the challenges are environmental in nature, the solutions must be met by people acting either individually or through public and private institutions. A combination of technology and an understanding of biophysical processes and economic and political factors is crucial in identifying and effecting solutions.

The challenges faced by cities often have the same underlying cause, but they may be manifested differently and occur in different cultural and biophysical contexts: thus city-specific solutions will be required. For example, the water quality issue for cities in low-income nations is primarily one of water supplies contaminated with human wastes. Water quality is limited in cities in high-income nations too, but by toxic and hazardous wastes rather than human wastes. An urban dweller in high-income cities may have a ready supply of safe drinking water, but this has probably been achieved by a large input of money and energy to treat contaminated waters — inputs not readily available in low-income nations.

Low-income countries

Much of the future urban growth will take place in Africa, Asia and Latin America. Despite large rural–urban migration and natural growth of urban populations, Africa in particular will also maintain a sizeable rural population and must thus deal with environmental crises in both the rural sector and the rapidly growing urban areas. Some particular urban problems are discussed here, specifically in the forms in which they occur in low-income nations.

Clean air

Air pollution is a problem in and around the cities of low-income nations. Even in African cities, where one would expect fewer industrial sources of air pollution, air quality is limited by dust and weak regulatory controls on existing manufacturing plants. High-income nations and transnational corporations also export their environment-damaging manufacturing industries to countries where environmental regulations are often lax, land and labour are cheap, and employers are not required to provide working conditions even close to the equivalent demanded in the corporations' countries of origin. Technology that has been superseded in the wealthier nations often continues to be used in these poorer cities.

Reducing atmospheric pollution can only be achieved by some combination of curbing emissions, developing technology to treat or control emissions, and optimising atmospheric ventilation to enhance dilution (Section 4.5). Modifying and reducing emissions at the source requires technology, financial incentives and government regulations. It also requires an ability to monitor emissions and pollution concentrations and to enforce standards. Such resources are typically unavailable, unless provided by high-income countries. However, some improvement can be achieved at relatively low cost with immediate benefits: for example, a reduction in suspended particulate matter from power stations can be achieved at a cost of only 1–2 per cent of the cost of electricity supply. Changing to natural gas and clean-coal technology can also reduce particulate matter and CO emissions by 99 per cent, and SO_2 and NO_2 emissions by more than 90 per cent.

Energy issues

Energy use could be reduced through pricing policies that reflect the real costs of providing and using oil, coal and electricity, encouraging efficiency in those cities where consumption is high. In low-income nations, underpricing of energy appears to be widespread, but whether the energy savings achieved in OECD countries as a result of price increases would be repeated in poor countries is unknown. Furthermore, any policy leading to a slowing down of development is likely to be resisted. Encouraging energy efficiency and alternative energy options, along with the necessary transfers of technology, are also key approaches to reducing atmospheric pollution. Any technology transfer, however, must be done in consultation with local people to ensure that it is appropriate for local conditions, that it works, and that the local population can use and further develop the technology (Section 7.6).

A reliance on coal (either for direct heating or for electricity generation) and biomass as energy sources is expensive to human health and environmental capital. Fossil fuel consumption contributes to the greenhouse effect (Chapter 5) and generates atmospheric pollution that impairs the health of the urban system. Reliance on artificial energy sources, and hence energy consumption, can be reduced by exploiting the local climate, and intelligent urban design can achieve considerable energy savings (see Section 4.4).

Water and sanitation

Water quality and quantity are linked, so a continuous and adequate supply can improve quality. Even in poor cities, people are often willing to contribute more to the total cost of water supply if reliability is assured. Hence one solution is to provide greater access to a reliable water supply and levy a charge which adequately covers supply costs but is weighed according to the ability to pay.

The development of adequate sanitation facilities is the other obvious need. It would be beyond the economic means of many poor cities to provide every urban dweller with a flush toilet connected to a city-wide sewerage system. What is needed is a means of disposing of human wastes that is functional yet economical to install, such as biocomposting toilets, biogas units, and properly installed conventional septic systems. Other problems and solutions are described in Section 2.5.

Appropriate and safe shelter

Shelter that is both appropriate and safe can only be achieved through careful planning, determining where people and industry should be located, and making available cheap and appropriate building materials. The term 'appropriate' is used to indicate materials that are both cheap and locally available (so that transport and energy costs are reduced) and that optimise local environmental conditions so that the microclimate can be controlled passively rather than through the use of anthropogenic energy sources.

Zoning areas for residential development requires an understanding of urban geomorphology, including an understanding of the processes that lead to slope instability, subsidence, flooding and other problems. To be effective, the planning must involve local participation and build on local knowledge. Many cities are sited on flood plains or in coastal zones that are often inundated by floods, but the reasons for the flooding must be understood. If it is part of a natural cycle there may be no practical solution, but if flooding has been exacerbated by deforestation or other human activities, there may be practical, though very long-term, solutions to the flooding problem.

The impact of urban development on the water balance is such that urban flooding is a probable by-product of urbanisation. Measures to reduce runoff, and thus peak flows, can be introduced. (These are reviewed later in this section in relation to high-income countries.) Simpler, low-cost solutions could also include planting vegetation and leaving areas aside for retention basins. Discouraging urban development on unstable slopes will not only reduce mass movement (such as landslides) but also reduce sedimentation rates in urban channels and rivers that contribute to and worsen the flooding problem.

Adequate food supplies

Urban populations are often more fortunate than rural dwellers in that they have easier access to food, water and health care. While the urban food supply is not limited to produce from the immediate hinterland, access to other sources requires an adequate transport and distribution system, adding to the cost of food for the urban dweller; access to fresh food may thus be limited by economics rather than availability. One approach to ensuring an adequate supply of fresh fruit and vegetables is to encourage the development of gardens within urban areas. These would have multiple benefits: a ready supply of fresh fruit and vegetables without high transport costs, greenspace which allows infiltration of rainfall, and a natural cooling mechanism through evaporative cooling. There are some barriers to this solution, however, including providing an adequate water supply (although suitably treated waste water could be used) and making enough land available (certainly not a trivial problem).

Institutional reform

A number of institutional changes are required if these urban challenges are to be addressed:

- participation in the development of solutions by people at a local level;
- better planning which is mindful of the whole urban system but also has local participation;
- improved efficiency of public utilities, and possibly greater involvement of the private sector; and
- improved international co-operation (Chapters 6 and 7).

High-income countries

High-income cities consume large amounts of energy, water and food per capita and generate large quantities of liquid, gaseous and solid waste, much of which is toxic. But these cities also tend to have the cleanest water and air and can thus transfer valuable knowledge and technology to lower-income countries. If we characterise the major crises of cities in low-income nations as 'fouling their own nest', leading to enormous health and environmental costs, then the high-income cities have this problem as well as that of over-consumption. The latter leads to the generation of large amounts of waste, much of it hazardous to both people and the biophysical environment, and it also places considerable strain on the regional resources and economies of these cities.

Conserving energy

High per capita consumption of fossil fuels contributes to many global environmental problems. Encouraging efficient and cleaner use of these fuels will also encourage the use of alternative fuels. The following are some ways of achieving such efficiencies:

- Consumption can be limited by either setting prices that accurately reflect the real cost of the fuel, or adding a tax that is then used to finance research into alternative-fuel technologies and to provide improved pollution monitoring and vehicle inspection. Increased fuel prices do reduce consumption (as found for petroleum products during the 'oil crisis' of the 1970s); and higher pricing, if carefully applied, should encourage a shift to less-polluting fuels and potentially reduce air pollution. But pricing regimes encourage greater use of equally polluting fuels or even more polluting fuels; for example, a shift from oil to coal must be avoided.
- Modern cars burn fuel more cleanly, use unleaded petrol and are more fuel-efficient than older cars. Incentive schemes, possibly including buy-back schemes for old cars funded by governments or private industry, would encourage people to upgrade to newer

vehicles. This would reduce fuel consumption and improve air quality.

- Appropriate building materials and designs should be used, and the layout of suburbs planned, to manipulate the local climate and thus conserve both energy and water. The planning measures could also optimise hydrological changes to minimise runoff, channel erosion, flash flooding and sedimentation.
- Urban consolidation can reduce transport costs and help with energy conservation and pollution reduction, but will only achieve its full potential if accompanied by transport innovations offering alternatives to the motor vehicle. With urban consolidation, public transport may become more viable and non-motorised traffic should be encouraged. However, urban consolidation may also have other environmental costs (see below).
- The use of alternative energy sources, particularly renewable and non-polluting sources such as solar energy, should be encouraged by incentives, along with changes to the pricing of fossil fuels.

Reducing water use

The quality of drinking water in high-income countries is fairly high despite pollution of freshwater rivers and lakes. Two overriding problems remain: chemical pollution and high consumption levels. Expanding urban populations have a large demand for water, which leads to a continual search for more and more sources, including perhaps exploiting the groundwater supply or building more dams that are often larger and further from the cities. A reduction in overall water consumption is thus highly desirable. The large volume of waste water generated in high-income cities points to the possibility of recycling as a means of conserving water.

Reducing atmospheric pollution

Many of the measures listed above under 'energy conservation' will also reduce atmospheric pollution. Reducing vehicle use or switching to alternative fuels are the only satisfactory solutions to photochemical smog, although there is some scope for reducing hydrocarbon and NO_x emissions from industrial sources. Newer cars have better emission controls and probably represent close to the lowest level of emissions possible from the internal combustion engine. Unfortunately the present layout of cities, with their dependence on the car, will mean that vehicle ownership and use will continue to increase, and this may largely or entirely offset gains from emission controls. In the many cities that are not amenable to an efficient, affordable and adequate public transport system, alternative fuels and modern cars are the only (partial) solution to vehicle-based atmospheric pollution.

A knowledge of the local meteorology, along with an understanding of the factors that determine photochemical smog levels, can be used by city planners and engineers to locate new roads and industries in areas that minimise the potential to generate photochemical smog. Planners can also design road networks that minimise vehicle congestion, although this should not be taken as an argument for an overall increase in road length, as the gains from reduced congestion will quite likely be offset by increased vehicle use.

Key ingredients in any strategy to reduce industrial emissions include incorporating new emissions-control technology, introducing strict market-based or financial incentives or government regulations, understanding the local and regional meteorology, and having sophisticated monitoring capabilities.

Waste water

Improving the quality of waste water so that it can be re-used or so that it is not hazardous to aquatic ecosystems is crucial. Reducing waste water quantities means reducing both water consumption and urban runoff. Reducing urban runoff will improve water quality in urban waterways and reduce flash flooding, channel sedimentation and coastal pollution. This requires the provision of:

- small-scale retention ponds and infiltration basins (which can reduce inputs of pollutants by 80 per cent);
- porous pavements to allow infiltration rather than runoff;
- vegetative strips, including urban gardens, that allow for infiltration; and
- on-site storage for urban stormwater, seen as a resource for future non-consumptive uses in gardens, swimming pools, toilet flushing, and the like.

In some countries, creative means have been found to treat and use sewage. Since 1892, most of Melbourne's sewage has been purified by land and grass filtration and in lagoons on an 11 000 ha treatment farm at Werribee. This farm is also run as a grazing enterprise, and high-quality beef production has offset much of the cost. By the mid-1970s urban expansion had exceeded the farm's capacity, and conventional treatment plants and ocean outfalls now serve Melbourne's south-eastern suburbs. In some inland Australian cities (for example, Dubbo and Alice Springs), tree plantations are irrigated with effluent, while at Broken Hill and in the Hunter Valley effluent is used to irrigate stabilised mine dumps.

Sydney's problems have been greater because the bulk of its sewage has until recently only received primary treatment before being discharged into the ocean. Eventually the volumes of sewage exceeded the capacity of this ocean 'sink', and coastal pollution became a serious problem which was addressed by constructing deep-ocean outfalls. This was recognised as only a partially adequate response, and a Clean Waterways Program was initiated by the Sydney Water Board to further improve the handling of Sydney's waste waters. Improvements have included a 26 per cent reduction in phosphorus in effluent discharged into the Hawkesbury–Nepean River; recycling 74 per cent of sludge for compost, agriculture, forestry and mine-site restoration; and the investigation of new treatment technologies such as the membrane filtration system and magnetite flocculation. In mid-1994, however, this program was in doubt for unclear political reasons.

Reducing solid and hazardous wastes

The safe disposal of solid and hazardous wastes generated in cities is an enormous problem. There are really only four ways to reduce solid wastes: burning, dumping, conversion into something else, or reducing the input. Incineration, of course, can lead to air pollution problems. Recycling combines the last two solutions. Landfill sites are becoming very scarce and must be regarded as a finite resource, so improved methods of burning and recycling will be sought, requiring a change in our attitudes to packaging and 'throw-away' convenience and a return to more durable products and re-use.

Reducing urban sprawl

One of the major challenges for high-income nations is to control urban sprawl. Urban sprawl consumes and degrades lands on the urban periphery and incurs huge capital costs in developing the necessary infrastructure (roads, water supply, sewerage pipes, etc.) and services that are a drain on the region's economy. The demand for more land for urban development is a legacy inherited from earlier times. The 'great Australian dream' of home ownership, combined with private car ownership, has contributed to sprawling cities typified by Melbourne and Sydney. The roots of this dream lie in the desire for a quality of life merging rural with urban lifestyles, while the removal of technological and economic limits to urban growth have made its realisation possible for so many.

This expansion has come at an immense environmental cost. Vehicle emissions contribute around 75 per cent of Sydney's atmospheric pollution, for example. The separation between places of residence and places of work, together with the lack of a comprehensive public transport system, leads to high vehicle use and large distances travelled: high vehicle emission levels and photochemical smog are the result. Urban and agricultural runoff have led to a deterioration of water quality in the river systems surrounding many large cities. Urban sprawl is an inefficient use of agricultural lands on the periphery of the city, as the land is taken out of production and only has value as suburban real estate.

An alternative to urban sprawl is the process of infilling inner areas — urban consolidation. This concept usually refers to the residential sector; that is, to increasing the density of dwellings in the suburbs and re-using vacant land and buildings in the inner city, although it could also be applied to other urban land uses. Some of the costs and benefits of urban consolidation are as follows:

- A reduction in the rate of urban development on the urban–rural fringe will mean reduced infrastructure, service and environmental costs. Market gardens and production sites for other inputs required by cities may then remain, improving the sustainability and the transport and energy costs of the urban system. These areas can also provide valuable recreation space and fill other non-economic needs.
- Increasing the density of dwellings may enhance the urban heat island effect, which could reduce energy demands for heating but increase energy demands for cooling unless accompanied by strict planning controls to maximise passive energy sources and natural ventilation. Unless urban consolidation is accompanied by increases in alternative forms of transport (motorised and non-motorised), high concentrations of CO and photochemical smog may result, especially if car ownership and vehicle use remain static.
- Vacant land must be available and affordable. Much of the land in inner cities is expensive, either to purchase or to develop. A better option is to develop vacant government-owned land which is no longer needed, or to convert land from obsolete non-residential uses. This requires approval from local government authorities to alter land-use zones.
- Redevelopment of inner-city areas can displace the existing population and remove rental properties, an important form of shelter for many urban dwellers, particularly those on lower incomes. The housing needs of these people must not be overlooked.

4.7 CONCLUSION

Urban land use occupies a smaller area than most other forms of land use. Consequently, it might be thought that urban environmental problems would affect so little of the Earth's surface that they could hardly be termed 'global'. Yet a large and increasing proportion of the world's population lives in, or very near to, major urban centres. Furthermore, urban growth has very real impacts on land, water, the atmosphere, forests and the ocean near large cities, particularly because the large pollution loads in both air and water transfer the effect of urban activities over long distances. Finally, cities in many parts of the world are merging to form very extensive metropolitan regions or megalopolises. Taken in aggregate, urban environmental problems are truly global problems, and cities around the globe share broadly similar problems and may benefit from sharing experiences and judiciously applying lessons learnt elsewhere.

FURTHER READING

Douglas, I., *The Urban Environment*, Edward Arnold (London, 1983). [Although now more than a decade old, this book is still one of the few to provide an integrated and systematic analysis of the urban environment, showing the links between the economic functions of a city and its physical environment. The book provides an excellent framework for understanding urban environmental problems in addition to many Australian and overseas examples and case studies.]

Gupta, A. and Pitts, J. (eds), *Physical Adjustments in a Changing Landscape: The Singapore story*, Singapore University Press (Singapore, 1992). [A detailed study by means of a series of specialist essays on various aspects of Singapore's physical environment and the relationship between the city and that environment.]

Hardoy, J.E., Mitlin, D. and Sattherwaite, D. (1992), *Environmental Problems in Third World Cities*, Earthscan Publications (London, 1992). [A comprehensive survey of environmental issues in 'Third World' cities, illustrating many of the myths and providing very detailed factual information and case studies.]

Myers, N. (ed.), *Gaia Atlas of Planet Management: For today's caretakers of tomorrow's world*, Pan Books (London, 1985). [This text has sections on environmental issues that have an urban dimension, such as water and air quality. It contains some useful graphics and statistics on the scale and costs of these environmental problems.]

Oke, T.R., *Boundary Layer Climates*, 2nd edition, Methuen (London, 1987) and Landsberg, H. *The Urban Climate* (Academic Press, 1981). [Both these texts have excellent sections (in Landsberg's case, the whole book) devoted to a detailed description of the effect of cities on local-scale climate and hydrology. Oke's text provides a more process-oriented approach, providing a physical explanation for urban climate effects. Both authorities have researched in this field for several decades, and the texts have numerous examples from their research.]

UNEP/WHO, *Urban Air Pollution in Megacities of the World*, Blackwell (Oxford, 1992). [This provides detailed analyses of air quality data from the world's largest cities plus descriptions of the unique features of each city that contribute to their air quality problems. This is an excellent reference and resource text.]

NOTES

1 Most of the statistics referred to in this chapter are from either Hammond, A.L. (ed.), *World Resources 1992–1993: A guide to the global environment*, Oxford University Press (New York, 1992); or World Bank, *Development and the Environment: The World Development Report, 1992*, Oxford University Press (New York, 1992).

2 United Nations, *Prospects of World Urbanization, 1988*, Population Studies 112 (1989), 13.

3 Hosier, R.H., Mwandosya, M.J. and Muhanga, M.L., 'Future energy development in Tanzania: the energy costs of urbanization', *Energy Policy*, **21** (1993), 524–43.

4 Australian Bureau of Statistics (ABS), *Australia's Environment: Issues and facts*, ABS (Canberra, 1992).

5 Douglas, I., *The Urban Environment*, Edward Arnold (London, 1983), 153.

6 *Time Magazine*, 11 January 1993.

7 Oke, T.R., *Review of Urban Climatology 1968–1973*, World Meteorological Organization Technical Note 134 (Geneva, 1979).

8 Oke, T.R., 'The surface energy budgets of urban areas', *Progress in Physical Geography*, **12** (1988), 471–508.

9 Changnon, S.A., 'METROMEX: a review and summary, *Meteorological Monographs*, **18** (1981).

10 Bell, F.C., 'The acquisition, consumption and elimination of water by the Sydney urban system', *Proceedings of the Ecological Society of Australia*, **7** (1972), 160–76.

11 Grimmond, C.S.B. 'The suburban water balance: daily, monthly and annual results from suburban Vancouver B.C.', Unpublished M.Sc. Thesis, University of British Columbia (1984).

12 World Bank, *Development and the Environment: The World Development Report, 1992*, Oxford University Press (New York, 1992), 5.

13 Hammond, A.L. (ed.), *World Resources 1992–1993: A guide to the global environment*, Oxford University Press (New York, 1992), 197.

14 ibid., 164.

5

THE GLOBAL ATMOSPHERE

5.1   INTRODUCTION

P EOPLE HAVE HAD a number of impacts on the atmosphere, ranging from the local-scale influences of houses or watered
gardens, through the effect of urban areas on regional-scale
climates (Chapter 4), to impacts on the global climate. The two most
important impacts on the global atmosphere are the enhanced greenhouse effect and the depletion of the ozone layer, both of which have
the potential to affect many other aspects of the Earth's physical,
chemical and biological systems. The enhanced greenhouse effect, for
instance, modifies the Earth's energy cycle, which in turn affects the
hydrological or water cycle (see Section 1.3). The depletion of ozone
affects both the energy cycle in the upper atmosphere and the amount
of radiation reaching the Earth's surface, while the increased ultraviolet radiation may adversely affect parts of the biosphere.

This chapter explores the likely consequences of the enhanced
greenhouse effect and ozone depletion. The consequences of the
greenhouse effect depend on the size of the 'additional warming' (or
how large the change in the Earth's energy cycle will be), how fast the
amounts of greenhouse gases in the atmosphere increase, and what
measures are employed to counter the effect. The greenhouse effect
and ozone depletion are physical processes, but the solutions are
political, economic and technical.

5.2   OZONE DEPLETION

Atmospheric chemistry and the ozone 'hole'

Ozone is a naturally occurring gas which is concentrated in the stratosphere between 10 and 50 km above the Earth's surface. It is formed

by the reaction of ultraviolet (UV) radiation at wavelengths of less than 0.19 μm with molecular oxygen (O_2) which is split in the presence of **catalysts** and recombines to produce ozone (O_3). Ozone plays a major role in the Earth's biophysical system, absorbing virtually all the UV radiation entering the atmosphere from the Sun. This 'global sun-screen' protects life forms which would otherwise be destroyed or adversely affected by exposure to the intense UV radiation entering the top of the atmosphere.

Ozone is destroyed naturally in the atmosphere in three ways: it reacts with UV radiation at wavelengths of 0.23–0.29 μm to produce an oxygen atom (O) and an oxygen molecule (O_2): it reacts with nitric oxide (NO), the concentration of which is linked to the release of nitrous oxide (a greenhouse gas); and it reacts with chlorine (Cl) which is produced naturally by volcanic activity.

The natural rate of ozone depletion in the stratosphere is, however, being accelerated by the release of **chlorofluorocarbons** (CFCs). CFCs do not break down in the lower atmosphere; they gradually diffuse into the stratosphere where there is a high level of UV radiation. This radiation breaks down the CFC molecules, releasing chlorine, which is extremely chemically active at that altitude. Initially the chlorine reacts with ozone in a **photolytic reaction** to produce chlorine monoxide (ClO) and oxygen:

$$Cl + O_3 \rightarrow ClO + O_2$$

The chlorine monoxide then reacts with atomic oxygen to produce chlorine and oxygen:

$$ClO + O \rightarrow Cl + O_2$$

This is a catalytic reaction leading to a chain of further reactions that effectively remove two molecules of ozone but does not result in the destruction of the chlorine, which is therefore available for further reactions and the destruction of more ozone. Because ozone is the main UV-absorbing gas, a reduction in the amount of ozone will significantly increase the amount of UV radiation reaching the Earth's surface. This presents a number of human health problems as well as ecological problems.

Ozone depletion was first observed above Antarctica, but it is not restricted to that area; significant declines in ozone are occurring in the mid to high latitudes and possibly over the Arctic. In 1992, for instance, the spring warming over the North Pole probably occurred just in time to prevent an Arctic ozone hole (an area of low concentration of ozone) forming. The **World Meteorological Organization** (WMO) confirmed in 1993 that the lowest ever recorded amounts of ozone between 45°N and 65°N (a region covering parts of North

America, Europe and Siberia) had been measured. In fact, since 1969 there has been a 14 per cent decline in ozone levels overall. Given that global ozone depletion between 1979 and 1986 was about 5 per cent, and given that the amount of CFCs in the atmosphere continues to increase and that they stay in the atmosphere for a long time (that is, they have long **residence times**), the global decline in ozone will continue to be a cause for concern for many years, even if the most ambitious targets for CFC reduction are met.

While significant ozone depletion is occurring over the populated continents, most attention has been concentrated on high-latitude ozone depletion and, in particular, on the Antarctic ozone hole. Measurements in 1985 showed that a huge loss of ozone was occurring over Antarctica during each Southern Hemisphere spring, and these results were subsequently confirmed by NASA using the Total Ozone Mapping Spectrometer (TOMS) satellite. Figure 5.1 shows the October ozone concentration over Halley Bay in Antarctica from 1958 until 1994: the loss of ozone in spring is particularly evident after about 1970. Plate E shows how the Antarctic ozone hole expanded between 1980 and 1992.

The formation of the Antarctic ozone hole requires a polar vortex — a region of strong winds which effectively cuts Antarctica off from the rest of the Earth's atmosphere — to form around the continent during winter. This leads to a pool of stagnant air over Antarctica together with very low light levels and atmospheric temperatures. The

Figure 5.1
October ozone concentration over Halley Bay in Antarctica, 1958–94, showing the dramatic depletion in ozone after about 1970 and the formation of the ozone 'hole'. The 1994 value shows a slight increase, but the geographical extent of the 'hole' was the greatest on record. (Recent data were provided by J.D. Shanklin of the British Antarctic Survey.)

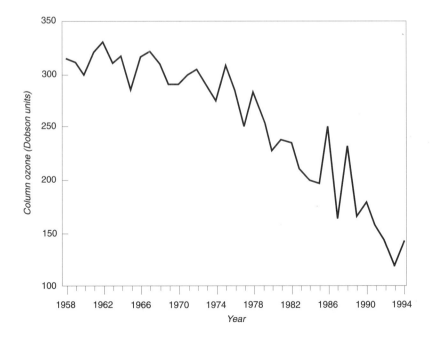

very low temperatures combine with the formation of significant amounts of polar stratospheric cloud to produce low moisture levels in the atmosphere and remove active nitrogen oxides by the adsorption of nitric acid onto the clouds. Because the nitrogen oxides have been removed from the air, they are no longer available to neutralise chlorine. The polar stratospheric clouds also provide a reaction surface for transferring inactive chlorine to an active state, ready to react once UV radiation levels begin to rise in spring.

The overall effect of all these processes is to predispose the atmosphere over Antarctica for the rapid **photodissociation** of ozone when increasing amounts of UV radiation are available in spring. This in turn leads to a rapid decline in the ozone concentration until the polar vortex breaks up because of increased heating in late spring. As the vortex breaks up, pockets of ozone-depleted air move northwards as far as Australia: a particularly bad example was in December 1987 when such an air pocket passed over Hobart, Melbourne and Perth.

On 6 October 1993 an ozone concentration of 88 **Dobson units**, the lowest ever recorded on Earth, was measured over Halley Bay. This extremely low value may be related to causes other than the amount of chlorine in the atmosphere, such as volcanic eruptions and unusually cold temperatures over the Antarctic in October 1993. However, the continued release of CFCs also probably played a role. When this ozone hole decayed in spring, ozone-depleted air masses drifted northwards. Measurements over Macquarie Island and southern Tasmania showed that some of these pockets would have passed over populated areas, leading to short-term reductions of 30 per cent in ozone levels above those locations.

Because of concerns over ozone depletion, the Montréal Protocol was formulated in 1987 (see also Section 6.4). This aimed at achieving a 50 per cent reduction in CFC emissions by 1999, but the decline in ozone over the Antarctic soon indicated that this reduction would be insufficient to adequately deal with the problem of ozone depletion. A review of the Protocol in 1990 imposed a total ban on the production of CFCs by AD 2000. The 1990 meeting also promised financial and technical aid to low-income countries to assist them in moving from CFCs to non-CFC technology. Unfortunately, recent evidence suggests that ozone depletion might be due, at least in part, to bromine-based chemicals not covered by the Montréal Protocol and still being used and released into the atmosphere without controls similar to those placed on CFCs.

186 Effects of ultraviolet radiation

Global ozone depletion over the decade 1983–93 has led to a 10 per cent increase in the UV radiation reaching the Earth's surface. It has been estimated that every 1 per cent decrease in ozone concentration will produce a 2 per cent increase in the UV radiation reaching the Earth's surface and an 8 per cent increase in the frequency of skin cancer in Caucasians. For example, a 5 per cent decrease in ozone concentrations could lead to a 10–15 per cent increase in skin cancer in Australia, which is already experiencing extreme levels of skin cancer. UV radiation also affects our immune systems, reducing our ability to fight common viral, fungal and protozoan infections: the **World Health Organization** (WHO) has warned that people with suppressed immune systems (for example, people with AIDS or other viral infections) will be particularly at increased risk. UV radiation also causes eye diseases such as cataracts, ocular lens damage and retina damage: a 1 per cent increase in UV light, for example, will increase the incidence of some eye diseases in Australia by 2.5 per cent in Aborigines and 14 per cent in non-Aborigines (see also Section 2.1). There are also warnings that the effectiveness of measles and tuberculosis vaccines might be reduced: measles and tuberculosis are very serious diseases in many countries, and although they can be controlled by vaccination programs, our ability to control outbreaks could be affected by ozone depletion.

UV radiation also has a detrimental effect on plants and animals. Plant leaves are damaged by UV radiation, and it is likely that this will lead to a reduction in agricultural yields. In addition, simple organisms with one or a few cells (**phytoplankton**, for instance) are highly susceptible to increases in UV radiation. We simply do not know how these simple organisms will be affected by changing amounts of UV radiation, but if they decline markedly, one of the most important **sinks** for CO_2 (the oceans) might be adversely affected, as might population levels of many marine species, including human food species, as phytoplankton are at the base of crucial oceanic food chains.

5.3 THE ENHANCED GREENHOUSE EFFECT

In 1988 the UN General Assembly asked the world's atmospheric science community for advice on the seriousness of the threat posed by the enhanced greenhouse effect. The resulting report from the Intergovernmental Panel on Climate Change (IPCC)[1] stated:

We are certain that emissions resulting from human activities are substantially increasing the atmospheric concentration of the greenhouse
gases . . . These increases will enhance the greenhouse effect resulting on
average in an additional warming of the Earth's surface.

The greenhouse effect is a natural process which makes the Earth
about 33°C warmer than we would otherwise expect it to be at its
distance from the Sun. It is a global phenomenon caused by naturally
occurring gases in the atmosphere (the so-called greenhouse gases),
has existed for millions of years, and has acted like a blanket around
the Earth, keeping the planet from becoming entirely covered by ice.
The greenhouse effect is not specific to the Earth, as both Mars and
Venus are affected by a greenhouse effect, although in the case of
Venus the effect is severe, warming the planet by 523°C.

While the greenhouse effect is a natural process, industry, land-use
change and other human activities are changing the amounts of greenhouse gases in the atmosphere, leading to a change in the natural heat
balance. This amplification of the natural greenhouse effect is known
as the 'enhanced greenhouse effect': it is this enhancement of the
natural process that has caused concern over the last decade.

People have always interacted with their environment, including the
atmosphere. When people first set fire to a forest or grassland they
began to upset the natural chemical and energy balance of the atmosphere. The effects became much greater, however, with the Industrial
Revolution in Western Europe (and later elsewhere), as large amounts
of wood and coal were burnt, releasing the energy stored in those
materials. When burnt, the carbon they contain is oxidised and carbon
dioxide (CO_2), a greenhouse gas, is released into the atmosphere at
rates greater than rates of removal by natural processes. But CO_2 is not
the only greenhouse gas: the rate of build-up of all the greenhouse
gases, particularly CO_2, methane (CH_4), nitrous oxide (N_2O) and the
chlorofluorocarbons (CFCs) was accelerating in the mid to late twentieth century, with little sign of the rate of acceleration declining. By
about 2030 enough greenhouse gases will have been added to have
effectively doubled the quantity of greenhouse gases in the atmosphere when compared with the levels which existed before the Industrial Revolution.

What happens in the atmosphere?

Everything emits radiation within a range of wavelengths determined
by temperature, explained by a relationship known as Planck's Law:
the hotter an object, the shorter the wavelengths at which it will emit
radiation. The Sun, with a surface temperature of about 6000°C, emits

radiation (solar radiation) at short wavelengths between about 0.15 and 5 μm, most radiation being emitted at 0.5 μm. Part of this shortwave radiation is visible light (Figure 5.2). Greenhouse gases in the atmosphere do not absorb this shortwave radiation very well (Figure 5.3), so most of it passes through the atmosphere to be absorbed by the Earth's surface. Because the Earth's surface is cold compared to the Sun, it emits terrestrial radiation in the thermal infra-red wavelengths

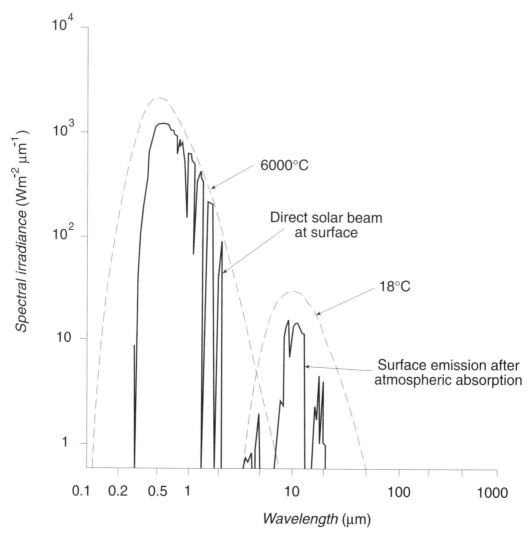

Figure 5.2
Theoretical Planck (or black body) curves (dotted lines) and actual radiation (solid lines) for the Sun (approx. 6000°C) and the Earth (−18°C). The vertical axis is scaled so that the two curves have the same vertical range. The peak of the solar curve is 0.5 μm, while the peak of the curve for the Earth is about 11.4 μm.

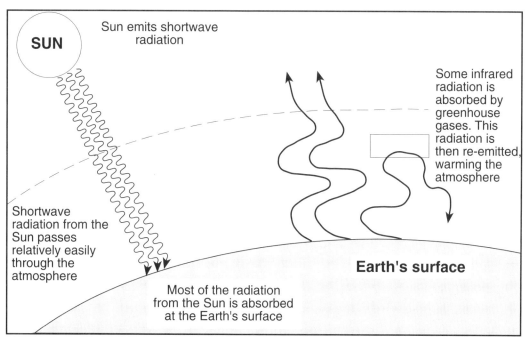

Sun emits shortwave radiation

SUN

Some infrared radiation is absorbed by greenhouse gases. This radiation is then re-emitted, warming the atmosphere

Shortwave radiation from the Sun passes relatively easily through the atmosphere

Earth's surface

Most of the radiation from the Sun is absorbed at the Earth's surface

Figure 5.3
A diagram illustrating the greenhouse effect (Source: Adapted from Houghton, J.T., Jenkins, G.G., and Euphrams, J.J. (eds), *Climate Change Working Group I: Scientific assessment*, Cambridge University Press (Cambridge, UK, 1990).)

of 3–50 μm with a peak at 11.4 μm (right-hand side of Figure 5.2). It is important to note that the surface *absorbs* the shortwave radiation, as radiation which is *reflected* remains at the same wavelength and can pass back out of the atmosphere just as easily as it passed in.

Some gases in the atmosphere, the greenhouse gases, are very efficient at absorbing the thermal infra-red radiation emitted by the Earth's surface as it is emitted into the atmosphere. The major gases in the Earth's atmosphere, nitrogen (N_2), comprising about 78 per cent of the atmosphere, and oxygen (O_2), comprising about 20 per cent, are not greenhouse gases. In contrast, greenhouse gases — mostly water vapour (H_2O), carbon dioxide (CO_2), methane (CH_4), nitrous oxide' (N_2O), ozone (O_3) and the CFCs — allow the Sun's energy to pass downward easily, but do not allow the Earth's radiation to pass back out easily, absorbing energy emitted from the Earth's surface and acting as a 'lid' on the atmosphere. As their concentration increases, the lid closes a little, catching more of the energy directed up through the atmosphere towards space. More energy trapped in the atmosphere means more heat in the atmosphere, and therefore warmer temperatures.

Figure 5.3 shows how the greenhouse effect occurs. Shortwave radiation from the Sun passes through the atmosphere and is absorbed at the Earth's surface. It is then re-emitted as thermal infra-red radiation, which is efficiently absorbed by the greenhouse gases: when the gases absorb radiation they become warmer and then emit radiation in all directions, the radiation emitted downwards warming the Earth.

Different greenhouse gases in the atmosphere absorb radiation at different wavelengths, as shown by Figure 5.4. Recall that Figure 5.2 shows that radiation at wavelengths from 0.1 μm to about 100 μm exists in the atmosphere, encompassing UV radiation, visible light, near infra-red radiation, and thermal infra-red radiation. In the shortwave part of the electromagnetic spectrum, and particularly in the wavelength region in which the Sun emits most radiation (around 0.5 μm), the atmosphere is essentially transparent, with almost no absorption. At longer wavelengths near the peak of the Earth's emission, the atmosphere exhibits much higher absorption — by the greenhouse gases. At the very short wavelengths of UV radiation, oxygen and

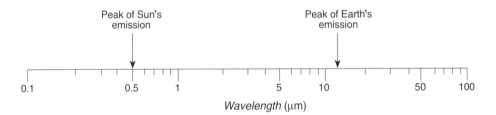

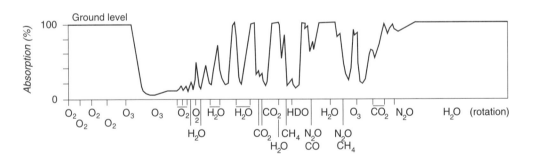

Figure 5.4
The electromagnetic spectrum showing the important wavelength regions for climatology (0.1 to <100 μm). The lower part of the diagram shows atmospheric absorption from 0.1 to <100 μm. In the visible part of the spectrum the atmosphere is partially transparent, but it exhibits high absorption by ozone (O_3) in the ultraviolet, and by water vapour (H_2O), carbon dioxide (CO_2), and other gases in the infra-red part of the spectrum. (Source: Modified from Henderson-Sellers, A. and Robinson, P.J., *Contemporary Climatology*, Longman (London, 1986).)

ozone absorb almost all radiation, thereby acting as a shield and preventing it reaching the Earth's surface (Section 5.2).

There are many greenhouse gases in the atmosphere which overlap in the wavelengths they absorb, and therefore some gases do not contribute as much to the greenhouse effect as might be expected. If a greenhouse gas 'blocks' one of the wavelength regions which the Earth's atmosphere does not otherwise block effectively (3 or 10 μm in Figure 5.4, for instance), then the importance of this gas will be greater than that of gas which absorbs radiation at a wavelength such as 6 μm where all the radiation is already absorbed by the atmosphere. Releasing a gas which absorbs at the latter wavelength will have less of an effect.

The most important greenhouse gas in the Earth's atmosphere is water vapour, while CO_2 is also a significant greenhouse gas with a major absorption band centred at 15 μm. The next most important greenhouse gas is CH_4, which overlaps the water vapour absorption bands. As we have seen, when gases absorb in the same regions, their joint heating is less than if they absorbed in different regions. The same is true of N_2O, which has absorption bands overlapping both the water vapour and CO_2 bands. The CFCs and ozone in the lower atmosphere, however, cover an area of the thermal infra-red region not covered by any of the other greenhouse gases; hence, although there are only small amounts of CFCs in the atmosphere, they contribute greatly to heating.

Table 5.1 lists the main greenhouse gases. The radiative absorption potential describes the effectiveness of a particular gas relative to CO_2. The table also shows what the natural concentrations of the major greenhouse gases 'should' be, the current concentration, and the residence time. So adding, for example, one metric tonne of CO_2 to the atmosphere has a relatively small effect because there are already large quantities present. In contrast, releasing the same amount of CFCs or N_2O has a much greater effect because these gases have long residence times and large radiative absorption potentials. Indeed, one metric tonne of CFCs has a massive effect because one CFC molecule is about 10 000 times more effective as a greenhouse gas than is one molecule of CO_2.

Overall, however, Table 5.1 shows that in the early 1990s far more CO_2 was released each year than all the other greenhouse gases combined — 7 Gt (7 gigatonnes or 7000 million tonnes) compared to less than 0.5 Gt. So even though CO_2 does not have as high a radiative absorption potential as the other gases, it was still the most important anthropogenically released greenhouse gas (Figure 5.5). Between 1965 and 1990, CO_2 contributed 61 per cent of the greenhouse effect

Table 5.1 Anthropogenically enhanced greenhouse gases and their concentrations (c. 1991)

Gas	Natural level	Current level	Current annual rate of increase	Residence time in atmosphere (years)	Radiative absorption potential	Annual release (Gt/year)
CO_2	280 ppmv	356 ppmv	1.8 ppmv (0.5%)	100	1	7.0
CH_4	0.8 ppmv	1.73 ppmv	0.015 ppm (0.9%)	10	32	0.45
CFC–11	0	280 pptv	9.5 pptv (4%)	65	>10 000	0.000058*
CFC–12	0	484 pptv	17 pptv (4%)	130	>10 000	
N_2O	288 ppbv	310 ppbv	0.8 ppbv (0.25%)	100–200	150	0.04
O_3		variable	2%	0.1–0.3	2000	

*The amount of CFC–12 and CFC–11 released is based on 1988 data and the two gases are combined to give a single total.

Figure 5.5
Greenhouse gases
that were the main
contributors to the
greenhouse effect (a)
from 1965 to 1990,
and (b) from 1980 to
1990. Note the
increasing
importance of
chlororfluorocarbons.
Stratospheric water
vapours (SWV) is
shown, but
tropospheric water
vapour is omitted
because it is a highly
variable quantity.

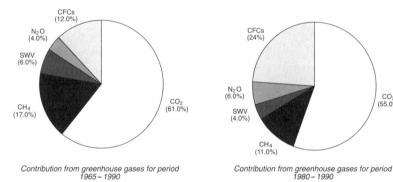

Contribution from greenhouse gases for period
1965–1990

Contribution from greenhouse gases for period
1980–1990

(excluding water vapour in the **troposphere**) and CH_4 was the second most important (17 per cent), followed by CFCs, stratospheric water vapour and N_2O. In the decade 1980–90, CO_2 was still the most important greenhouse gas (55 per cent), but its relative importance had declined. The gases which had grown in importance are clearly the CFCs. Although only small quantities of CFCs were released (Table 5.1), their radiative absorption potential is huge and their overall importance to the greenhouse effect was still increasing in the mid-1990s.

Sources and sinks of greenhouse gases

When greenhouse gases are emitted into the atmosphere they are dispersed around the world. Greenhouse gases do not stay in the atmosphere forever, being recycled back to the Earth's surface or into some other gas in the atmosphere. The 'places' from which the gases are emitted — industry, deforestation, cars and so on — are called sources, while the places they are removed to are called sinks. The length of time the gas stays in the atmosphere is known as the **residence time** (see Table 5.1). Finally, the rate of movement of a gas between sources and sinks is known as its flux. All of these parameters are extremely important in understanding the greenhouse effect, and form the framework for the following sections which consider each greenhouse gas in turn, beginning with the most important greenhouse gas of all, water vapour.

Water vapour (H_2O)

Water vapour enters the atmosphere through evaporation and through **transpiration** by plants, while the sink for water vapour is condensation into droplets, forming clouds and ultimately falling to earth as precipitation (see Figure 1.4). The key to the importance of water vapour to the greenhouse effect is that the amount that can be held in the atmosphere is closely coupled to air temperature. As the atmospheric temperature rises, more water can evaporate, so that as the atmosphere warms slightly due to increasing amounts of other greenhouse gases, it can hold more water vapour. Water vapour is a very efficient greenhouse gas, and more of it in the air leads to more absorption of radiation emitted by the surface, producing a temperature rise that in turn leads to yet more water vapour. This positive feedback (Figure 5.6) is a natural but very important component of the greenhouse effect, and is typical of the role of feedbacks in the climate system.[2]

Carbon dioxide (CO_2)

Carbon dioxide is the most important greenhouse gas that humans have directly added to the atmosphere (Figure 5.5): Box 5.1 summarises its key sources and sinks. The pre-industrial level of atmospheric CO_2 was 280 ppmv (parts per million by volume), but by the early 1990s there were 356 ppmv in the atmosphere. It is increasing by 1.5 ppmv each year, or 5 per cent per decade (Figure 5.7). Burning substances containing carbon (C) in an oxygen (O_2) atmosphere produces CO_2 and, as most fuels are carbon-based, burning almost any fuel releases CO_2. In addition, cutting and burning trees releases CO_2 immediately, while leaving trees to decay eventually releases it into the atmosphere. Deforestation is therefore doubly bad, as it also removes growing trees, a major sink for CO_2 (Section 3.3). In the mid-1990s, people put 6.7–9.3 Gt of carbon into the atmosphere each year, made up of about 5.4 Gt per annum of carbon from fossil fuel burning and

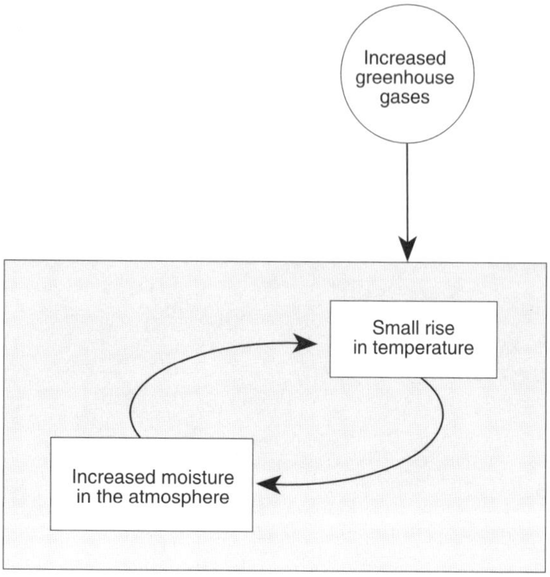

Figure 5.6
The positive feedback effect between water vapour and temperature. This feedback makes water vapour the most important greenhouse gas.

about 1.6 Gt per annum from deforestation and land-use change. CO_2 emitted into the atmosphere has a residence time of about 100 years.

Measurements of the concentration of CO_2 in the atmosphere over Hawaii (Figure 5.7) show an overall upward trend, superimposed on which is an annual oscillation in the concentration of CO_2 due to an imbalance between the northern and southern hemispheres in the amount of CO_2 seasonally taken up and released by plants. The overall increase is due to burning fossil fuels and deforestation.

In many low-income nations (for example, in Latin America and tropical Africa), there is considerable CO_2 release due to forest clearing for agriculture. Many high-income countries (for example, in North America and Europe) have stopped clearing land and are allowing land to revert to its natural state or are implementing reafforestation programs to reclaim degraded farmland or, more rarely, to remove CO_2 from the atmosphere: whether or not CO_2 removal is the primary purpose, it has the effect. Although reafforestation will have no long-term impact on the enhanced greenhouse effect, it will slow the process in the short term and help reduce many other environmental problems.

Because CO_2 is a natural component of the Earth's system, there are many natural sinks. The most important of these are the oceans, which take up about 50 per cent of the CO_2 emitted annually. Much of this becomes part of the shells and skeletons of oceanic animals, which

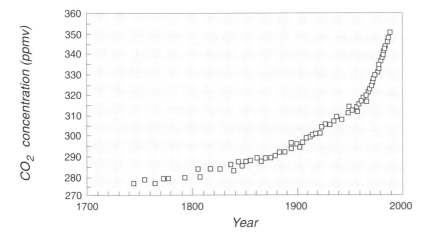

Figure 5.7
The changing atmospheric CO_2 concentration based on measurements from Mauna Loa (Hawaii).

may ultimately form carbonate rocks such as limestone. This is a slow process which acts as a sink only on geological time-scales, and not in all oceanic environments. It is not nearly fast enough to compensate for the increased amount of CO_2 released by people.

The other major sink for CO_2 is growing plants in which **photosynthesis** converts the CO_2 into carbon compounds needed for growth. However, a mature forest removes very little net CO_2 from the atmosphere because uptake in photosynthesis is more or less balanced by release in respiration and litter decay. So, while it is important to retain tropical rainforest and other natural vegetation for environmental reasons (for example, to preserve genetic diversity) this preservation does not counter the enhanced greenhouse effect. To mitigate the enhanced greenhouse effect in the short term, new forests must be grown. Of course, tropical deforestation does add CO_2 to the atmosphere, thereby contributing to the enhanced greenhouse effect (Section 3.3).

Methane (CH_4)

Methane is a significant greenhouse gas (Figure 5.5) and is produced by fermentation, a process which occurs in any environment where there is no oxygen (that is, under anaerobic conditions); for example, marshes and ponds release CH_4 due to rotting vegetation. Figure 5.8 shows how levels began to increase slowly in the atmosphere around 1850 and more rapidly after about 1900, while Box 5.2 summarises the sources and sinks of methane.

One of the major reasons that CH_4 is increasing in the atmosphere is because we have increased the amount of land covered by marshes,

BOX

5.1

Sources and sinks of CO_2, 1980–89 (Gt C per year)

Sources

Burning fossil fuels	5.4 ± 0.5
Deforestation and land-use change	1.6 ± 1.0

Sinks

Accumulation in the atmosphere	3.4 ± 0.2
Uptake by the ocean	2.0 ± 1.0
Uptake by the biosphere	$1.6 \pm 1.5*$

*The size of this sink is based on subtracting the 'known' sinks from the 'known' sources. A sink of 1.6 ± 1.5 Gt C (gigatonnes of carbon) per year is probably far too large, implying that we do not know the carbon cycle well.

particularly the artificial marshes we know as paddy fields. These are a significant source of CH_4, which is produced under the water used to flood the paddies; the rice plants acts as wicks, efficiently pumping the gas into the atmosphere. So the increase in the rice-growing area necessitated by the rapid increase in the human population, especially in low-income countries (90 per cent of harvested rice paddies are in Asia), has resulted in an increase in atmospheric CH_4.

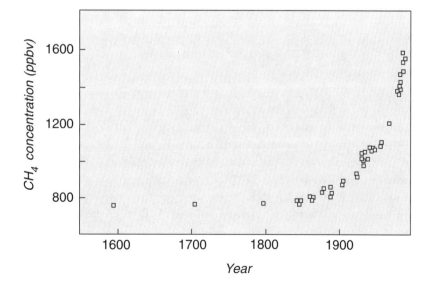

Figure 5.8
Atmospheric methane variations from 1600, based on ice-core samples.

Another important source is animals which use anaerobic digestion, especially ruminants. The total CH_4 production from domesticated animals is about 0.08 Gt per annum: of this, cattle contribute about 73 per cent, buffalo about 8 per cent, sheep about 9 per cent, and camels, mules and pigs most of the remainder.[3] Termites also produce CH_4, and agricultural intensification following deforestation seems to increase the number and size of termite colonies. Although it is almost impossible to produce reasonable estimates of how much termites produce, the amount is probably about 0.04 Gt per year. If correct, this would be a significant contribution to the increase in the atmosphere.

Anaerobic decay in garbage tips, direct leakage from underground coal and gas deposits, leaking gas mains (claimed to be an important source in the UK, for example), and fossil fuel burning are all additional sources, while another possibly important source is the **tundra** of northern North America and Eurasia. There is a possibility that global warming, for whatever reason, could melt regions of permafrost within which huge quantities of CH_4 are stored. While the best estimate of current release from the permafrost is only 0.005 Gt per annum, there is the possibility that an additional release of 0.1 Gt per annum could occur with permafrost melt. If this does occur, it would be another important example of a positive feedback operating in climate change.

A final, newly identified possible source is of considerable concern. Recent evidence suggests that hydro-electric power schemes which allow large lakes of water to form behind dams result in large emissions derived from the rotting of drowned vegetation. If this does prove to be a large source, it could mean that hydro-electric power generation does contribute to the greenhouse effect after all.

The sinks for CH_4 are not well understood. However, the main sink comprises chemical reactions in the atmosphere in which sunlight breaks up the complex molecules in the presence of the hydroxyl radical (OH^-) to create active chemicals which then break down further. Part of the reason CH_4 has been increasing in the atmosphere is that the hydroxyl radical may have been depleted due to emissions of carbon monoxide (CO), the main anthropogenic source of which is biomass burning. CO emissions are therefore important in contributing indirectly to the enhanced greenhouse effect, even though CO is not itself a greenhouse gas.

CH_4 has a residence time in the atmosphere of about 10 years, the shortest of all the greenhouse gases. This means that if we could stop the enhanced emissions, the amount in the atmosphere should fall to its natural level in a decade.

BOX

5.2

Sources and sinks of methane (Gt CH$_4$ per year)

Sources

Natural wetlands	0.115
Rice paddies	0.110
The guts of ruminant animals	0.08
Leakage from coal and natural gas deposits	0.08
Termites	0.04
Garbage tips	0.04
Biomass burning	0.04
Oceans	0.01
Fresh water	0.005
Permafrost areas	0.005
Total	0.525

Sinks

Photochemical reactions in the atmosphere	0.5
Removal by soils	0.03
Total	0.53

Atmospheric increase	0.044*

* Adding the sources and then subtracting the sinks does not give a figure of 0.044 Gt because the sources and sinks are only approximately known. The atmospheric increase is the most reliable of all these numbers.

Nitrous oxide (N$_2$O)

Nitrous oxide contributes about 6 per cent to the total greenhouse effect. (Box 5.3 summarises the sources and sinks of N$_2$O.) It is exceedingly difficult to quantify the size of the individual sources, but total production is probably about 0.004–0.01 Gt per year, approximately 60 per cent coming from natural emissions from the ocean and soils. The remainder is produced anthropogenically, with approximately 15 per cent from fossil fuel burning, 10 per cent from biomass burning, and 10 per cent from the application of nitrogenous fertilisers to soils. The primary source of N$_2$O is believed to be **denitrification** in **aerobic** soils. The contribution from biomass burning, including forest clearance and natural bushfires, may be greater than previously thought because fire seems to stimulate soil microbial production, which continues for many months after the fire.

Figure 5.9 shows how N_2O levels have increased in the atmosphere. This increase began in the eighteenth century as agriculture began to become more intensive, but it is the increase in the last few decades that is most important. The increased release of N_2O due to the intensification of agriculture, through the application of nitrogen-based fertiliser (some 0.07 Gt of nitrogen are applied to crops each year), is a serious issue. Both natural and artificial fertilisers can lead to enhanced N_2O production, mainly through denitrification; the overuse of nitrates in the soil also leads to the pollution of groundwater.

The sink for N_2O is the upper atmosphere (stratosphere) where sunlight decomposes it into nitrogen and oxygen. N_2O has a residence time in the atmosphere of 100–200 years, one of the longest of all greenhouse gases. Even if we could control the sources of N_2O immediately, it would thus take a very long time for it to fall to its natural level.

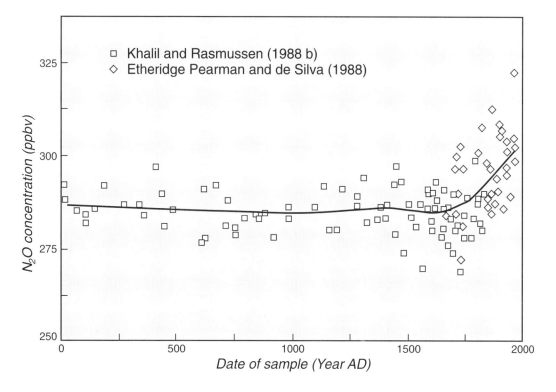

Figure 5.9
Nitrous oxide concentrations in the atmosphere over the last 2000 years.

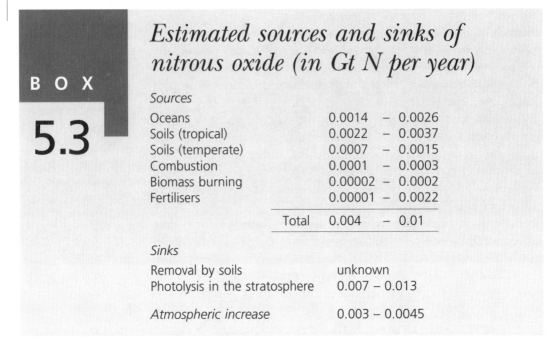

BOX

5.3

Estimated sources and sinks of nitrous oxide (in Gt N per year)

Sources

Oceans	0.0014	– 0.0026
Soils (tropical)	0.0022	– 0.0037
Soils (temperate)	0.0007	– 0.0015
Combustion	0.0001	– 0.0003
Biomass burning	0.00002	– 0.0002
Fertilisers	0.00001	– 0.0022
Total	0.004	– 0.01

Sinks

Removal by soils	unknown
Photolysis in the stratosphere	0.007 – 0.013

Atmospheric increase	0.003 – 0.0045

Chlorofluorocarbons (CFCs)

There is a whole family of chemicals within the atmosphere, collectively known as halocarbons, which variously contain fluorine, chlorine, or bromine. The most important of these are referred to by the generic term chlorofluorocarbons (or CFCs), and sometimes by trade names such as Freon. CFCs are major greenhouse gases and were manufactured by people: the most common CFCs (CFC–11 and CFC–12) were increasing in the atmosphere at about 4 per cent per year in the early 1980s (Figure 5.10).

CFCs were designed to replace ammonia (a hazardous chemical in industrial and domestic locations) in refrigeration plants because they are effective in heat pumps, removing heat either from inside a refrigerator or from an air-conditioned room. Because they were designed to be inert (that is, not to take part in chemical reactions), they have also been used in many other manufacturing processes and products: for example, as the propellant in aerosol cans, in some fire extinguishers, and for cleaning electronic components. CFCs were also used as bubbling agents in some plastic foams. Articles such as foam-filled furniture, polystyrene cups, and foamed trays for fresh meat and pre-packaged vegetables in supermarkets, were originally manufactured by bubbling a CFC through them, the CFCs being released to the atmosphere during the manufacturing process. This is not true of refrigerators and air-conditioners, where the CFCs are contained within the machines: the release of CFCs could be reduced by collecting all old refrigerators and air conditioners with a view to recycling the CFCs, as is being done in some places, or by safely disposing of them.

CFCs are essentially inert in the troposphere and have extremely long residence times, probably taking 65–130 years to break down in the lower atmosphere, during which time they circulate around the Earth. However, some CFCs leak into the upper atmosphere (the stratosphere) and break down rapidly by photodissociation under UV radiation. This releases chlorine, which has led to a worldwide reduction in ozone and the formation of ozone holes. Ozone depletion and ozone hole formation are *not* part of the greenhouse effect — these topics are discussed in Section 5.2.

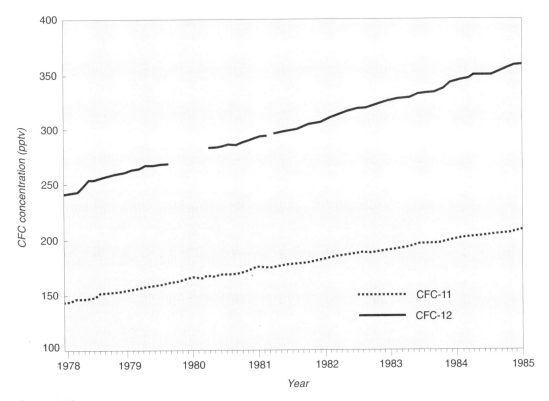

Figure 5.10
Concentrations of CFC–11 and CFC–12 in the atmosphere above Cape Grim, Tasmania from 1978 to 1985.

5.4 CONSEQUENCES OF THE ENHANCED GREENHOUSE EFFECT

Given that natural greenhouse gases in the Earth's atmosphere warm the Earth by about 33°C, it is logical to assume that the addition of more greenhouse gases would lead to further warming. This is likely to be the case, but identifying the amount by which the Earth's climate will warm and what other consequences will be experienced due to that warming is rather difficult and still controversial. There are already, however, data which show that some aspects of the climate system are undergoing change. None of these changes prove that the release of greenhouse gases by humans has caused climate change, because it is impossible to be sure whether the changes are caused by the greenhouse effect or by other aspects of the climate system.

Figure 5.11 shows the changes in the global temperature over the first 90 years or so of the twentieth century: the smoothed line shows the trend, while the individual bars show annual values. There are many fluctuations in the annual values and we do not fully understand why all of these have occurred. However, after about 1910 there appears to have been an upward trend in the Earth's average temperature broadly in line with what might be expected due to the enhanced greenhouse effect. It is, perhaps, circumstantial evidence that the additional greenhouse gases put into the atmosphere by people are warming the Earth.

If the Earth's temperature rises, the temperature of the oceans will also rise, although rather more slowly. If water is heated it expands, so if the upper levels of the oceans warm they will expand and cause the sea level to rise. Evidence suggests that the sea level has risen by about 0.12 m since the 1880s, but, as was the case with temperature, this is not proof that the release of greenhouse gases by human activity has been the cause.

More circumstantial evidence has been obtained from observations of snow and ice cover. If the Earth is warming we would expect that snow and ice sheets would melt and become smaller, and that glaciers would melt and become shorter. This appears to be happening: for example, observations show that many glaciers have become substantially shorter since about 1850. Similarly, there seems to have been a reduction in the extent of snow cover over the Northern Hemisphere since 1980.

Temperatures and sea level do seem to be rising, and snow and sea ice limits appear to be retreating. The changes in sea levels and snow cover are probably due to changes in the temperature, but we are not

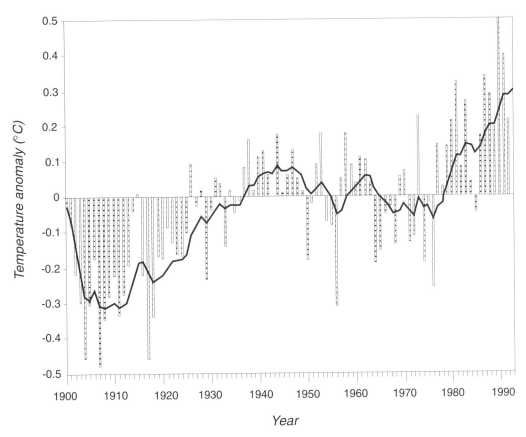

Figure 5.11
Changes in the global temperature from 1900 until 1992. The solid line is a
10-year running average, while the individual bars show the temperature
difference from the average 1951–80 temperature (positive numbers indicate
warming).

certain that this is caused by the enhanced greenhouse effect. There
are other plausible explanations. About 18 000 years ago the Earth
experienced the last glacial maximum of the Ice Ages. Since that time
the planet has gradually warmed as snow and ice have receded, and
the additional warming since the beginning of this century may be
part of that process. A second possible explanation for the apparent
warming is that most meteorological stations were originally located at
the edges of towns. As urban expansion occurred, these stations became surrounded by buildings, roads, and factories. Therefore, the
urban heat island effect (Section 4.4) might have seriously affected the
long-term temperature record. In addition, most meteorological stations are located in populated regions (that is, not in Antarctica,
Africa, tropical South America or the oceans). This makes the global

temperature record questionable, and the temperature increase observed since the 1850s unreliable. When all of these factors are accounted for in the temperature record, however, there is still a global temperature increase evident, suggesting that the apparent warming is not due entirely to urbanisation and the other factors mentioned above.

The temperature increase since the 1850s has been quite marked and the Earth's temperature is now warmer that at any time since 1300. If the Earth's climate warmed by a further 1°C it would be warmer than at any time in the last 20 000 years: and if the Earth warmed by 4.5°C (as it is predicted to do if there were an effective doubling of atmospheric CO_2), the Earth's climate would be warmer than at any time in the last 70 million years. In fact, if the Earth's temperature does increase at the predicted rate (about 0.3°C per decade), this rate of increase would be 10 to 100 times faster than the increase the Earth experienced at the end of the last glacial maximum. There are serious questions concerning the abilities of natural ecosystems to adapt to such rapid climate change.

The consensus of scientific opinion is that the temperature increase this century is due in part to urban expansion, and that about 0.3°C is due to the enhanced greenhouse effect. This does not sound very much, but it is a globally averaged figure which hides a lot of regional variability. While many climatologists believe that the temperature increase is due to the enhanced greenhouse effect, we cannot afford to wait for certainty before beginning to deal with the problems a global rise in temperature would cause. This, then, appears to be an area calling for the application of the precautionary principle (Section 7.8).

5.5 PREDICTING GREENHOUSE CHANGES

Global climate model predictions for an effective doubling of CO_2

The enhanced greenhouse effect will not lead to uniform climate changes: in fact, there will be major geographical variability in the climate changes that do occur. Climate models, or atmospheric general circulation models (GCMs), can be used to predict how the Earth's climate might change as the composition of the atmosphere changes.

Climate models are based on a numerical formulation of the physical laws which govern the behaviour of the atmosphere and, to a lesser extent, the oceans. Climate models attempt to represent all aspects of the Earth's energy and water cycles (see Figures 1.2 and 1.3). The processes which take place in the atmosphere are expressed as mathematical equations programmed into a computer — the climate 'model' only exists inside the computer. Climate modellers make predictions based on these mathematical models by organising the physical laws in a form that large computers can use. To do this the Earth's surface is divided into large rectangular areas, each about 300 km by 500 km at the equator. The atmosphere is also cut up into about ten horizontal slices which fit over the rectangular surface grid. The atmosphere can therefore be thought of as interlinked boxes through which air flows and within which temperatures change, clouds form and other meteorological processes occur. Moisture and heat move three-dimensionally between the boxes, allowing predictions to be made about climate change.

Climate models only predict a single value for each of temperature, rainfall, wind speed and other variables for each box, so they cannot give us accurate regional-scale predictions. For example, since the whole of Australia is covered by only a few dozen surface blocks, a region like New South Wales has only about five blocks, which is not enough to give reliable regional or local predictions. In addition, climate models are far from perfect. They are extreme over-simplifications of the real world and do not take account of many important processes. In particular, they use coarse resolution; they simulate clouds poorly; the ocean component is imperfect; and the representation of the Earth's surface, especially topography, is simplistic. These weaknesses may be very important and may undermine the reliability of climate predictions. Despite the simplifications, climate models work rather well in the sense that they produce apparently realistic simulations of the winds, temperatures and rainfall around the globe. They are, however, global-scale models designed to compute global-scale circulations. These models are run on the largest supercomputers in the world, but it still takes a long time to undertake a five or ten-year simulation of the atmosphere; so at present it is not feasible to sharpen the resolution.

Many GCMs have been used to predict the changes in climate which might result from greenhouse-induced warming. There is broad consensus among climate modelling groups about the effects of the additional greenhouse heating at the global scale. Temperatures are believed to be likely to increase by 1.5–4.5°C for an effective doubling of CO_2, the 'best-guess' estimate being 2.5°C. All of the models agree that doubling CO_2 will increase the amount of evaporation and change the amount of precipitation (that is, rain and snow together) leading to an intensification of the global water and energy cycles.

Some simulated results from one climate model are presented in Plates F and G. This GCM was developed at the Australian Bureau of Meteorology's Research Centre in Melbourne, and is one of the most respected climate models. The results shown in plates F and G come from a 15-year average simulation of what this model predicts will happen if CO_2 levels in the atmosphere are doubled. A 15-year simulation for the climate of today was produced, and then a 15-year simulation with everything kept the same except that the amount of CO_2 in the atmosphere was doubled. The results are expressed as a difference, with the key below the plate showing the simulated change.

Temperature

Plate F shows what would happen to the annual mean air temperature in the GCM if CO_2 were doubled. The Earth's temperature clearly increases under greenhouse conditions, with everywhere on the Earth's surface warming by at least 0.5°C. In some regions the air temperature rises by up to 6°C (near Antarctica) and by more than 4°C in large parts of Eurasia, North America and the Arctic. It is important to note that many of the biggest changes occur at high latitudes (near the poles), a phenomenon also seen in other climate models. Over the land nearer the Equator (Africa, South America and Australia) the temperature increases are usually smaller, but still 1–3°C. This model predicts temperature increases over most of Australia of 2–3°C, although the northern areas warm by 1–2°C.

Precipitation

Plate G shows the effect on annual total precipitation if the amount of CO_2 were doubled. In contrast to changes in temperature, changes in precipitation are much more variable, with many areas showing increases and others showing decreases. The changes over the continental surfaces are generally quite small (increases or decreases of 0.5 mm per day). Over North America and Eurasia, rainfall is reduced by about 0.5 mm per day, with larger reductions over parts of Africa. The east coast of Australia receives slightly less rainfall, although the rest of Australia experiences slightly increased amounts. Northern Eurasia and Canada also become slightly wetter. Reductions in precipitation of 0.5 mm per day do not sound very dramatic, but for many parts of eastern Australia a decrease of 180 mm in annual rainfall would make agriculture significantly more difficult.

Predictions for Australia

The results from the Bureau of Meteorology's Research Centre's GCM shown in plates F and G are one possible consequence of the enhanced greenhouse effect for Australia. Climate models are not well suited to regional-scale prediction, but it is still possible to draw some very broad conclusions concerning the effects of global warming on the continent. Figure 5.12 shows the consensus annual temperature increase predicted by a number of climate models. The simulations of the present day were checked against observed data by the CSIRO and considered reasonable. Agreement between these models and the present does not mean that the prediction of warming due to the enhanced greenhouse effect is necessarily correct, but it does increase its perceived reliability. For Australia, the consensus from the climate models is that temperatures over the entire continent will increase by at least 0.5°C. Along the southern coast the temperature is likely to generally increase by up to 2.0°C, while along the northern coast temperatures are likely to increase by up to 1.5°C. However, Figure 5.12 only shows one possible scenario for Australian temperatures in a warmer world, and it should not be considered to be an accurate forecast.

Changes in rainfall are harder to predict than changes in temperature. Predicted summer rainfall changes due to the enhanced greenhouse effect range from no change to a 20 per cent increase by 2030. Changes in winter rainfall (Figure 5.13) might include decreases of up to 10 per cent in inland southern Australia, possible changes of −10 per cent to +10 per cent in the east and south-west, and an increase of 10 per cent in Tasmania. However, Figure 5.13 shows only one possible scenario for Australian rainfall in a warmer world, and it should not be considered to be an accurate forecast. There is also a possibility of a general increase in rainfall intensity and heavy falls, with more and longer dry spells and fewer days with rain. There is also a chance of more very hot days, fewer frosts, more floods, and more dry spells; in other words, more extreme weather generally.

However, there is at least one great unknown: all these scenarios depend on how the **El Niño–Southern Oscillation** (ENSO)[4] phenomenon is affected by greenhouse warming. If the frequency, duration or intensity of ENSO changes, then the climate scenarios for 2030 could be greatly changed. It is also important to realise that all these predictions are seriously flawed by the weaknesses inherent in all climate models, so that the suggested changes are a warning of what might happen rather than a prediction of what will happen.

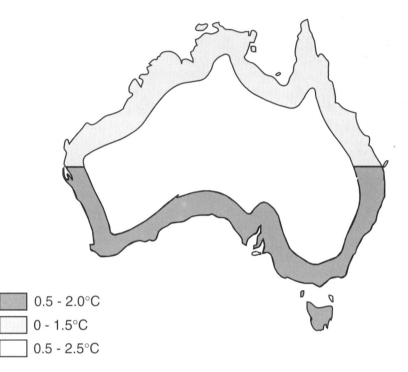

Figure 5.12
Temperature
increases predicted
by a number of
climate models for
Australia. This figure
shows one possible
scenario; it is not a
prediction with high
confidence levels.

0.5 - 2.0°C
0 - 1.5°C
0.5 - 2.5°C

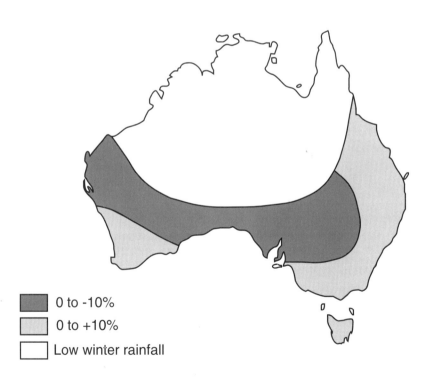

Figure 5.13
Winter precipitation
changes predicted by
a number of climate
models for Australia.
This figure shows
one possible
scenario; it is not a
prediction with high
confidence levels.

0 to -10%
0 to +10%
Low winter rainfall

Other effects of greenhouse change

Assuming that the climate model predictions are correct, it is possible to make some preliminary estimates of how other phenomena might be affected. While this section concentrates on Australian examples, there are clear implications for other nations, especially low-lying island states.

Sea level

The sea level is expected to rise by 0.08–0.29 m by 2030 and 0.21–0.71 m by 2070 due to the enhanced greenhouse effect. Sea-level rise will affect Australia by shoreline changes, saltwater intrusion into coastal lands, increased temporary flooding of coasts and structures, and changes in coral reef structure. In recent decades the sea level has risen around parts of Australia's coast: some areas show major increases in sea level (for example, west of Adelaide) while many other areas show little change. These changes may or may not have been caused by the enhanced greenhouse effect, but it should be realised that the enhanced greenhouse effect is expected to lead to sea-level rise in addition to changes which are happening naturally. It has also been suggested that greenhouse-induced sea-level rise might have a detrimental effect on the Great Barrier Reef, but it could also be argued that the dynamics of this environment are such that coral growth can easily keep pace.

Tropical cyclones

If surface ocean temperatures increase, tropical cyclones could form further south than at present and increase in intensity and frequency, while sea-level rise and ocean warming could reduce the return period of severe cyclones from 10 000 to 100 years. Indeed, it has already been observed that the minimum pressure of Australian cyclones is falling by 1 hectopascal (10 millibars) per annum — cyclones are apparently becoming more intense. Tropical cyclones have killed about 1600 people in Australia since 1830 and have cost Australia more than A$1715 million. However, they are also the primary source of rainfall in some parts of Australia, so although they can cause major damage they also bring advantages. The current scientific assessment is that the regions affected by tropical cyclones will not change. In part, this conservatism is due to our lack of understanding of how ocean temperatures will be affected by greenhouse warming.

Human health and safety

Changes in the frequency of severe thunderstorms, tropical cyclones, flooding and the like will all affect our health and well-being to some degree. Global warming will affect humans most in areas that are sensitive to climate change: many of these areas are already prone to weather extremes and these extremes may simply become more common. The areas particularly at risk include those near coasts (especially islands), near rivers (especially where two rivers join), in areas susceptible to tropical cyclones, in areas susceptible to landslides, in areas susceptible to drought, in poor but densely populated areas, and in areas where subsistence agriculture is practised. The most important aspect of the enhanced greenhouse effect is perhaps not how big the changes in climate might be, but where the changes occur and the sensitivity of the environment and local communities to change in each particular region. Most low-income countries are potentially very sensitive since they cannot afford to plan for change. Globally, the biggest factors are likely to be sea-level rise and the increased frequency or severity of droughts, storms and floods. In Australia all these effects are likely to occur, but because Australia is a relatively rich country the results are likely to be far less dramatic.

Temperature seems to be important in the frequency of death due to stroke. As temperature increases from very cold levels (−30°C) there is a reduction in the frequency of death until about 27°C, after which there is a dramatic rise. With enhanced greenhouse temperatures and possible heat waves, we could be faced with a recurrence of the conditions of January 1939, when 368 people died from heat stress in Australia — 145 died in just two days in Melbourne alone. Heat stress does not affect all people to the same degree: it particularly affects old people; people in the poorer sectors of society; the physically and mentally handicapped; sufferers of cardiovascular disease, diabetes or hypertension; the obese; the unfit; alcoholics; and people in strenuous occupations. Sudden changes in temperature are also important because they place stress on our bodies, and the people at risk tend to be those who have bodies which cannot respond quickly to changes. The enhanced greenhouse effect may lead to more heat stress simply because the average temperature will be warmer, and therefore very warm or hot days will be that much warmer and occur that much more often.

The distribution of disease-carrying mosquitos is generally controlled by temperature and precipitation, so changes to these under greenhouse conditions may well lead to changes in the areas at risk from mosquito-borne diseases such as malaria. The distribution of malaria is limited by the 10°C average minimum isotherm in July (so areas in Australia which are colder than 10°C in July are not currently at risk), but because the enhanced greenhouse effect is expected to increase temperatures, more of Australia will be at risk from malaria-carrying mosquitos. If rainfall also increases, the present lack of moisture in central Australia may be replaced by enough water for mosquitos to breed. Encephalitis, which cause headaches, vomiting, stiffness and giddiness, is also carried by mosquitos and is partly controlled by climate. Areas affected are limited by winds, temperature and rainfall patterns, but more areas could be at risk under greenhouse conditions. Another mosquito-borne disease is Ross River virus, also known as epidemic polyarthritis as it causes general pain, particularly in joints, and leads to arthritis. This disease is more common during warmer and wetter summers, conditions which could become more widespread under the enhanced greenhouse effect.

The prevalence of asthma is also likely to be affected by enhanced greenhouse conditions. Asthma affects 10–15 per cent of adults in Australia; in fact, Australia and New Zealand have the highest prevalence in the world. The amounts of general pollution and particulates (dust, pollen, etc.) in the air are important factors in the prevalence of asthma. Asthma is likely to be more common under enhanced greenhouse conditions because more rain and warmer temperatures may increase the pollen output of many plants, while damper conditions could be ideal for moulds. In contrast, less rain and warmer temperatures would lead to much drier soils, increasing the amount of dust in the air. Figure 5.14 shows the likely effects of a variety of climate events on asthma. It is clear that in some places a climate change will lead to some unpleasant side effects for sufferers. In particular, warmer temperatures and higher humidity can lead to a much higher incidence of asthma. Heat stress (which will become a more significant problem if temperatures rise) and high humidity with higher rainfall could lead to many more asthma attacks.

Implications for Agriculture

Plants are sensitive to climate, in part because agricultural crops have become highly specialised over hundreds of years so that farmers now plant a specific variety to best suit their soil and the average climate in their area (Section 2.2). The enhanced greenhouse effect is likely to lead to warmer temperatures, changed precipitation patterns, changed evaporation levels and, overall, a change in the growing season.

While these changes might make it harder for a farmer to know which crop varieties to use and may well lead to reduced yields, the

Direct climatic effects

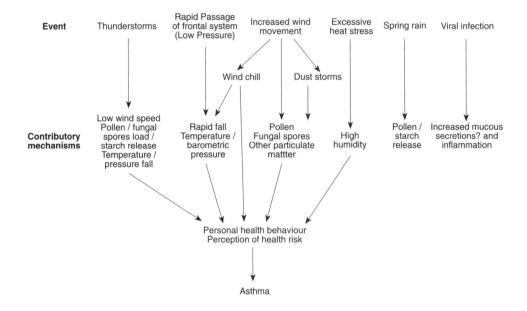

Indirect climatic effects

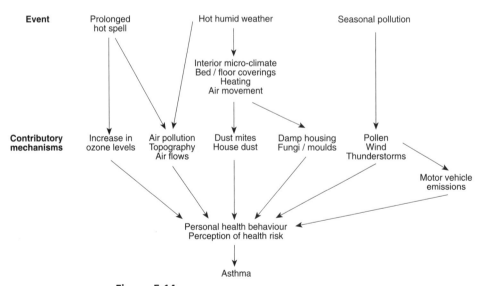

Figure 5.14
Direct and indirect climatic effects on asthma (after Curson, P., 'Climate and chronic respiratory disease in Sydney — the case of asthma', *Climatic Change*, **25** (1993), 405–20).

greenhouse effect might also bring some benefits. Increasing amounts of CO_2 in the atmosphere mean that plants can use water more efficiently and grow faster and larger. Plants may thus grow better because CO_2 enhances growth: by 10–15 per cent for some types such as wheat, rice, barley, fruits and vegetables; and perhaps by 10 per cent for other crops such as corn, sorghum and sugar cane. The enhanced greenhouse effect may also mean that less irrigation is required in some areas, because when CO_2 increases plants do not lose as much water by transpiration. This could produce higher crop yields or allow some detrimental effects of irrigation to be reduced (Section 2.4). Farmers who receive enough reliable rainfall may therefore achieve improved yields and incomes. If rainfall becomes less reliable or rainfall amounts are reduced, then even less of Australia's farm lands will be usable for sustainable agriculture. At the present time, the annual variation in the value of crops to Australia attributable to weather effects is about A$36 billion. This year-to-year variability is likely to increase, making it even more important that the agricultural industry formulates plans for dealing with climate variability.

However, agriculture is highly dependent on climate and weather, particularly the precise timing and distribution of rainfall and temperature. As it is impossible to predict how these will change because of the enhanced greenhouse effect, it is impossible to provide reliable forecasts for the farming community. However, in many regions of the world, wheat, rice or other crops cannot be grown for reasons that are not linked to climate: soils might be infertile, salty, or waterlogged, for example. The enhanced greenhouse effect might make these regions *climatically* suitable for wheat or rice, but we still could not grow those crops in these areas. So the solution to the agricultural consequences of enhanced greenhouse conditions is not simply to grow crops elsewhere.[5]

RESPONSES 5.6

Even if the enhanced greenhouse effect does lead to severe climate change, there is time to develop strategies to cope with this change. Implementing solutions is the job of planners, policy-makers and politicians. In developing a planning response it is useful to draw a decision tree of possible choices, which might be composed of three branches (Figure 5.15). The planning response begins with the realisation that the enhanced greenhouse effect is a problem and that some response is needed; the next stage is to decide whether to do nothing, take preventative action to stop the consequences, or prepare for the consequences.

Do nothing

Ignoring the enhanced greenhouse effect is a genuine planning option. We could choose to do nothing for the moment and wait until more information becomes available — a valid response if we believe there is serious doubt about the predictions of climate change and if we are sure that the consequences of the enhanced greenhouse effect, if they do occur, will not be too severe.

The enhanced greenhouse effect may have a variety of impacts on our environment and we cannot accurately predict these, leaving us with a rather difficult issue to be addressed. Taking preventative action or preparing for the consequences requires considerable political will. The political decisions are extremely difficult and can easily be avoided by claiming that we cannot do anything until the scientists are certain that there will be an adverse climate change. However, most scientists agree that the enhanced greenhouse effect is already happening and that it will lead to climate change. Many believe that we must act now and plan for the consequences, and try to reduce their impact by reducing our emissions of greenhouse gases; that is, take preventative action.

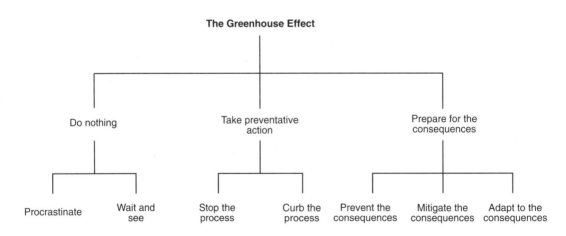

Figure 5.15
Possible planning responses to the greenhouse effect (after Bowie, I.J.S. and Goldney, D.C. (eds), *The Planning Implications of Greenhouse*, Open Learning Institute, Charles Sturt University — Mitchell (Bathurst, 1992)).

Figure 5.15 suggests that preventative action can take two forms: stopping the process or curbing the process. In the case of the enhanced greenhouse effect, it is too late to stop the process. Due to the long residence times of some greenhouse gases, we will experience some of the consequences even if we stop the release of all greenhouse gases today. However, we can reduce the effect by reducing the volume of greenhouse gases entering the atmosphere.

Although it is theoretically possible to remove greenhouse gases from the atmosphere, it is more practical to reduce the emissions at the sources. Table 5.2 shows the considerable cuts in emissions that are necessary to stabilise greenhouse gases at their present levels. Although it might be possible to cut CFC emissions by 100 per cent, there is no likelihood that the required cuts in CO_2, CH_4 or N_2O could be made without significant economic and social impact.

Cuts might be achieved in part by favouring nuclear energy, even though this could lead to other environmental problems, and we might look at renewable or 'alternative' energy sources to reduce rather than replace our use of fossil fuels. For example, solar panels are becoming common in Australia, and we are in a good position to utilise this technology because our per capita solar energy resource is more than thirty times the global average. At present about 20 per cent of the world energy demands are provided from renewable sources, mainly in the form of biomass and hydroelectric power. The potential for renewable energy is huge and far exceeds the energy available from fossil fuels. Indeed, it has been argued that using biomass as a fuel source has more potential in slowing the enhanced greenhouse effect than does reafforestation. Biomass, while growing, will absorb carbon dioxide in roughly the amounts that will be returned to the atmosphere when it is burnt, and so the net long-term effect will be negligible, unlike the case with fossil fuels. However, it requires invest-

Table 5.2 Cuts in emissions needed for stabilisation of greenhouse gases at present atmospheric levels according to IPCC and the US Environmental Protection Agency (c. 1990).

Greenhouse gas	IPCC estimated cut (%)	EPA estimated cut (%)
CO_2	>60	50–80
CH_4	15–20	10–20
N_2O	70–80	80–85
CFC–11	70–75	75–100
CFC–12	75–85	75–100

ment and development at a time when the energy required for many countries is already available from cheap fossil fuels.

Because the cuts in greenhouse gas emissions required to stabilise the atmospheric concentrations are substantial (Table 5.2), we really need to use less energy. Energy conservation has the advantage that it is good for the environment even if the enhanced greenhouse effect is subsequently proven not to exist. Transport accounts for about 27 per cent of primary energy use in Australia and a higher proportion of fossil fuel use; road transport accounts for about 77 per cent of the total transport energy use. Per head of population, Australians use about twice as much petrol as Europeans and about four times as much as the Japanese. Land-use planning has a significant bearing on the fuel efficiency of cities and regions, and therefore on the production of CO_2 and other greenhouse gases (see Section 4.6). We need to reassess our attitude towards the Australian urban sprawl and the role of the private car; future policies should perhaps give greater weight to urban consolidation and promotion of a more compact and efficient urban form. We might start by implementing policies which discourage the use of the private car for the journey to work.

If all the presently available energy-efficient products in Australia were actually used in homes, it would reduce domestic energy consumption by about 75 per cent. Using energy-efficient light globes, which also last longer than the usual globes, would save about 1 tonne of CO_2 emissions over the life of the globe. Multiply this by the number of light globes in Australia and you will see that energy conservation is not necessarily difficult. In addition, if we employed the best available technology for conserving oil and gas, Australia could cut its use of these fuels by 75 per cent. Energy efficiency also leads to less pollution being emitted and would help reduce air pollution problems in our cities (see Chapter 4). In mid-1994, discussions were proceeding toward introduction of a special, relatively low-interest credit scheme to encourage people to install solar hot-water systems and use energy-efficient appliances in their homes.

Tradeable emissions and emission charges

At the national or international scale, there are many ways preventative action could be taken to reduce greenhouse gas emissions. The concept of tradeable emissions has been suggested: a limit on the total global emissions of greenhouse gases is set and a limit on each country's contribution to these emissions is agreed on (a similar scheme can be applied to firms in a nation or region). Australia, the USA, Canada and many European nations might be told, for example, that they could only emit 50 per cent of their current emissions. A country which contributes less to global pollution would also be given an allocation for greenhouse gas emissions, but that allocation might require smaller cuts or even allow an increase.

Under a tradeable emissions scheme, a nation which emits only 30 per cent of its limit could trade the remaining 70 per cent for technology, aid or defences against rising sea levels. This would encourage the implementation of efficiency measures because it would become increasingly beneficial to improve efficiency, to invest in non-greenhouse energy sources, and to protect the interests of the world's poorest nations by helping them acquire appropriate technology (see Section 7.6).

The application of emissions charges is an alternative strategy. At present, the amount we each pay for electricity is based on the amount it costs to produce the electricity, plus a profit margin for the electricity supplier. No part of this charge is related to the environmental cost of production: in other words, the cost of the damage we cause to the environment when we use electricity is never recouped from the user. This must eventually change because, until the full costs of electricity are passed on to the consumer, alternative energy sources which do not damage the environment as much will not be as cost-effective as they ought to be. It has been suggested that consumers should pay these costs in the form of a 'carbon tax'. If Australia imposed a carbon tax on its own products, its exports could become more expensive and possibly non-competitive. However, if Australians were charged for electricity based on the cost to the environment, then Australia would be setting an international lead, helping its own environment, and contributing to the solution to a global problem.

Reafforestation

Deforestation contributes about 15–20 per cent of the global carbon release, so reducing the rate of deforestation would be a very positive step. Furthermore, more trees means more CO_2 removed from the atmosphere, at least in the short term, so major afforestation is a possible response to the enhanced greenhouse effect (see Section 3.3). However, there are some significant caveats which, although they do not mean we should not grow more trees, do indicate that reafforestation is not the whole answer to the greenhouse problem. The major problem with reafforestation is finding enough land. If US power companies built all the new fossil fuel power plants they have planned for the next decade, 4.5 million ha of new forests would have to be planted to absorb the additional CO_2 emissions. To do so would be a positive step in land management, because adding vegetation cover to areas of eroded agricultural land would help control soil erosion as well as balancing the projected CO_2 emissions, and the cover would also help regulate river flow, improve water quality and reduce soil salinity.

Reafforestation, however, is only a short-term solution to the enhanced greenhouse effect. It might buy us time, but eventually all the available land will be used up and we will have the problem of what to do with the trees. They cannot be allowed to decay (as the CO_2 would be released), and if we kept planting and harvesting trees the soil would eventually be exhausted. Finally, massive reafforestation fails to tackle the problem at the source: we are trying to solve a human-induced problem by using nature. Reafforestation may buy us time, but it will not solve the problem.

Prepare for the consequences

Preventive action can help reduce the enhanced greenhouse effect, but it cannot prevent all the consequences. We must therefore begin to plan our response. Figure 5.15 indicates three ways of doing this: preventing the consequences (this does not include preventing the enhanced greenhouse effect itself, since this is not possible), mitigating their effects, and adapting to them.

Preventing the consequences of the enhanced greenhouse effect requires that the processes which cause the problem are solved or curbed. For example, if an increased prevalence of a particular disease is likely to be a local consequence, an immunisation campaign might be undertaken; or if climatic changes are likely to affect local agriculture, a switch to new crops could be the answer. In most cases, however, it will be more appropriate to find ways to mitigate the effects or to adapt to the consequences. These approaches require major long-term plans to be put in place.

Mitigating the consequences of the enhanced greenhouse effect is very similar to preventing them. Many of the strategies discussed earlier in this chapter also apply here. One is to build bigger, stronger structures to cope with extreme weather events and hazards. Another is to provide integrated land-use planning to better cope with likely greenhouse problems: in other words, to foresee the problems and lessen their impact. Such an approach would recognise, for example, that coastal and flood plain environments are dynamic zones where the costs of protection by physical structures are often greater than the benefits. More suitable land uses, ones that can absorb the ill-effects of natural processes, would be planned for such areas. Some government authorities in Australia have already begun to formulate plans to help mitigate the consequences of the enhanced greenhouse effect (see Section 5.7).

Adapting to the consequences is the general strategy favoured by most economists. We could allow society to adjust to environmental changes without attempting to mitigate or prevent changes in advance. Adaptation might include strategies such as the development of new crops and the planned migration of people and relocation of agricultural areas. It is inevitable that people will have to adapt to the enhanced greenhouse effect because the prevention and mitigation strategies will not work perfectly. Ultimately, the difficulty in adapting depends on the specific effect under consideration. Although it appears callous to say so, it would be easy to adapt to the destruction of the Maldives that would be caused by a small rise in sea level, though it would be extremely disruptive for the local population. That population is small and the people could be moved to other countries. But the global community will have much more difficulty coping with perhaps 20–30 million refugees being forced from Bangladesh. Or consider the implications of a repeated harvest failure in the USA, or the failure of the Gulf Stream in the North Atlantic that would plunge Western Europe into much cooler conditions. These are all possibilities rather than probabilities. The point is that the enhanced greenhouse effect has the potential to stretch the adaptive capabilities of people, so it is not sensible to limit our response entirely to adaptation. We should attempt to prevent or mitigate the consequences of the enhanced greenhouse effect as a priority of the highest order.

If we are to adapt to enhanced greenhouse conditions, we must begin the planning process now. Such a policy has little to recommend it to politicians, who are usually interested only in short-term acclaim and the next election. In the longer term, though (say, the forty years of rising sea levels and higher floods), the cost advantages of implementing immediate change may be considerable, especially when compared with the continuing costs of maintaining large and inappropriate engineering structures.

PLANNING FOR THE ENHANCED GREENHOUSE EFFECT 5.7

International agreements

International agreements to protect the environment are very hard to negotiate, as it takes years of discussion, planning, and the gathering of extensive scientific evidence before governments will commit themselves. The Montréal Protocol signed in 1987 took a decade to negotiate, yet almost as soon as it was signed it was realised that the reductions in CFC emissions called for by the Protocol were insufficient, and even tighter controls were agreed to (see also Section 5.2 and 6.4). The Toronto Conference (1988), which called on governments and industry to reduce CO_2 emissions by 20 per cent of the 1988 levels by the year 2005 and, subsequently, the Hague Summit (1989) on the protection of the environment, resulted in the Hague Declaration of March 1989. Australia signed this Declaration, but the USA, the UK, China and the former USSR did not; those four countries release about 60 per cent of the total CO_2 emissions from fossil fuels. The Australian Government believes that Australia can do little to ameliorate the enhanced greenhouse effect while these four countries fail to join any initiatives. However, per capita, Australia is one of the worst polluters, and could take an environmental lead on the greenhouse issue.

The Australian response

It is worth asking whether Australia is actively addressing the issue of global warming. In 1990 the Federal Government announced that it had set an 'Interim Planning Target' to stabilise emissions of all greenhouse gases. This decision was endorsed by state and territory governments and subsequently included in the (Australian) Intergovernmental Agreement on the Environment endorsed in May 1992. The policy is as follows:

> to stabilise greenhouse gas emissions (not controlled by the Montréal Protocol on Substances that Deplete the Ozone Layer) based on 1988 levels, by the year 2000 and to reduce these emissions by 20 per cent by the year 2005 ... subject to Australia not implementing response measures that would have net adverse economic effects nationally or on Australia's trade competitiveness, in the absence of similar action by major greenhouse producing countries.[6]

The Federal Government also introduced an energy-efficiency package which aimed, over time, to:

> reduce the release of greenhouse gases in Australia, in particular to reduce energy-related carbon dioxide by about 4% of projected levels by the year 2005, and by then to save about $1.5 billion annually on energy use.[7]

This represented a first step toward the possibility of achieving the Interim Planning Target. A longer-term response, envisaged as a path to developing a policy to achieve that target, was also initiated through the National Greenhouse Response Strategy released by the Federal Government in December 1992 after endorsement by the Council of Australian Governments. Subsequently, on 31 December 1992, Australia ratified the Framework Convention on Climate Change (see Section 6.4).

The Response Strategy is written in the terms of 'no regrets' actions and says that:

> equity considerations should be addressed by ensuring that response measures meet the broad needs of the whole community and that any undue burden of adjustment potentially borne by a particular sector or region is recognised and accounted for.[8]

This let-out clause means that any industry or geographical region should not be economically burdened by responding to the enhanced greenhouse effect. The Strategy has evolved into a plan of least possible change. Overall, the Strategy concentrates on reviewing the initiatives of the various tiers of government already under way and stating that these will continue. It only commits governments to relatively small and fragmented new initiatives, and federal and state governments are not required to define time-frames or targets to reduce greenhouse gas emissions. This is despite the Interim Planning Target being described as 'a yardstick against which the implementation of greenhouse measures can be assessed' and as 'a focus for action in Australia to help mitigate human caused global climate change and associated impacts'.[9]

The Response Strategy identified the following priority areas for special attention:
* identifying sources and sinks of greenhouse gases in Australia;
* identifying mechanisms for involving the community in strategy implementation and development;
* establishing a National Greenhouse Advisory Panel; and
* implementing measures to address the issue of greenhouse gas emissions.

This fourth priority area includes planning, changes in energy pricing, new standards for appliances, improvements in fuel efficiency for new vehicles and provision of information for energy users.

There are many obstacles to overcome with respect to Australian domestic greenhouse policy if the nation is to fulfil its obligations as a signatory to the Climate Convention of the Earth Summit. As a high-income country, Australia is expected to aim to reduce greenhouse gas emissions to 1990 levels by the year 2000 and to report on progress toward this stabilisation in the meantime. The barriers to achieving this goal for Australia include the following:

- So long as we cannot predict with certainty the impacts of climate change, the political impetus to implement policies to counter the greenhouse effect will be hampered. There are also uncertainties with respect to the costs and benefits of greenhouse policy options to counter the effects of climate change.
- The implications of reducing greenhouse gas emissions in Australia, given our economic dependence on the energy sector, is a concern for politicians. The emission cuts needed to achieve the reduction in emissions to 1990 levels by the year 2000 would involve more than the 'no regrets' reductions of the National Greenhouse Response Strategy. The obvious concern is that Australia could suffer economically. The nation could also suffer economically if other countries make significant reductions in energy use, as coal and natural gas are important Australian exports.
- The division between federal and state powers in Australia has caused political and bureaucratic problems in formulating an effective national strategy and can easily be used as an excuse for inaction.
- It is hard to maintain the political will to cut greenhouse gas emissions when environmental issues are receiving less media coverage in Australia. The media coverage of the enhanced greenhouse effect tends to focus on the scientific uncertainty, in contrast with the more positive coverage at the time of the Earth Summit.

Despite obstacles to Australia meeting the aims of the Framework Convention, there are several reasons which make it rational for Australia to comply with them.

- Several of the impacts of climate change could cause considerable economic loss. Other potential impacts offer commercial opportunities, and we would be wise to prepare for both negative and positive consequences.
- Australia has a record of actively supporting co-operative solutions to international environmental issues (see Sections 6.2, 6.3 and 6.9), which it should seek to maintain.
- Many responses will have benefits for Australia regardless of whether greenhouse impacts occur or not, and cautious action would be a wise investment.

Overall, the enhanced greenhouse effect can be regarded as an opportunity rather than a threat. The challenge to produce energy without burning fossil fuels will generate a vast demand for new technologies which, for example, produce electricity while emitting less CO_2 and other pollutants, utilise renewable resources such as the Sun, wind, oceans and biomass, and encourage energy-efficient buildings, transportation, lighting and manufacturing. Other innovations may include alternatives to CFCs, improved agriculture requiring less nitrogenous fertiliser, and dryland rice cultivation reducing methane emissions. These are merely indicative of the huge range of opportunities presented by the possible consequences of the enhanced greenhouse effect. As the 'clever country', with expertise in agriculture, biotechnology, solar energy, and advanced manufacturing, Australia is well positioned to take advantage of some of the opportunities. Unfortunately, our continued reliance on fossil fuels and the Federal Government's intention to adapt to greenhouse in ways which do not affect the Australian economy may mean that we remain one of the worst atmospheric polluters while our competitors, particularly in South-east Asia, adapt to the inevitable economic consequences of the enhanced greenhouse effect and reap the economic benefits.

In the first report on progress toward implementing the National Strategy, prepared by the National Greenhouse Steering Committee in December 1993, it was concluded that 'considerable progress has been made in implementing the first phase national greenhouse response measures'. It was not clear, however, just what had actually been achieved; rather, it appears that state and federal governments had been biding their time. Some of the achievements claimed are that:

- several state power authorities (ACT, NSW, Northern Territory, Queensland) have developed 'buy-back' initiatives within the electricity generation sector in which excess power generated by solar, wind or hydroelectric means could be supplied to the main grid;
- large sub-divisions within the ACT had to undergo energy audits;
- the ACT was investigating the possibilities of making more use of natural gas, while South Australia (a natural gas producer) was promoting gas-fired electricity generation;
- many states were investigating the potential for using renewable energy sources;
- improved appliance labelling to indicate energy efficiency had been introduced;
- legislation aimed at improving the fuel efficiency of motor vehicles had been introduced; and
- funding for scientific investigations into greenhouse issues had been increased.

While there seemed to have been a wide range of initiatives addressing the greenhouse problem, the overall strategy has not attempted to actively solve the underlying problems. Scientists still appeared unable to convince politicians of the seriousness of those problems.

A national Australian meeting on the enhanced greenhouse effect in June 1994 did not give any more cause for optimism. Most states and territories were not represented at ministerial level, giving an indication of the difficulties encountered in having the issue taken seriously on a political level. Nor was there more than the minimum of attention paid by the media. From what little information was available, it seems that business interests had persuaded the Federal Government (and presumably state governments) that Australia should pull back from previous commitments because not to do so would hurt Australia economically. Another argument used was that Australia's cuts should not be expected to be as large as those made by other OECD nations because it depended so much on fossil fuels (both domestically and as exports). It would be equally as logical — much more so from an ecological perspective — to argue that this means that Australia should make more cuts than other nations, not fewer, to bring it into line with some internationally acceptable level of CO_2 emissions. The financial press, in particular, echoed the concerns of business, industry and mining interests and reported their call for Australia to place economic interests above environmental interests, and to attempt to form strategic alliances with like-minded nations to strengthen Australia's negotiating position at the Berlin meeting in March 1995 that will consider extending the Framework Convention and tightening its provisions, a development supported by the USA. The strong implications is that Australia should either oppose that move or demand special consideration promised under a 'burden-sharing provision' to 'economies that are vulnerable to the adverse effects of the implementation of measures to respond to climate change'.

Dealing with the enhanced greenhouse effect and providing a sustainable future require planning. In developing a strategy for the future, planners normally require scenarios which they believe reliably describe possible and probable futures. Planners also tend to work at the local scale, the scale of states, territories or possibly a country. In the case of the enhanced greenhouse effect, plausible and defendable future scenarios are extremely difficult to produce for an individual country and are largely impossible at state scales. In any case, the scenarios tend to evolve as the climate models improve and the processes involved become better understood. Standard planning usually requires a scenario to be stable in time, so that designs can be produced, considered and implemented over a decade or so. The greenhouse problem therefore provides a challenge to planners in that they are required to formulate a strategy which can evolve over time as the information base improves. Box 5.4 considers the NSW response in greater detail.

One state's response: planning in New South Wales

B O X

5.4

The planning response in NSW is an example of practical action at a local level. While the state contributes only about 0.3 per cent of the Earth's total CO_2 emissions, a greenhouse policy has been developed, and many of the state's planning policies show an awareness of the problem, taking account of the points listed in the table below. Indeed, in 1990 the NSW Government solicited a discussion paper published as *A greenhouse strategy for New South Wales*. However, we need to make a clear distinction between making plans and actually controlling development. In NSW, as elsewhere, all of the points listed in the table should be taken into account, but many of the plans which take vegetation conservation, coastal protection, and environmental impact assessment into account do so only tentatively. Making statements to guide planning helps, but plans need to be prepared, backed by legislation, and followed by action.

Planning for the greenhouse effect in NSW

Reducing greenhouse emissions	
City planning	Sydney Metropolitan Strategy provides for urban consolidation, an integrated transport policy and design guidelines in urban areas
Building design	Energy efficiency guidelines
Vegetation conservation	Green space preservation policy
Environmental impact assessment	Requirements being implemented to account for greenhouse change

Adapting to unavoidable climate change	
Coastal zone planning	Coastline management policy
Floodplain hazard	Policy under review to take greenhouse into account
Drainage and sewerage	Greenhouse is not taken into account in planning
Environmental impact assessment	Policy being implemented to take greenhouse into account

The NSW Government has identified four priorities: set up an administrative structure to co-ordinate a response to greenhouse; collect information on climate change and potential impacts; evaluate and implement reduction strategies; and evaluate adaptation strategies. The aim to evaluate and implement reduction strategies included labelling all electrical appliances with their energy efficiency, and a series of programs leading toward more energy-efficient housing, transport and industries. Unfortunately, all these 'reduction strategies' were phrased in terms of 'encouraging', 'supporting', or 'promoting' various activities: there is no suggestion of 'enforcing'. In 1994, more than three years after the NSW discussion paper was released, there had not been any obvious achievements by the NSW Government in relation to the greenhouse problem.

The state plans to adapt to the greenhouse future in a variety of ways. Because the predicted rise in sea level could affect the shoreline, the State Government is reviewing planning and building standards along the coast. The state is also threatened by changes in rainfall patterns and the frequency of extreme weather events, so the government is re-evaluating its design standards for water supply systems to determine whether these systems could withstand or be adapted to cope with the changes caused by the enhanced greenhouse effect. The government has also identified changes in urban design which may be required to counter the greenhouse effect: plans for land use, building design, water supply, sewerage, and drainage systems, as well as transport and other infrastructure, may all need to be adapted.

Source: *A Greenhouse Strategy for New South Wales: Discussion paper*, New South Wales Government (Sydney, 1990).

5.8 CONCLUSION

This chapter has described two major atmospheric global crises: the enhanced greenhouse effect and stratospheric ozone depletion, both of which are human-induced. They are both likely to have significant impacts on the Earth over the next few years to decades.

The greenhouse effect is a real, natural, physical phenomenon. It warms the Earth by 33°C and enables life to exist on the planet. The enhanced greenhouse effect, brought about by the release of additional greenhouse gases, is increasing that natural warming. The consensus in the early 1990s was that this enhanced effect had already warmed the Earth by about 0.5°C and would warm the Earth by a further 2°C by 2030. The impacts of this warming may be substantial (sea-level rise, more flooding and droughts, and a more variable climate with larger extremes), or the impact may be negligible. The consensus is that the impacts will probably be significant in both high latitude and temperate regions. The impacts will have significant social and economic consequences: the task for politicians is to develop an environment where technological advances can be made to offset the consequences.

The basic causes of the enhanced greenhouse effect are intimately linked with our production of energy and food. Sustainable mechanisms for reducing the release of greenhouse gases must, therefore, affect our economy and society in a major way, at least in the short term. This could cause real economic difficulties, and governments, including the Australian Government, do not willingly enter into economically damaging agreements or policies. Ultimately, the enhanced greenhouse effect will have to be addressed both scientifically and politically.

The ozone 'hole', and the more general phenomenon of global ozone depletion, are more immediate concerns. The increasing amount of UV radiation reaching the Earth's surface is a significant health hazard. More importantly, it is also a more widespread hazard due to the interactions of this radiation with plant and animal life. The ozone problem appears to be easy to remedy: banning CFCs is rather straightforward (the method for achieving this ban, the Montréal Protocol, is discussed in Section 6.4). International political pressure has led to further technological innovation, resulting in replacements for CFCs. This represents the first real example of an effective interaction between politics, economics, technology and a physical process at the global scale that is leading to a potential solution to a major environmental problem. The solution to the ozone problem has been identified and there is considerable optimism that it will be implemented.

Before the success of the Montréal Protocol there was little optimism that an international agreement on either ozone or greenhouse could be negotiated. The ozone problem has been shown to be solvable, while the greenhouse problem is proving harder but is not impossible. The Framework Climate Convention signed at the Earth Summit is a very important step in reaching meaningful agreement on successful strategies for tackling global warming. The political options, and the mechanisms whereby international agreements such as these are forged, are addressed in the next chapter.

FURTHER READING

Henderson-Sellers, A. and Blong, R.J., *The Greenhouse Effect: Living in a warmer Australia*, New South Wales University Press (Sydney, 1989). [A good starting point for understanding some of the implications of the enhanced greenhouse effect for Australia.]

Houghton, J.T., Jenkins, G.G. and Euphrams, J.J. (eds), *Climate Change Working Group I: Scientific assessment*, Cambridge University Press (Cambridge, UK, 1990). [This volume, and that by Teggart et al. (see below) are reports from the Intergovernmental Panel on Climate Change. They were 'state of the art' in 1990 and remain hugely valuable sources of information. They were written for governments, and so contain executive summaries which are very straightforward to understand. The main body of each volume, however, contains vast amounts of detailed and very advanced information.]

Leggett, J., *Global warming: The Greenpeace report*, Oxford University Press (Oxford, 1990). [This is rather more advanced than Henderson-Sellers and Blong (see above). It contains separate chapters on individual aspects of the greenhouse effect and ozone depletion. It is not obviously written from Greenpeace's perspective, except for those chapters in which the organisation's point of view is consciously put forward; other chapters are written by experts in their respective fields. It is an excellent source from which to learn much more about the enhanced greenhouse effect and ozone depletion.]

Parry, M.L., *Climate Change and World Agriculture*, Earthscan (London, 1990). [An introduction to the effects that the changes in climate predicted as a result of the greenhouse effect are likely to have on agricultural productivity.]

Teggart, W.J.McG., Sheldon, G.W. and Griffiths, D.C. (eds) *Climate Change Working Group II: Impacts assessment*, Australian Government Publishing Service (Canberra, 1990). [See the comments for Houghton et al. above.]

Thompson, R.D., 'The changing atmosphere and its impact on planet Earth', in Mannion, A.M. and Bowlby, S.R. (eds.), *Environmental Issues in the 1990s*, Wiley (Chichester/New York, 1992). [A useful source of information on the greenhouse effect and ozone depletion.]

1 The IPCC was composed of many of the most accomplished atmospheric and ecological scientists and planning specialists. It produced three initial reports, all in the 1990s. The first deals with the theory of the greenhouse effect, the second with impacts of the effect, and the third with how governments might respond. Subsequent update reports are being produced. The three initial reports are very advanced in parts, but still provide the best source of information. The quotation is from the first of these: Houghton, J.T., Jenkins, G.G. and Euphrams, J.J. (eds), *Climate Change Working Group 1: Scientific assessment*, Cambridge University Press (Cambridge, UK, 1990), ix.

2 Leggett, J., *Global Warming: The Greenpeace Report*, Oxford University Press (Oxford, 1990) discusses the role of feedbacks and their importance in the climate system.

3 You may see this referred to in some of the scientific literature as 80 Tg. A Tg is a teragram or 10^{12} grams.

4 El Niño is a warm current which flows along the western coast of South America. It is associated with the Southern Oscillation, which is a fluctuation in the circulations of the Indian and Pacific Oceans. The combination of El Niño and the Southern Oscillation is known as ENSO. The climate and ocean patterns that occur during an El Niño event cause serious droughts in eastern Australia and higher than average rainfall in Western Australia.

5 Much more information on the potential impacts of climate change on global agriculture can be obtained from Parry, M., *Climate Change and World Agriculture*, Earthscan (London, 1990).

6 *Intergovernmental Agreement on the Environment*, Australian Government Publishing Service (Canberra, 1992).

7 Ibid.

8 *National Greenhouse Response Strategy*, Australian Government Publishing Service (Canberra, 1992).

9 Ibid.

6

INTERNATIONAL
CO-OPERATION

GLOBAL COMMONS

IN MEDIEVAL BRITAIN, villages had areas of land called 'commons' on which people could graze their livestock. Commons were intended for the benefit of the local population in general, not for the greater benefit of a few at the expense of the majority.

Antarctica and the oceans beyond territorial waters are global commons, areas of the Earth which are not 'owned' by any particular country. Nations have long battled for supremacy over these areas but, perhaps because of this conflict, these same areas have seen some of the most successful international co-operation on environmental issues. Australia has a special interest in both realms — it is located in the 'water hemisphere', it has always depended greatly on the oceans surrounding the continent, it is close to Antartica, and has had a long-standing major involvement in that continent. The atmosphere is another realm that contains no firm international boundaries, while forests, although clearly occurring within national borders, are seen by many as having a global importance transcending national inter-ests. Further important attempts at international co-operation have therefore occurred in relation to atmospheric and forest issues. These four examples — Antarctica, oceans, atmosphere and forests — are used to introduce the broader kinds of international consultation and debate on global environmental issues, climaxing in the Rio de Janeiro Earth Summit (or UNCED) of 1992 and continuing in follow-up negotiations.

Garrett Hardin, writing in 1968, made the analogy between medi-eval commons and modern examples of common property, and fore-saw potential tragedy in the conflict between individual and group benefits.[1] If individuals (commoners) are to maximise their returns, it will be at the expense of other individuals, and ultimately to the detriment of all as the commons become over-exploited and total returns decline. In the case of the global commons — Antarctica, the oceans and the atmosphere — nations are tempted to increase their returns from a limited resource without regard for the common good that might be better served by husbanding that resource; they try to gain exclusive control over sections of the commons; and they throw their wastes onto the commons. Any such nation may, in the short term, receive a disproportionately large share of the total benefits of that action, while many nations will jointly suffer the consequences. Furthermore, benefits are likely to be unsustainable. But extending private ownership is not necessarily always the best answer. A more recent interpretation suggests an alternative paradigm: careful, co-operative regulation and protection of a resource in common owner-ship can lead to wise, long-term, sustainable use for the benefit of all.

Academics, politicians, and ordinary citizens alike are increasingly interested in following the path suggested by this new paradigm. It is for this reason that some world leaders and United Nations (UN) representatives want the resources of the oceans and Antarctica de-clared world resources to be shared among all peoples. It is also why world leaders have attempted to reach, and have sometimes succeeded in reaching, international agreements. Such agreements are often an important step toward the careful, co-operative regulation and protec-tion needed. In these examples, as in other global environmental issues, there is a desperate need for co-operation between high-income and low-income nations and between powerful and weak na-tions, for the sake of humanity as a whole. These issues are central to this chapter and Chapter 7. A time-line of major agreements, includ-ing those mentioned in this chapter, is given in Figure 6.1.

THE OCEANS 6.2

The need for international co-operation

Concern over control of the oceans has led to many international disagreements, while nations have extended their territorial waters, especially since World War II. These concerns and actions have led to the growth of a comprehensive body of agreement known as the Law of the Sea, arrived at through three UN conferences (1958, 1960 and 1973–82), a process outlined in the following section. There have also been more specialised agreements, however, concentrating on re-gional seas or on particular aspects such as fishing, whaling and pollu-tion control. Some of these are dealt with later in this chapter.

We should all share a concern about the state of the oceans, a very vulnerable but poorly understood part of the planet. They have long

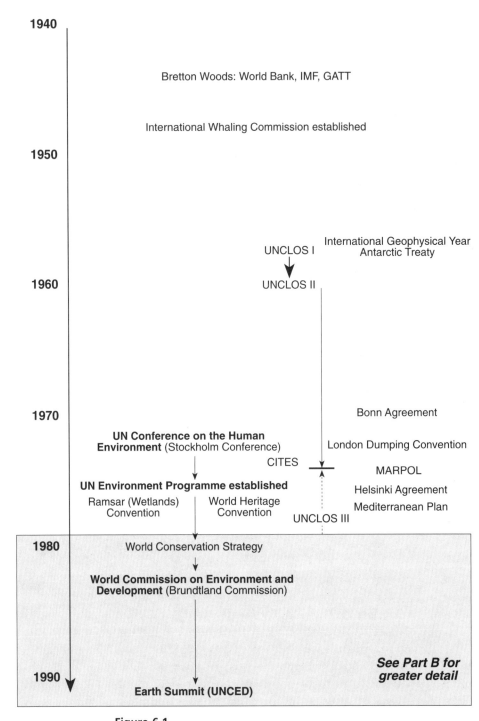

Figure 6.1
Time-line of international environmental agreements since World War II,
including those covered in Chapter 6. (Continued on opposite page.)

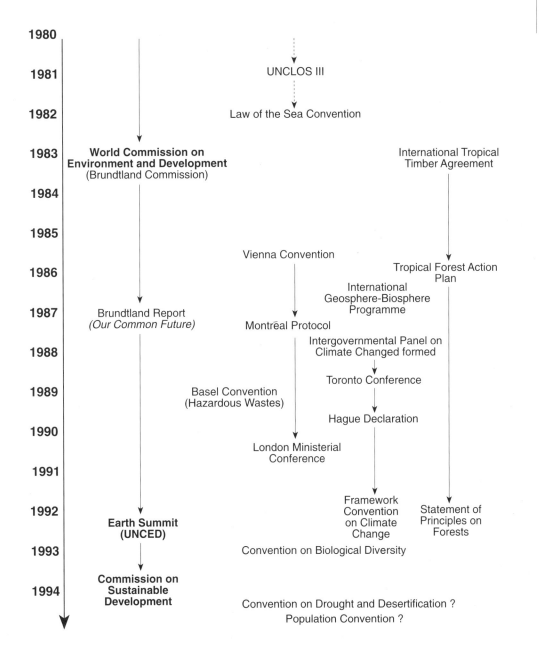

Figure 6.1 (continued)

been an important source of food, especially protein, and many people pin a great deal of hope on them as one important source in overcoming current and future food shortages (although other people claim that we have already reached, and possibly surpassed, the overall **sustainable yield** on a global basis). Perhaps some regions and some species may provide scope for higher yields; but if that is to be the case, extremely careful management of marine biological resources and prevention of pollution will be necessary. Indeed, it will be necessary if we are to merely maintain anything like present yields. The extreme vulnerability of the marine realm was recognised in 1993 in *Global marine biological diversity*, a joint report of the Center for Marine Conservation in Washington D.C., the **World Conservation Union** (IUCN), the **World Wide Fund for Nature** (WWF), the United Nations Environment Programme (UNEP) and the **World Bank**.

Sustainable yields of marine biological resources depend on management plans based on sound knowledge, as well as on regulation and co-operation. Important elements of management usually include limits on the total catches of individual species, closed seasons, and restrictions on taking juveniles and breeding females. Limits and other restrictions also need to be sensitive to seasonal and year-to-year variations in conditions and to population dynamics, as well as being set for specific places. Constant feedback from population monitoring is essential, as is international co-operation. After all, fish and other marine animals are no respecters of national borders, nor are the currents that carry both life and pollution with them. But often a mix of ignorance and pressure from vested interests leads to ineffective regulations, or ones that even make the situation worse, as the European Court of Auditors in 1993 claimed to be the case in relation to European fishing agreements.

One factor that has made fisheries management imperative is the change almost everywhere from local, indigenous fishing to large-scale, mechanised, commercial fishing. The technology has become increasingly sophisticated and fishing correspondingly more 'efficient'. For example, the 1993 European Court of Auditors' report claimed that 'improvements in technology have given the Community's fishing boats the capacity to catch about 40 per cent too much fish' (that is, 40 per cent above the sustainable yield). Such changes in technology usually lead to a short-term increase in takes but can very easily result in over-exploitation, declining populations and, consequently, reduced catches in the longer term. There have also been many cases of conflict when modern fishing techniques, often used by foreign fishing operators, have interfered with the livelihood and food supply of native people, who are unable to compete on equal terms, particularly in low-income nations.

One example of many factors mentioned above was the use of driftnets, a modern method of fishing on a gigantic scale with nets up to 60 km long and stretching from the surface to a depth of ten metres or more. The major users of this technique in the South Pacific were Japan, South Korea and Taiwan. It was certainly not a selective fishing method, as just about any form of marine life, including seabirds and dolphins, became entangled in the nets and died or were discarded. In the late 1980s and early 1990s, widespread protests, including protests from the Australian Government, focused on the indiscriminate nature of driftnetting and on concern over the adverse effects of the very large catches on populations of commercial species and on the local fisheries of South Pacific island nations.

In 1988–89, the USA and Canada were drawn into the controversy when they realised that driftnetters in the North Pacific were taking large numbers of salmon and steelhead trout, species which spawned in North American streams. The USA went so far as threatening bans on imports of Japanese marine products, a threat that ran into trouble with the **General Agreement on Tariffs and Trade** (GATT). In late 1989, Japan agreed to comply with a ban on very long driftnets in the South Pacific, as did Taiwan in mid-1990 (to take effect a year later). All driftnetting nations were to have banned the practice by their fleets on the high seas by the end of 1992, and they largely, if not entirely, adhered to that date. In early 1994, the European Union nations agreed to restrict driftnets used in European waters to 2.5 km in length and wanted to ban their use altogether after 1997. In June 1994, however, Italy was seeking an exemption allowing its ships to use driftnets up to 9 km in length until 2004, even though Italian nets had just entangled four sperm whales, among the most endangered species in European waters, and the two youngest had drowned as a result.

The International Law of the Sea

Discussions on the rights of nations to exploit various parts of the oceans perhaps began formally in the seventeenth century when the notion of '**freedom of the seas**' was first promulgated. A band of coastal water three nautical miles (nm) (5.6 km) wide and known as the 'territorial sea' was, however, reserved as in effect an extension of national territory. The situation remained like this until the major conflicts over foreign fishing in the 1950s between the United Kingdom and Iceland, and between the USA and Peru, Ecuador and Chile. In 1952 these three South American nations declared a 200 nm (370 km) limit within which only their boats or ones they had licensed would be allowed to fish. This declaration, not recognised by the USA and most other countries, led to the First Law of the Sea Conference called by the UN in 1958.

This first Conference accepted the concept of a contiguous zone extending another 9 nm (16.7 km) beyond the territorial sea, and this zone was generally considered to be an exclusive fishing zone. Additional reserved rights were also attached to **continental shelf** waters to a depth of 200 m. Participating nations also agreed on the need to co-operate in conserving the living resources of the **high seas** beyond these limits. Some nations, however, continued to claim territorial seas 200 nm wide: the Second Law of the Sea Conference in 1960 also failed to resolve these differences. By that time, too, increasing interest in the potential for winning hydrocarbons and other minerals from the ocean bed had made a resolution more pressing.

The Third Conference on the Law of the Sea (1973–82), also known as UNCLOS III, resulted in the Law of the Sea Convention, which allowed for four zones: a 12-nm wide territorial sea; a contiguous zone to 24 nm (44.4 km) from the coast; an **exclusive economic zone** (EEZ) to 200 nm; and the continental shelf to a depth of 200 m. This meant that about 40 per cent of the oceans could come under the direct control of coastal states (Figure 6.2). Some 42 per cent of the total, the high seas, was designated as the 'common heritage of mankind' and would be controlled by the International Seabed Authority.

By 1984, 134 nations had signed the Convention, while 35, including such important ones as the UK, the USA and West Germany had

Figure 6.2
Area of the oceans covered by actual and potential 200 nm Exclusive Economic Zones.

refused. Many low-income countries strongly support the Convention and, in particular, the concept of an EEZ. They wish to control their offshore areas in case they contain hidden wealth that they may be able to exploit in the future, rather than having high-income nations continue to grow richer on 'their' off-shore resources. At the same time, they emphasise the 'common heritage of mankind' concept as they cannot presently hope to compete with the high-income countries in exploiting deep-sea resources.

The Convention did not come into force until November 1994 as it had not been **ratified** (as distinct from signed) by the required 60 countries until November 1993, although another 101 nations had signed it by then. There had been, and still is, much reluctance to sign and especially to ratify it, because if a state disagrees with one aspect it tends to reject the entire package. For example, the USA objects to the international regime for the seabed, largely because it does not want to share its deep-sea mining technology with other nations through the International Seabed Authority, and hence had not signed, let alone ratified, the Convention by late 1993. Despite this slowness and only partial success in having the Convention implemented, the situation is much less confused than it was in the 1960s and 1970s.

Australia, the Law of the Sea, and fisheries agreements

In 1979 Australia declared a 200-nm Australian Fishing Zone (AFZ) surrounding the continent and its island territories (Norfolk, Lord Howe, Christmas, Cocos, Macquarie and Heard islands). This effectively doubled Australia's national territory (Figure 6.3). Although the Australian Government had signed the UNCLOS III convention in 1982, it did not ratify it until October 1994. Australia was an original party to the Convention when it came into force on 16 November 1994. Australia had previously converted its AFZ to an EEZ in August 1994.

Australia has also entered into a number of international fisheries agreements and has been involved in achieving others. One of the most important of these is the South Pacific Forum Fisheries Agency Convention (1979) which established the Agency (FFA) to build a pool of expertise and knowledge to help South Pacific nations protect and further develop their fisheries resources. One of the major achievements of the FFA has been the conclusion of a treaty with the USA to allow the licensing and regulation of US fishing boats in the waters of member nations, including Australia. In 1979 Australia also entered into a bipartisan agreement with Japan and, in 1990, reached a similar agreement with the former USSR. In 1990 Australia also signed the

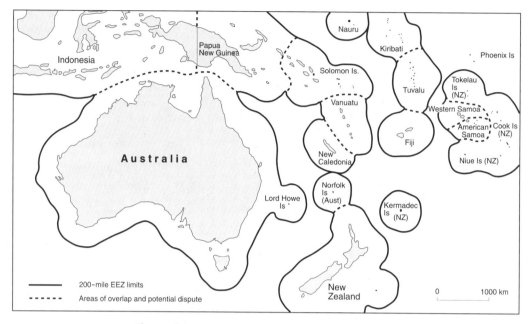

Figure 6.3
Actual and potential Exclusive Economic Zones in the Australian and South
Pacific regions.

Convention for the Prohibition of Fishing with Long Driftnets in the
South Pacific. This Convention was a very significant source of pressure on East Asian nations to cease this type of fishing in the region.

On the other hand, difficulties have arisen in relations between
Australia and Indonesia with respect to the indigenous people of
Sulawesi fishing within the AFZ in the Timor and Arafura seas. The
Sama Bajo people (or 'sea gipsies') have been fishing in Australian
waters for trepang, possibly for many generations, and more recently
for trochus shell and shark (for the fins to sell in Asia, the rest of the
fish being thrown back). This is a very poor group of people with a
total population of about 1.2 million and illiteracy levels exceeding
80 per cent. Fishing is their way of life and they are finding it increasingly difficult to maintain this in the face of competition from western
Indonesia, Japan and Taiwan. In addition, changes in Australian maritime law have denied them legal access to parts of their traditional
waters and they are regularly arrested, their catches confiscated, and
their boats burnt by Australian authorities.

Until 1974 Indonesians were free to fish within 3 nm of the Australian coast. In that year Australia and Indonesia signed a memorandum
of understanding which continued to allow traditional reef fishing
using sail-powered boats without modern equipment (including
radios) within a defined area around several reefs in the Timor Sea.

The declaration of the AFZ in 1979 forced the shark-fishing boats into the same area, even though these are not good shark-fishing waters. It is common for boats to drift out of the defined area and to be intercepted by the Australian authorities. In the five years to 1993, over 200 boats were seized and destroyed and over 3000 crew members gaoled and eventually repatriated to Indonesia. The costs of enforcement are considerable, both to the Australian authorities and to the crews. While it is true that the boats present potential quarantine, customs and illegal immigration risks, there is surely a better way of resolving the conflict.

One obvious suggestion would be to initiate an Australian aid program which would enable the Sama Bajo to upgrade their fishing technology, increase their income, and thus allow them to pay licence fees to use the Australian resource and to do so on a more equal basis. Furthermore, the assistance of the Sama Bajo could be enlisted in co-operatively researching the nature and extent of the fisheries resources in Australia's northern waters. We need that knowledge if we are to seriously manage the marine resources of those waters.

The International Whaling Commission

Whaling is another form of exploitation of the oceans that has entailed international conflict and a search for resolution. Whales have been hunted for over 1000 years for meat and oil, but for most of that time on a small scale and by indigenous peoples for their own local consumption. That changed in the late nineteenth century when whale catches increased markedly for two reasons. Firstly, improved technology, especially the use of steamships, made larger catches further from land possible. Secondly, demand for whale-based products increased rapidly as general wealth increased and industrial applications appeared.

Two effects of those changes are clear. Firstly, there is a recurring history of the most commonly hunted species becoming extremely scarce and whalers then turning their attention to other species (Figure 6.4). Secondly, the average size of whales caught decreased: for example, the average weight of whales caught in 1932 was 67 tonnes, but by 1978 that had decreased to 20 tonnes. This size reduction was due to two factors: the change to different and generally smaller species and the fact that whales often no longer grew to full adult size before capture. In addition, when larger animals were available, smaller, younger ones were often not taken, but purposely left to grow and reproduce.

The International Whaling Commission (IWC) was established in 1948, by which time it was clear to many people that some species of

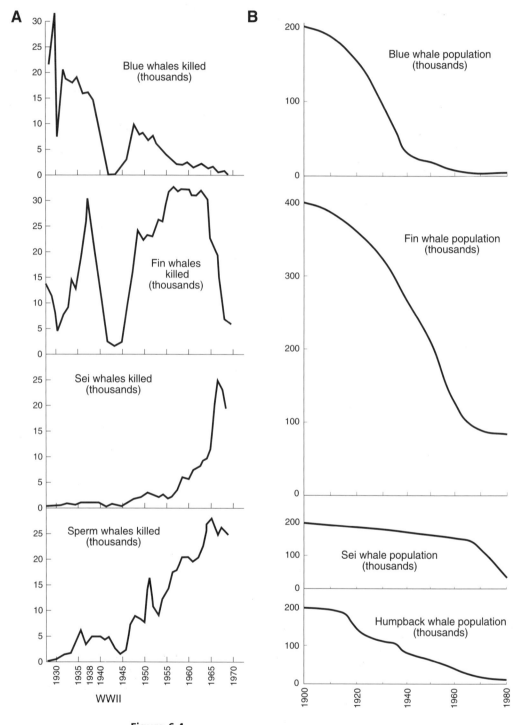

Figure 6.4
(a) Number of whales killed by species, 1925–1970; and (b) estimated whale populations in the Southern Ocean 1900–1980.

whales were almost extinct and others endangered. The IWC has met regularly to establish quotas for the catch of each species by each country, but a quota is not binding on a nation that formally objects to it. In other words, while quotas have moral force, and even reluctant nations are often persuaded to co-operate, they have no legal standing. Since 1978 most countries have, in fact, stopped whaling. Australia did so after a Commonwealth Government decision in 1977, and banned the import of all whale products from 1980. Furthermore, at IWC meetings Australia has consistently voted against resumption of commercial whaling. Apart from aboriginal catches (by Inuit people), virtually all of the greatly reduced catch in the early 1990s was taken by Japan, the USSR, Norway and Iceland. Even those catches were meant to be only for scientific purposes, but it is amazing how many carcasses Japan, in particular, needed for research. It is also interesting that whale meat sells for up to US$350/kg in Tokyo. During the first seven years of the general moratorium on commercial whaling (1986–93), an estimated total of 15 000 whales were killed worldwide.

In the late 1980s and early 1990s the IWC has continued to hear pleas to both relax and continue bans on commercial whaling. Japan, Iceland and Norway asked, in 1990, for the ban on minke whales to be lifted because they claimed the species was no longer in danger of extinction. When the ban was not lifted, Japan threatened to leave the IWC because the organisation had 'caved in to pressures from environmental groups'. Iceland did leave in 1992, and Norway said it would recommence commercial catching of minke whales in 1993 regardless of the IWC's continuing refusal to lift the ban. Meanwhile, the IWC agreed in principle, but not in detail, to a revised management procedure (RMP) that would allow limited takes at minimum risk. Despite this, bans on whaling were maintained as a result of the IWC's 1993 meeting, although in the face of stern opposition from Japan and Norway. It seemed certain that both of these nations would continue to take minke whales despite the moratorium: declared goals are 300 for 'scientific purposes' by Japan (2000 commercial catches were also sought, but refused by the IWC) and 800 admittedly commercial catches by Norway. The USA has threatened sanctions against Norway if it goes ahead with its plans, though GATT regulations could once again prove to be a stumbling block (see Section 6.2). In mid-1994 some scientists argued that Norway's calculation, using the RMP, that it could safely take 301 minkes per year was based on an incorrect estimate of population numbers, and that the safe catch was, in fact, one whale!

Meanwhile, France and Australia pushed for a Southern Whale Sanctuary that would include all waters from the Antarctic coast north to latitude 40°S, the latitude of Bass Strait. This would give remaining whale populations — perhaps as small as 2000 right whales, 4000 blue whales and 5000 humpbacks — a chance to recover to sustainable levels. This proposal was a key item of debate at the IWC scientific meeting on Norfolk Island in late February 1994, and was agreed to with some compromise at the full general meeting of the IWC in Mexico at the end of May 1994. Figure 6.5 shows the agreed boundaries, dipping south to 60°S to avoid Chilean waters and to 55°S to coincide with the boundary of an existing whale sanctuary in the Indian Ocean. Commentators felt that the Japanese would respect the decision, but that the viability of populations of dolphins and other smaller cetaceans might suffer as those species were caught to replace whale meat on Japanese restaurant menus.

Ocean pollution

The nature of the problem

Pollution can have three main effects on the oceanic environment: it can directly destroy organisms within the polluted area or lead to

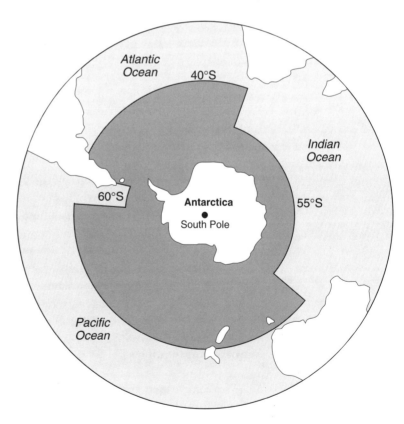

Figure 6.5
The Southern Whale Sanctuary agreed to by the International Whaling Commission in May 1994.

disease, low fertility rates, and genetic defects; it can alter the physical and chemical properties of the environment, thus favouring or excluding particular species and altering amenity values; and it can introduce substances that may become biologically concentrated and pose health risks to higher forms of life, including humans.

Pollutants reach the oceans by several pathways, the most obvious being rivers, sewer outfalls and deliberate or accidental dumping. Large quantities of pollutants also enter the sea by way of rainfall or atmospheric fallout: for example, it is estimated that as much as 40 000 tonnes of lead per annum from industrial emissions enter the marine environment by these means. All types of pollution are far more serious when they occur in sheltered waters where mixing and dispersal are slow, as the concentrations of pollutants are likely to be much higher and those high levels will be maintained for longer periods. A large part of human activity takes place on or near sheltered bays and estuaries and along coastlines with shallow seas offshore, further exacerbating the problem (see also Section 4.2).

Any change in the marine environment may lead to dramatic changes in the populations of given species. As many people are largely dependent on marine food, any decrease in the quality or quantity of favoured species is likely to have far-reaching economic and nutritional consequences. There can also be serious and even fatal effects from eating marine organisms from polluted waters, as was the case with mercury poisoning from contaminated fish ('Minamata disease') in Japan and illnesses from oysters contaminated by sewage in New South Wales. Many substances, such as mercury, lead and other heavy metals, DDT and other pesticides, and radioactive materials, become concentrated in marine food species and pose risks for humans. For example, oysters exposed continuously to waters with a DDT concentration of 0.1 ppbv have been found to have a tissue concentration of DDT of 7.0 ppmv, 70 000 times that in the water.

Less obvious pollutants can also cause problems. Excess nutrients can lead to an accelerated growth of some species, especially algae, leading to discoloured water, foul odours, clogged intake pipes and the production of toxins by some fish and shellfish. If growth is excessive and high rates of decay follow, the available oxygen in the water will be depleted and other marine life will die. Recent research on the Great Barrier Reef indicates that excessive amounts of nutrients from agricultural run-off from the mainland (Section 2.4) and sewage from tourist developments on the Reef are damaging some coral colonies. An excessive discharge of sediments can also have adverse effects on marine life, particularly when human activities lead to very sudden and very large increases in the rate of sedimentation.

Two sources of oceanic pollution have given rise to particular concern: intentional dumping of waste at sea and oil spills from ships and other sources. Both have been the subject of international agreements.

Many cities, even whole nations, have viewed the oceans as large, convenient and inexhaustible garbage dumps. As landfill sites have become harder to find (see Section 4.3), many municipal authorities and private contractors alike have turned to the oceans. Another form of dumping is the disposal of containers of toxic and radioactive waste materials, substances notoriously difficult to dispose of safely on land or into the atmosphere. Those advocating offshore disposal argue that the containers will last forever at the bottom of the ocean, but many others are extremely sceptical. If a container should rupture for any reason, its contents will almost certainly have a devastating effect on the marine environment. International condemnation and grave concern followed Russian admissions (in 1993–94) concerning large-scale marine disposal of radioactive wastes over previous decades.

Probably the most publicised marine pollution, though, is from oil spills resulting from tanker accidents (Box 6.1) and other incidents. However, almost as much petroleum reaches the sea through runoff in small but fairly continuous quantities originating from motor vehicles, industrial machinery, refineries and petrochemical plants. Indeed, a great deal of the oil from ships also comes from numerous small accidental releases or the purposeful washing out of tanks at sea. Figure 6.6 highlights some of possible pathways oil may take when spilt into the sea.

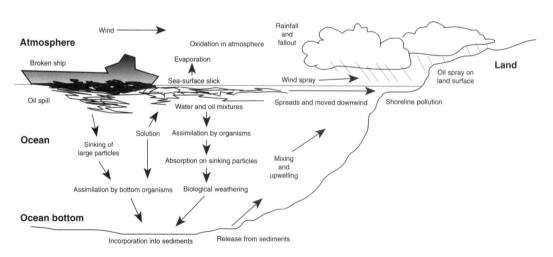

Figure 6.6
Pathways taken by oil released in a marine spill.

Spills from two oil tanker accidents

B O X

6.1

Major tanker spills have a devastating effect on local marine environments because of the sheer quantities of oil released in a limited area. In the *Exxon Valdez* accident in Alaska in March 1989, for example, 41.6 million litres of crude oil poured into the sheltered waters of Prince William Sound. The slick covered 80 km² and, according to US government researchers, had an extremely serious impact on both wildlife and the local fishing industry. Scientists hired by Exxon, however, produced many studies which contradicted those findings. A heated exchange between the two groups occurred in mid-1993. The latter group claimed that the effects on the local fishing industry were negligible and that some of the worst-hit species had recovered well, and that recovery of the fouled parts of Prince William Sound was almost complete. The former group accused the latter of being selective with their data and 'making sweeping statements about recovery based on a few selected sites' while 'ignoring "hot spots" of contamination' (*New Scientist*, 8 May 1993, 4). If nothing else, this difference of opinion demonstrates the complexity of this case, typical of environmental issues generally, and the lack of true objectivity in scientific studies into environmental matters. There is so much we do not yet know.

Five years after the event, in mid-June 1994, a US Federal Court did, however, rule that Exxon was liable for the environmental damage, opening the way for law suits claiming US$15 billion in punitive damages and US$1.5 billion in compensatory damages against the company. Exxon had already spent about US$3 billion on clean-up programs and civil settlement costs (to state and federal governments) by that date, although almost half of that was said to have been recouped through insurance (US$700 million) or written off as tax liabilities (US$700 million of the US$900 million in civil settlement costs).

More recently, the *Braer* ran aground in the Shetlands, northern Scotland, releasing 85 000 tonnes of light crude (twice the amount released by the *Exxon Valdez*) that seriously affected marine life and island communities as wind-borne oil coated vegetation and human settlements (see Figure 6.6 for possible pathways that oil can take after a spill; the figure on the next page shows some aspects of the *Braer* accident). Fortunately, a major oil slick was prevented from forming by a combination of three factors: the type of oil, the strong and persistent winds and waves, and the nature of the coastline. Good fortune is no excuse for complacency, especially given the controversy that arose in subsequent reports. The UK Marine Pollution Control Unit's report exposed flaws in emergency plans to deal

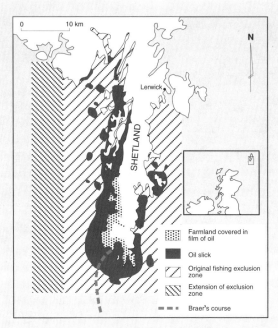

Effects of the oil spill from the wreck of the *Braer* in the Shetlands, 5 January 1993. (Based on material in the sources mentioned for this Box.)

with such incidents. The computer models of oil dispersal and the aerial surveillance equipment proved inadequate. The use of chemical dispersants was particularly criticised and, with hindsight, deemed unnecessary and harmful to the environment. The report agrees that it was mainly through good luck that the incident did not have much more serious consequences. While there has been much on-going disagreement as to just how serious the consequences were, there has been almost complete agreement that they could have been very much worse.

These are only two of a large number of similar accidents. Those in enclosed waters or near coastlines with onshore winds blowing do the most obvious damage, while open ocean spills are dispersed much more rapidly. It seems that such accidents will continue despite everyone's best intentions to stop them: in about 1980 it was claimed that 360 tankers each year were involved in collisions or groundings. It is also clear that we need much more basic knowledge if we are to be able to adequately deal with those accidents.

Sources

New Scientist, 8 May 1993, 4; 8 January 1994, 34–7.
Sydney Morning Herald, 15 June 1994.
Ritchie, W., 'The short-term impact of the *Braer* oil spill in Shetland and the significance of coastal geomorphology', *Scottish Geographical Magazine*, **109** (1993), 50–56.

Accidental spillage from offshore drilling and production platforms and blowouts during exploration are not uncommon. Some of the accidents have been gigantic. The blowout of the Mexican *Ixtoc I* well spilt an unknown amount of crude oil into the ocean: it released oil and gas from 3 June 1979 until 23 March 1980, peaking at a rate of about 30 000 barrels (4.8 million litres) per day. One consequence of the *Ixtoc I* incident was an international row between Mexico and the USA (into whose waters some of the oil drifted) over responsibility, cleanup methods and compensation. The possibility of such accidents has been the main argument used against petroleum exploration rights being granted over areas of the Great Barrier Reef.

We are probably most aware of marine pollution, however, when it affects our enjoyment of swimming, surfing and sailing, as it has along the coastlines of Melbourne and Sydney in recent decades. Beach pollution has also certainly led to human illness, but at least some of the effects mentioned above are far more serious in global terms. The most important long-term effect of all might well be changes in the role of the oceans in various natural cycles and in affecting climate (see Chapter 5). We know relatively little about the complex relationships between the oceans and the atmosphere or about the feedback mechanisms involved, but there may be serious consequences if the composition of the oceans or the nature of life in them is affected in a major way of pollution.

International agreements

The Convention on the Prevention of Marine Pollution by Dumping of Wastes and Other Matter (the London Convention) of 1972 was the first international attempt to regulate the dumping of radioactive and toxic wastes in the world's oceans. In 1983 a ten-year voluntary moratorium on the ocean dumping of radioactive materials was signed. When this came up for renewal in November 1993, only forty-two of the seventy-one signatories to the London Convention attended, the absentees including some nations suspected of having nuclear weapons. Thirty-six of those present, including the USA, voted for a permanent ban, but five nations, including the other four acknowledged nuclear powers (UK, France, Russia and China) abstained and are now unlikely to obey the ban — the UK, France and the former USSR are all known to have been major ocean dumpers of radioactive material. The meeting did agree, however, to phase out the dumping of industrial waste, but not sewage sludge and dredgings, by the end of 1995.

In 1973 the Convention for the Prevention of Pollution from Ships (MARPOL) set minimum distances from land for the discharge of treated garbage, treated sewage, untreated sewage or garbage, some toxic wastes and oil (Figure 6.7). Ships of over 400 tonnes were required to carry tanks for retaining oil residues, while ports handling oil were required to have proper disposal facilities. MARPOL granted greater protection to a number of partially or completely land-locked seas where flushing and mixing is reduced and pollution poses a more serious threat: the discharge of toxic wastes is prohibited in the Baltic and Black Seas, and the discharge of oil is prohibited in those seas and the Mediterranean, the Red Sea and the Persian Gulf.

The most blatant disregard for MARPOL was shown by Iraq during the Gulf War of 1989–90 when huge amounts of crude oil were allowed to flow into the Persian Gulf from deliberately damaged installations, although recent evidence suggests that much of the oil may have resulted from Allied bombing. Whatever the truth in this particular case, it is true that war can have devastating effects on the environment as well as on people — just one more reason to seek peaceful solutions to international conflicts.

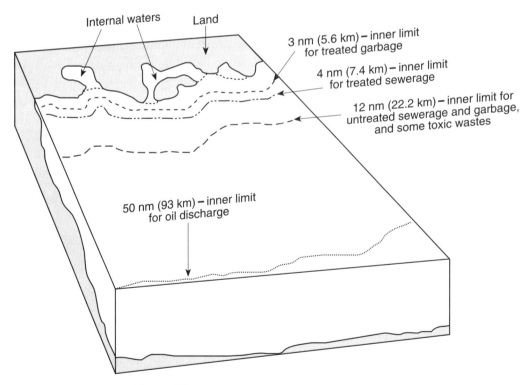

Figure 6.7
MARPOL limits for ocean dumping.

A number of other comprehensive but areally limited agreements have also been reached. The 1969 Bonn Agreement focused on the control of oil pollution in the North Sea, while the 1974 Helsinki Agreement was a comprehensive approach to both sea and land pollution affecting the Baltic Sea. Building directly on this experience, the Regional Seas Programme of UNEP led to the establishment of ten regional schemes to clean up and prevent marine pollution between 1974 and 1984, mostly in particularly vulnerable coastal waters. The first of these, the Mediterranean Plan (1975), overcame long-running national rivalries to institute concerted action to clean up this land-locked sea (Figure 6.8). The most pressing problem was that of land-based pollution (sewage, industrial waste, agricultural fertilisers and pesticides); this was dealt with in a 1980 protocol which completely banned the discharge of 'black' substances (for example, heavy metals and DDT) and licensed and controlled the discharge of 'grey' substances.

Since the early 1990s, Australia has led an international campaign to regulate the discharge of ballast water from ships in coastal waters. Just as land plants and animals introduced into other ecosystems can have far-reaching effects, so can exotic marine life. In 1993, for example, a destructive starfish from the northern Pacific was well established in Tasmanian waters. Released in ballast water from a Japanese ship, it spread rapidly, causing widespread damage to indigenous species.

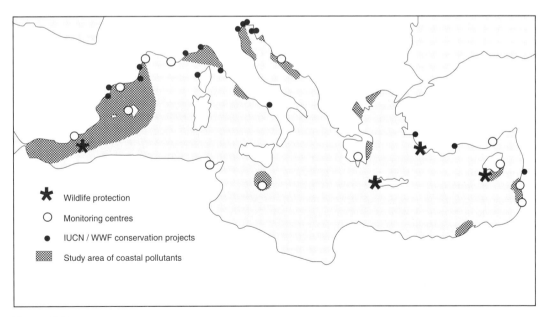

Figure 6.8
Location of some key facilities under the Mediterranean Plan.

There is also concern around the world at the possibility of human diseases such as cholera being transferred in this fashion. The problem was considered in late 1993 by the Marine Environment Protection Committee of the International Maritime Organization (IMO). At the same time, the Resource Assessment Commission of Australia recommended revised practices in Australia waters for both domestic and international shipping.[2]

6.3 ANTARCTICA

Antarctica is the second component of the global commons over which there has been considerable successful international co-operation. As with the oceans, a brief discussion of the processes involved in attempting to reach agreement will highlight the difficulties of reconciling national and international interests.

Antarctica is unique in that is has never been governed as part of a nation or nations, despite a rash of territorial claims in the first half of the twentieth century. Australia, Norway, France, New Zealand, the UK, Chile and Argentina have all claimed control over sections of the continent (Figure 6.9). These claims were usually, but not invariably, based on the nation's exploration efforts. All claims remain unrecognised by much of the world community and have very little practical meaning.

The Antarctic Treaty

Antarctica experienced a year of unprecedented international scientific co-operation during the International Geophysical Year (1957–58), and nations with interests in Antarctica, including Australia, looked for ways of making such co-operation permanent. The resultant Antarctic Treaty was signed in 1959 by twelve nations with an active interest in Antarctica — the seven claimants together with the USA, USSR, Belgium, Japan and South Africa. By early 1990 there were twenty-five full or consultative members. Acceding nations (another seventeen nations in mid-1989) promise to abide by the Treaty's provisions, but cannot vote. The Treaty was intended, among other things, to defer the question of claims, limit the use of Antarctica to peaceful purposes, promote co-operative scientific research, and conserve biological resources (see Box 6.2).

The objectives of the Treaty have been met to varying degrees. Freedom of access to the entire continent by all nations has been guaranteed, and a great deal of scientific research covering a wide

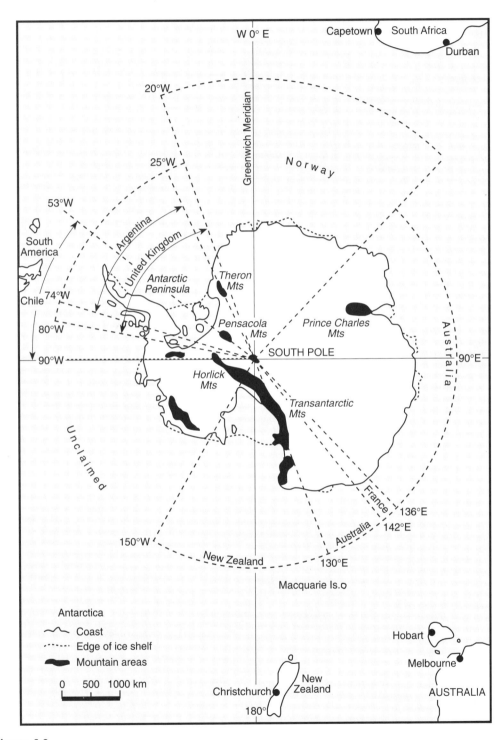

Figure 6.9
Territorial claims and major topographical features of Antarctica.

Major provisions of the Antarctic Treaty

Some of the major Articles, in abridged form, are as follows:

I   Antarctica shall be used for peaceful purposes only.

II Freedom of scientific investigation and co-operation in scientific endeavours is to continue.

III Scientific information and personnel are to be exchanged freely.

IV Territorial claims are neither accepted nor rejected by the Treaty.

V   Nuclear explosions and the disposal of radioactive waste are prohibited.

VI The provisions of the Treaty shall apply to the area south of 60°S, including all ice shelves, but do not affect rights to use the High Seas in that area.

VII Observers of each Contracting Party shall have the right to inspect all Antarctic facilities and equipment; and each Contracting Party must inform the others of expeditions, stations, etc.

IX Representatives are to meet regularly to exchange information, consult on matters of mutual interest, and formulate measures to further the objectives of the Treaty, including the preservation and conservation of the living resources of Antarctica.

XI The Treaty can be modified or amended at any time by unanimous agreement of the Contracting Parties. If any Party requests it, a thorough review will be held after the Treaty has been in force for thirty years, and amendments may be made on a majority vote.

range of disciplines has been carried out in a co-operative spirit. Much has also been achieved in the area of conservation, particularly conservation of living resources. The Scientific Committee on Antarctic Research (SCAR) has played a central role in environmental issues in Antarctica, acting as an informal advisory body to Antarctic Treaty governments and co-ordinating and exchanging information about scientific activities on the continent and in surrounding waters. On the other hand, there are large numbers of military personnel at Antarctic bases, radioactive waste has had to be removed, and some claimants have gone to great lengths to establish the trappings of sovereignty to strengthen their claims. Finally, the consultative parties have been accused of acting like a private club, keeping their meetings closed to the public, the press and **non-governmental organisations** (NGOs) like **Greenpeace**. A review of the Antarctic Treaty was to be held after 1991 — that is, after the Treaty had been in force for 30 years, if any of the consultative members so demanded. That was a major reason for the intense lobbying over possible mining between 1990 and 1992.

World Park or mining lease?

At the 1976 Consultative Meeting a resolution called for all nations to refrain from commercial mineral exploration and exploitation in Antarctica until a legal regime could be established. This voluntary restraint remained in force in 1994. A recommendation from the 1979 meeting provides that any agreed regime should include means to assess the possible impact of mineral resource activity on the Antarctic environment and establish rules for its protection. It was also agreed that the 'interests of all mankind' should not be prejudiced. On the other hand, the Second World Conference on National Parks, held in 1972, had recommended that Antarctica should become the first World Park under the auspices of the UN. In 1981 the IUCN specifically urged that 'no mineral regime be brought into operation until such time as full consideration has been given to protecting the Antarctic environment'.

The 1981 Consultative Meeting began to consider an Antarctic mineral resources regime to control any future exploitation. A committee formulated the Convention on Regulation of Antarctic Minerals Resource Activities (CRAMRA, or the Wellington Convention) in 1988. For that Convention to take effect, all seven claimant nations and a minimum of nine of the other fifteen full members had to ratify it by November 1989, or it would lapse. In April 1989 Australia stated its refusal to sign CRAMRA and its support for the World Park idea: France joined Australia in June 1989. In early 1990, New Zealand changed its mind and announced support for a ban on mining. This stance brought heated opposition from the USA, supported by the UK, Uruguay and Argentina. Those in favour of CRAMRA argued that mining with strict rules was better than an unenforceable outright ban, as Australia, France, and New Zealand wanted, though it was never made clear how the 'rules' could be enforced any more adequately then the ban. The Antarctic Treaty meeting of October 1989 agreed to hold a special meeting in 1990 to consider the World Park proposal, and CRAMRA lapsed. Eventually, in October 1991, the Treaty nations voted for a 50-year ban on mining. Environmental rules in the protocol are voluntary, but each nation must provide detailed information on its environmental management procedures. New activities, including tourism, are meant to be subject to **environmental impact assessment**.

6.4 THE ATMOSPHERE

The atmosphere is a third component of the global environment over which international agreement has been reached, although more recently than in the cases of the oceans and Antarctica. Although the most recent example of a global atmospheric agreement was a document from the Earth Summit, that convention is discussed here for completeness, rather than in Section 6.6. We have also separated discussion of the atmosphere from the general Earth Summit section because atmospheric concerns have figured so prominently in other chapters of this book (Chapters 4 and 5 in particular). Agreements on forests and desertification are treated in similar fashion in the next section for similar reasons.

The Montréal Protocol

After a decade of increasing awareness of the detrimental effects of **chlorofluorocarbons** (CFCs) in the atmosphere (see Sections 5.2 and 5.7) and a decade of negotiations, the Vienna Convention was signed in 1985 by twenty nations, including the major CFC producers. The tougher and more inclusive Montréal Protocol was signed in 1987 by 242 countries, including Australia, and came into force in 1989 after ratification by the required number of nations. It required all signatory nations to reduce emissions of CFCs and other ozone-depleting gases such as halons: specifically, emissions of CFCs should be reduced to 50 per cent of 1986 levels by 1999. However, mounting scientific evidence suggested that the phase-out would be too slow. The London Ministerial Conference of 1990 agreed to eliminate the production and use of CFCs by 2000, with a reduction of 85 per cent by 1997. A fund of US$240 million was set up to help low-income nations acquire necessary technology from industrialised nations so that they could also reach the targets. This was the first time a specific international fund had been established for environmental purposes.

The Toronto Conference and the Hague Declaration

The Toronto Conference of 1988 called on governments and industry to reduce CO_2 emissions to 80 per cent of the 1988 levels by 2005 (see

Chapter 5 for the background to this decision). This goal was en-shrined in the Hague Declaration of 1989, signed by Australia but not by the USA, the UK, China or the USSR — four nations which together were then producing 60 per cent of the world's emissions of CO_2 from fossil fuel use. The Australian Government agreed to aim for this reduction, but only if such a policy did not harm Australia's interna-tional competitiveness. The Government also believed that Australia's actions would have little effect on world totals: probably true, but no reason for inaction. This is a good example of a nation waiting for competitor nations to act before it does: perhaps the only viable way forward is for all nations to agree to act in unison, something that could not be achieved at the Earth Summit (Section 6.6).

UNCED Framework Convention on Climate Change

This Earth Summit convention was prepared under UNEP sponsor-ship over fifteen months, being finalised in May 1992, and had been signed by 153 nations by 14 June 1992. The USA refused to sign until, in the last few months before the Summit, specific, legally binding targets and timetables were dropped and replaced by vague statements of intent. In this case the US Government chose to adopt the view of an influential minority of US atmospheric scientists who doubted the accuracy and seriousness of climate-change predictions, perhaps be-cause that allowed it to conveniently side-step issues seen as detrimen-tal to US business interests. In mid-1993 President Clinton expressed an intention to reconsider specific targets for emissions reductions but, when details were finally released in late October 1993, proposals to reduce CO_2 emissions were weak, especially those related to trans-port. At the same time, many other nations, including Australia, also seemed to be backing away from targets to which they had previously agreed.

The USA has, however, ratified the Convention, as have Japan, Canada, Sweden, Norway, China and Mexico, among others. Australia ratified the Convention in December 1992, the eighth nation to do so: the early ratification was intended to be a signal that Australia is taking the Convention seriously and sees it as a crucial international environ-mental agreement. The Convention came into force in March 1994, 90 days after fifty nations had ratified it. It calls for the protection of the Earth's atmosphere from the results of the build-up of anthro-pogenic gases leading to the enhanced greenhouse effect. The return of industrialised nations to their 1990 levels of greenhouse emissions by 2000 had been targeted as an initial goal. The final document does not provide any specific timetables, instead calling for a conference of signatory countries in 2000. Several countries, disappointed with the lack of definite targets or timetables and with the US position, have started initiatives to introduce protocols that do contain those omitted elements.

6.5 DEFORESTATION AND DESERTIFICATION

Forests

Tropical deforestation has been one of the major global environmental crises of recent times and has attracted considerable attention from governments, NGOs, the media and the public (see Chapter 3). Since the early 1980s there have been three major attempts to deal with the problem: the International Tropical Timber Agreement, the Tropical Forest Action Plan, and UNCED.

The International Tropical Timber Agreement

The International Tropical Timber Agreement (ITTA) was drawn up under the aegis of the **United Nations Conference on Trade and Development** (UNCTAD) in 1983 and came into effect in 1985. The general aim was to establish a system of consultation and co-operation between nations producing and consuming tropical timber, with the International Tropical Timber Organization (ITTO), based in Yokohama, established to administer the agreement. Specific objectives include promoting the expansion and diversification of international trade in tropical timber and improving the nature of the international market for timber; encouraging the development of national policies aimed at sustainable use and conservation of tropical forests and their ecological resources; and facilitating the achievement of 'Target 2000', through which member countries seek to ensure that all timber entering international trade will be produced from forests under sustainable management by the year 2000.

In practice, there have proven to be serious conflicts between these various objectives, and the Agreement has been the target of intense international criticism. In particular, there is not surprisingly a conflict between the ITTA's developmental and conservation objectives; a key response has been lengthy discussion of the concept of 'sustainability'. Unfortunately, the term has many meanings: to environmental groups it might refer to ensuring the survival of the ecological values of the forests; while for foresters 'sustainable yield' is essentially a commercial concept. A study commissioned by the ITTO showed in 1989 that substantially less than 1 per cent of the world's tropical forests were being managed for the sustainable production of timber. Clearly, huge advances were necessary if the 'Target 2000' was to be achieved, although during the 1990s the ITTO has been involved in the negotiated reduction in exploitative forestry practices in a few countries.

Tropical Forestry Action Plan

The Tropical Forestry Action Plan (TFAP) originated in two reports prepared in 1983 and 1984 by the **Food and Agriculture Organization** (FAO) and jointly by the **World Resources Institute**, the World Bank, and the **United Nations Development Programme** (UNDP). With the release of the reports in 1985, the TFAP was established under the FAO. Its intentions were to slow tropical deforestation and to serve as a blueprint for forest management. It provides a forum for development agencies to co-ordinate their forestry programs and a process for tropical countries to formulate forestry plans which might then be funded by those agencies.

From its early days, critics have challenged its diagnosis of the causes of deforestation, in particular its heavy focus on poverty and overpopulation, and the strategies proposed and the beliefs that lay behind them, notably the views that tropical forests will be conserved only if they have a commercial value, and that they can be logged sustainably without loss of **biodiversity**. Critics also deplored both the 'top-down' nature of the plan — ignoring the experiences and aspirations of ordinary people — and its neglect of hard-won lessons of previous attempts to improve management of tropical forests. By 1990 the TFAP was recognised as having failed to arrest tropical deforestation, and the FAO commissioned a review. To overcome some of the weaknesses, the review recommended the establishment of a legally binding international forest convention. This notion was taken up by US President George Bush, and became one of the antecedents of UNCED's deliberations over the world's forests: this may turn out to have been the greatest contribution of the TFAP! The fate of the TFAP does, however, illustrate the huge difficulties involved in dealing globally with an issue as complex as deforestation, where a wide range of processes create the problem and a wide range of groups have very different views on possible solutions, or indeed whether there is even a problem.

UNCED Statement of Principles on Forests

This was the only document relating to a particular environmental issue formally adopted by all the nations present at UNCED (Section 6.6). Even in this case, however, the difficulties encountered in reaching agreement are reflected in its title: *Non-legally Binding Authoritative Statement of Principles for a Global Consensus on the Management, Conservation and Sustainable Development of all Types of Forests.* Some countries certainly wanted a fully fledged convention with its greater legal and political weight, but the political sensitivities surrounding the issue made this impossible to achieve. Despite such scepticism, this document is the first global consensus on forests and does affirm the importance of forest management and conservation for sustainable development.

The negotiations on the forest principles illustrated the complex inter-linkages between environmental and developmental factors. Much of the negotiation was between low-income nations on the one hand and high-income nations on the other, and it took a number of paths. Firstly, claims of national sovereignty over natural resources, including forests, contrasted with claims that forests are the common heritage of humankind. Secondly, the dependence of many low-income economies on harvesting forest resources made the prospect of internationally imposed limits unacceptable in the absence of adequate compensation. Thirdly, some negotiators specifically contrasted calls by high-income nations for tropical forests to be conserved because of their importance in ameliorating climate change with the reticence of the same nations when called on to agree to limit their greenhouse gas emissions.

There were interesting connections made between the Climate Convention and the Forests Statement and between the two corresponding chapters in the *Agenda 21* document from the 1992 Earth Summit. The Arab Group of nations, particularly Saudi Arabia, asserted that the climate chapter and the Convention placed too much emphasis on energy conservation and efficiency in using fossil fuels. Some high-income nations, notably the USA, argued along similar lines while contending that preservation of tropical forests was more important (or more acceptable, perhaps) as a way of dealing with global climate change. Low-income nations, strongly led by Malaysia, took the opposite point of view, stressing the need for high-income nations to drastically cut their profligate use of energy. This is just one example of the manner in which the national concerns of individual governments can interfere with the search for international consensus. It is also a very clear example of the way in which social, economic, cultural and technological contexts can affect the perception of (and response to) environmental issues by nations and, for that matter, individuals.

Drought and desertification | 259

It was impossible to agree on the wording of a convention on desertification at Rio, but the process has begun as a result of Chapter 12 of *Agenda 21*. The first of five planned meetings of an intergovernmental negotiating committee was held in May and June 1993 in Nairobi; a second was held in Geneva in November 1993. Delegates to the second meeting agreed that desertification, drought and climate change are intimately linked and should be treated that way in the future (Section 2.3). Data collection and monitoring were singled out for attention and future strengthening. The meeting stressed the global nature of the problem, and a draft report emphasised its importance: more than 250 million people are claimed to be directly threatened by desertification; 36 per cent of the world's land area is arid, semi-arid or dry sub-humid; 18 per cent of the world's population lives in such regions; and over 100 countries have experienced dryland degradation. A formal convention was developed at a later meeting in June 1994, but the 'problem' of desertification remains ill-defined and pledges of money from high-income nations were not forthcoming. In addition, the Global Environment Facility (see Section 7.4) has refused to define desertification as a 'global' problem that is eligible for money from its resources.

The agreements and negotiations discussed so far have related to particular sections of the environment. At the same time momentum was building for international co-operation on environmental matters on an altogether broader and more all-encompassing scale. It is to that process that we turn in the next section.

THE EARTH SUMMIT (UNCED) 6.6

Events leading to the Earth Summit

The UN Conference on the Human Environment, held in Stockholm in 1972, was the first international environment conference to have a broad agenda covering virtually all aspects of the environmental and human actions affecting it. It grew out of an increasing awareness during the late 1960s and early 1970s of the seriousness of environmental and resource use issues at the global scale. It was a conscious effort to bring together low-income and high-income nations 'to delineate the "rights" of the human family to a healthy and productive environment'. Furthermore, it had the potential to promote global action, as any recommendations it made would be put before the UN General Assembly.

The Conference adopted a *Declaration on the Human Environment* and an Action Plan containing 109 recommendations. In late 1972 the General Assembly adopted several resolutions stemming from the Conference report, the main ones establishing a Governing Council for Environmental Programmes, a co-ordinating Board, the Environment Secretariat in Nairobi, and an Environment Fund. The Declaration included statements to the effect that:

- all people have the right to live in a quality environment;
- people have a responsibility to protect the environment for future generations;
- economic and social development is essential and the potential of developing countries should be enhanced;
- resources should be made available to preserve and improve the environment;
- rational planning is essential;
- demographic policies are needed; and
- states have the right to exploit their own resources.

These statements, and many others, are clearly precursors of statements in the Rio Declaration and *Agenda 21*.

One of the most important outcomes of the Stockholm Conference was the establishment in 1974 of the United Nations Environment Programme (UNEP). Its major tasks were to act as a source of environmental data, assessment and reporting on a global scale, and to become a principal advocate and agent for change and international co-operation. UNEP has worked in close collaboration with UN and outside organisations to establish and promote a large number of programs covering such topics as desertification, climate change, hazardous waste, oceans and global environment monitoring. Through its Environment Fund and extensive co-operation with other agencies, UNEP has played a key role in funding environmental programs, especially in low-income countries. Establishing international institutional frameworks has been yet another key area of activity: for example, UNEP's Earthwatch has become the leading agency for environmental risk assessment. Very importantly, UNEP, in conjunction with IUCN and WWF, produced a World Conservation Strategy in 1980 that contained many of the key ideas now incorporated in the concept of sustainable development (see Section 7.8).

In 1983 the UN established the independent World Commission on Environment and Development (WCED) to formulate a 'global agenda for change' that would include long-term strategies for:

- achieving sustainable development;
- achieving greater co-operation among countries at different stages of economic and social development;

- taking account of the interrelationships between people, resources, environment, and development; and
- dealing more effectively with environmental concerns at the international level.

Definitions of shared perceptions of long-term environmental issues, a long-term agenda for action, and the aspirations of the world community were to be sought. Two major practical outcomes resulted: the publication in 1987 of *Our Common Future* (also known as the Brundtland Report), which encapsulated the major themes of the Stockholm Conference as outlined above and stressed the need for sustainable development, and the Earth Summit in 1992.

UN Conference on the Environment and Development

After two and a half years of preparation, the Earth Summit finally took place in Rio de Janeiro in June 1992. The *Rio Declaration, Agenda 21* and the Forests Statement (see Section 6.5) were adopted and recommended for endorsement at the next session of the UN General Assembly late in 1992. Conventions on Biological Diversity (see below) and Climate Change (see Section 6.4) were opened for signatures, but were not adopted due to disagreement, notably on the part of the USA. UNCED was both the largest gathering of heads of state and government in history and by far the most important gathering ever of representatives of NGOs and social movements, along with major gatherings of indigenous peoples, women and youth from around the world. One important result was a heightened awareness of the importance of NGOs in the debate about the environment and development. Finally, UNCED was a major media event and focused world-wide public attention on environmental issues.

Rio Declaration on Environment and Development

According to a UN statement, 'the *Rio Declaration* is a set of 27 principles to govern the economic and environmental behaviour of both nations and individuals': an abridged version of the principles is given in Box 6.3. While they are, in a sense, a series of 'motherhood statements', they do give a philosophical basis upon which to build in the future. The Declaration is not, however, an action plan.

Agenda 21

Agenda 21 is UNCED's 'blue-print for action to the 21st century', notable for its extensive coverage of environment and development

The Rio Declaration: *abridged principles*

These are abridged, reworded and sometimes combined versions of the twenty-seven principles in the original document.

A People are at the centre of concerns for sustainable development and are entitled to a healthy and productive life in harmony with nature. In order to achieve sustainable development, environmental protection must constitute an integral part of the development process and cannot be considered in isolation from it. All states and all people should co-operate in the essential task of eradicating poverty as an indispensable requirement for sustainable development. The right to development must be fulfilled so as to equitably meet developmental and environmental needs of present and future generations.

B States have the sovereign right to exploit their own resources and the responsibility to ensure that activities within their jurisdiction do not cause damage to the environment beyond their borders. States should enact effective environmental legislation, reflecting their environmental and developmental circumstances. States should effectively co-operate to discourage or prevent the relocation and transfer to other states of any activities and substances that cause severe environmental degradation or are found to be harmful to human health. States should develop national law regarding liability and compensation for the victims of pollution and other environmental damage and co-operate to develop further international law regarding liability and compensation. States should immediately notify other states of any natural disasters or other emergencies that are likely to produce sudden harmful effects on the environment of those states and every effort should be made by the international community to help states so affected. States should provide prior and timely consultation, notification, and relevant information to potentially affected states on activities that may have a significant adverse transboundary environmental effect.

C The special situation and needs of low-income countries, particularly the least developed and those most environmentally vulnerable, should be given special priority. States should co-operate in a spirit of global partnership to conserve, protect, and restore the health and integrity of the Earth's biophysical systems. In view of the different contributions to global environmental degradation, states have common but differentiated responsibilities. The high-income countries acknowledge the responsibility that they bear in view of the pressures their societies place on the global environment, and of the technologies and financial resources they command. States should co-operate to strengthen local capacity for sustainable development by improving scientific understanding through exchanges of scientific knowledge and technology. To achieve sustainable development and a higher quality of life for all people, states should reduce and eliminate unsustainable patterns of production and consumption and promote appropriate demographic policies.

D Environmental issues are best handled with the participation of all citizens. At the national level, each individual should have appropriate access to information concerning the environment and states should facilitate and encourage public awareness and participation and provide effective access to judicial and administrative proceedings. Women have a vital role in environmental management and development and their full participation is essential to achieve sustainable development. The creativity, ideals and courage of the youth of the world should be mobilised to forge a global partnership in order to achieve sustainable development and ensure a better future for all. Indigenous peoples and local communities have a vital role in environmental management and development because of their knowledge and traditional practices. States should recognise and duly support their identity, culture and interests and enable their effective participation in the achievement of sustainable development.

E States should co-operate to promote a supportive and open international economic system that leads to economic growth and sustainable development in all countries to better address the problems of environmental degradation. Trade policy measures for environmental purposes should not constitute a means of arbitrary or unjustifiable discrimination or a disguised restriction on international trade, but should, as far as possible, be based on international consensus. National authorities should endeavour to promote the internalisation of environmental costs and the use of economic instruments, taking into account the user-pays approach to the cost of pollution, with due regard to the public interest and without distorting international trade and investment.

F In order to protect the environment, the precautionary approach should be widely applied by states according to their capabilities — where there are threats of serious or irreversible damage, lack of full scientific certainty must not be used as a reason for postponing cost-effective measures to prevent environmental degradation. Environmental impact assessment should be undertaken for proposed activities that are likely to have a significant adverse impact on the environment.

G Peace, development and environmental protection are inter-dependent and indivisible. Warfare is inherently destructive of sustainable development. States must therefore respect inter-national law providing protection for the environment in times of armed conflict and co-operate in its further development. States should resolve all their environmental disputes peacefully and by appropriate means in accordance with the Charter of the United Nations. The environment and natural resources of people under oppression, domination and occupation should be protected.

H States and people shall co-operate in good faith and in a spirit of partnership in the fulfilment of the principles embodied in this Declaration and in the further development of international law in the field of sustainable development.

matters as inextricably linked issues. Its ambitious goal is to cover all areas where environment and development intersect, something it attempts in forty chapters (Figure 6.10) and more than 100 program areas. It does not break a great deal of new ground, but it does bring together detailed statements on most of the important environmental concerns in the one document. While it is merely a blue-print which does not have the force of treaties, protocols or international agree-ments, it is nonetheless an important body of agreement by virtually all national governments on principles that may lead to such 'action' documents in the future.

The first section deals with the social and economic dimensions of sustainable development (Figure 6.10), focusing on both the impacts of human activities on the environment and the impacts of environ-mental degradation on human living conditions. It also deals with both the relationship between poverty and environmental degrada-tion and the negative impact which affluence, through unsustainable consumption patterns, has on the environment. The relative impact of poverty and affluence became a point of contention, the proposed statement meeting strong resistance from the USA. Agreement was finally reached and the following statement was included: 'While poverty results in certain kinds of environmental stress, the major cause of the continued deterioration of the global environment is the unsustainable pattern of consumption and production, particu-larly in industrialised countries, which is a matter of grave concern, aggravating poverty and imbalances.' (These issues are taken up in Chapter 7). Finally, this section consistently emphasises the need to

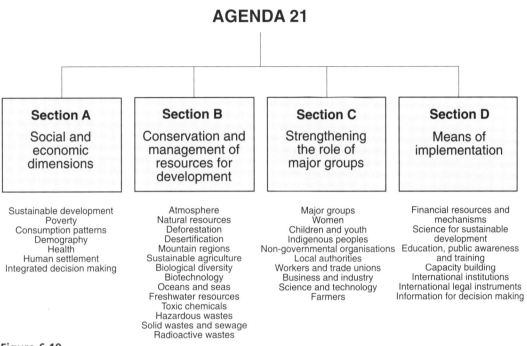

AGENDA 21

Section A	Section B	Section C	Section D
Social and economic dimensions	Conservation and management of resources for development	Strengthening the role of major groups	Means of implementation

Sustainable development	Atmosphere	Major groups	Financial resources and mechanisms
Poverty	Natural resources	Women	
Consumption patterns	Deforestation	Children and youth	Science for sustainable development
Demography	Desertification	Indigenous peoples	
Health	Mountain regions	Non-governmental organisations	Education, public awareness and training
Human settlement	Sustainable agriculture	Local authorities	
Integrated decision making	Biological diversity	Workers and trade unions	Capacity building
	Biotechnology	Business and industry	International institutions
	Oceans and seas	Science and technology	International legal instruments
	Freshwater resources	Farmers	Information for decision making
	Toxic chemicals		
	Hazardous wastes		
	Solid wastes and sewage		
	Radioactive wastes		

Figure 6.10
General structure of *Agenda 21*.

address economic, social, cultural, and political issues along with the more obviously 'environmental' ones.

Agenda 21's second major section deals with the conservation and management of resources for development, addressing the protection and management of various sectors of the environment, the conservation of biodiversity, promoting sustainable agriculture and managing various types of wastes. Although many of the chapters in this section have developmental dimensions, they are primarily on environmental issues. The length of the section, approximately equal to that of the three other sections together, is indicative of the concern of many low-income countries and NGOs that environment should receive more attention than development. Chapters on deforestation, biodiversity and the atmosphere were influenced by related conventions negotiated prior to UNCED (see later in this section, and Sections 6.4 and 6.5).

The third section is the most extensive and formalised recognition in any UN document of the potential contributions of NGOs and other independent-sector groups. The nine chapters outline the contributions of particular groups, such as women and indigenous peoples, and examine ways of strengthening them and further incorporating them into governmental and international work on environment and development.

The fourth and final section, on means of implementation, includes chapters on financial resources and mechanisms; transfer of technology; science; education, training and public awareness; capacity building in developing countries; international institutional arrangements; regional organisations; international legal instruments and mechanisms; and data and information. (Most of these topics are dealt with at greater length in Chapter 7.) The negotiations on finances, institutions and transfer of technology were particularly protracted, reflecting their significance in the implementation of *Agenda 21*. These final chapters are considered by many to be the most important, although it still remains to be seen whether or not nations have the will to deliver the goods in such respects.

Other documents

Two of the three official documents on specific topics have already been mentioned above: the Framework Convention on Climate Change (Section 6.4) and the Statement of Principles on Forests (Section 6.5).

The Convention on Biological Diversity, sponsored by UNEP, was under deliberation for nearly four years and was finalised in late May 1992. By the end of UNCED it had been signed by 153 states and the European Community, but not by the USA. President Clinton did, however, announce his intention to sign in April 1993. The earlier US objections were primarily in the areas of ownership of intellectual property rights and payments for genetic materials gathered from other nations, arising from the Convention's assertion that high-income countries must assist low-income countries both financially and with the transfer of technological know-how. Much emphasis is also placed on the role of natural reserves as the prime means of preserving biodiversity, and on the rights of indigenous peoples and rural communities to continue patterns of sustainable use which have existed over centuries (see Section 6.2 for an example). Indeed, such groups are also seen as vitally important in preserving biodiversity, especially in crop and livestock species. The treaty came into effect in December 1993 after having been ratified by the requisite number of nations, including Australia, by the previous October. It is, however, merely the first step in a long process.

The '*Earth Charter*' and NGO treaties emanated from the NGO Global Forum (billed by the media as the 'alternative summit') held in conjunction with UNCED. The proposed 'official' Earth Charter was dropped in favour of the *Rio Declaration* before UNCED began. The NGO Global Forum, however, adopted its own basic statement of principles, intent and commitment, which it proceeded to call the

Earth Charter. The Forum also agreed on treaties covering the same range of topics as *Agenda 21.* They tend, however, to be generally more critical of governments and of the international business community, and to envisage an even greater role for NGOs. While they often lack detailed suggestions for action, they do bring a significantly different perspective to the global environmental debate, and the role taken by NGOs generally in the Earth Summit proceedings clearly established them as important participants in that debate.

Achievements and failures of UNCED

While many commentators have expressed serious disappointment at particular shortcomings of UNCED, including the lack of agreement on crucial conventions and the rather vague wording of some of the documents, almost everyone agrees that the major achievement was to direct world attention, including the attention of governments and media, to questions of the environment and development. A briefing by the UN Non-Governmental Liaison Service, for example, claimed that

> [t]he Rio conference was not only a major historical event but also an illustration of changes in international economic and political relations. It contained manifestations both of the end of one era and the beginning of another. Many who hoped that it would demonstrate a new understanding of the fact that the threat to global security is environmental, economic and social degradation were disappointed . . . [T]he next three years leading to the 50th anniversary of the United Nations in 1995 . . . is being seen as the time to reshape national and international priorities and the structures and distribution of resources to serve those priorities . . . [3]

Although interest and media attention had obviously waned within a few months, UNCED did give a new and higher base level of interest, understanding and concern. For example, US Vice-President Al Gore wrote:

> [T]his meeting was criticized by many for producing weak and watered-down agreements with few meaningful commitments to change the behaviour of nations. But . . . the Earth Summit nevertheless marked a historic turning point in the long struggle to increase international awareness of the true nature of the global environmental crisis. And it effectively moved the world a long way down the road toward a better understanding of how and why future economic progress is inextricably linked to sound policies promoting the protection of the environment and wise stewardship of our natural resources . . .
>
> Indeed, there is little doubt that a powerful learning experience took place in Rio . . . The Earth Summit laid the groundwork for important shifts in policies throughout the world designed to stop the destruction of the global ecological system.[4]

Many of the specific disappointments have already been mentioned, or will be taken up in the next chapter. The failure to come to grips adequately with the issues of population growth, international debt and overconsumption in high-income nations are among them.

At its December 1992 session the UN General Assembly endorsed the outcomes of UNCED and recommended that the Commission on Sustainable Development (CSD) be established. The CSD was to be a 53-member intergovernmental body and would provide a forum for bringing together low-income and high-income nations, integrating development and environment issues, and ensuring accountability of international financial and trade institutions such as the World Bank, the **International Monetary Fund** (IMF) and GATT. Part of its mandate is to monitor progress in implementing *Agenda 21* and, in particular, progress toward the UN target of 0.7 per cent of the GNP of high-income nations being used for official development assistance (see Section 7.4). But the signs are not encouraging. Reflecting on the final agreement on finances, Brundtland commented:

> We are disappointed by the lack of adequate financial commitments made. The 20-years-old target of 0.7 per cent of GNP as official development assistance must be reached before the year 2000.[5]

6.7 AUSTRALIA'S ROLE IN THE UNCED PROCESS

Australia, unlike most other nations, was not represented at UNCED by its head of government. Its delegation was led by the Minister for the Arts, Sport, the Environment and Territories and comprised 49 members who all made active contributions to various aspects of the Summit, including negotiations on some of the more controversial issues. Australia is seen, at least by the Minister, as 'an "honest broker", positioned between the "Big Seven" industrial nations and developing countries'.[6] That, according to the Minister, meant that Australia is 'uniquely placed to provide direction and assistance in the ongoing process that flows from UNCED'. It remains to be seen if that eventuates. The Minister, in her report, further stated that

> . . . the Earth Summit has put in place a new dimension in international relations, a framework of which Australia must clearly be part. Just as trade and security are major global issues, so too will the environment now have that status . . . Australia is quite clearly part of this international process in which the environment is becoming an essential element of mainstream decision-making. If we are to benefit from this situation — then government, industry and the community must seize the opportunities which that brings. UNCED was not just a first step down the path of sustainable development — it provides a map of where we are going, both domestically and in the international arena.[7]

Australia signed both the Biodiversity Treaty and the Convention on Climate Change, along with the other official Summit documents, during UNCED, and the Australian Government has since ratified both. The Minister did state on her return that 'the [Australian] Government would be sticking to strict targets for the reduction of greenhouse gas emissions, although leaders at the summit endorsed a watered-down version'.[8] There are already, though, signs of weakening resolve (see Section 5.7). The Australian Government established a Consultative Committee on International Environmental Issues as the major mechanism to monitor and direct Australian post-Summit activity (but it soon became inactive), while local NGOs actively pursued issues from their perspectives.

It is of great importance in the longer term that Australia does make a positive response and builds on the momentum established in Rio. Australia could, and should, play a key role in its region. It has recently strengthened links of many kinds in the Asia–Pacific region, and this trend will continue. Australian academics and research scientists have long worked in the region, in many cases in close co-operation with local people and on 'small-science' projects. What is more, Australians have something of a reputation for innovative, low-cost, low-energy solutions to problems, including environmental problems.

At the same time, overt intervention by the Australian Government could easily be seen as paternalistic. There are, though, many low-key, less direct ways in which the Government can assist the implementation of *Agenda 21* programs by explicitly building on some of the document's recurrent suggestions. Regional meetings, conferences and workshops could be arranged or sponsored by Australia; Australia could take a leading role in data collection and analysis, the results of which could then be shared with other nations in the region; and Australia could play a key role in networking, information dissemination and environmental education. In recent years Australian aid programs have made substantial advances in focusing on environmentally acceptable projects, and the official policy is that environmental assessment and sustainable development issues are considered before a project is approved. Australian aid, however, remains well below the UN goal of 0.7 per cent of GNP. Ultimately, Australian assistance may be best directed through Australian and regional NGOs, minimising direct government-to-government assistance.

6.8 CONCLUSION

In many ways UNCED was merely another milestone on the road to genuine global cooperation to solve or prevent global environmental crises, but it was an extremely important milestone. To use a slightly different analogy, it was a major freeway sign-board pointing the way to an essential goal, rather than an insignificant finger-post at a street corner. But we certainly still have a long way to travel. The final chapter discusses some of the major obstacles and challenges the world community will have to deal with on its way to its destination.

FURTHER READING

Anon., 'UNCED', in Bissio, R.R., et al. (eds), *Third World Guide, 1993–94*, Instituto del Tercer Mundo (Montevideo, 1993), 101–13. [A succinct summary of the Earth Summit from the point of view of low-income nations.]

Barnes, J.N., *Let's Save Antarctica!*, Greenhouse Publications (Melbourne, 1982). [Contains text of most of the Antarctic treaties and conventions to 1980, as well as general, easily accessible material on the continent and its environmental concerns.]

Borgese, E.M., *Ocean Yearbook 9*, University of Chicago Press (Chicago, 1991). [A comprehensive overview of a very wide range of topics to do with the world's oceans. Yearbooks for other years, both before and since 1991, are also useful.]

Bramwell, M., et al. (eds), *Atlas of the Oceans* (1990 edn), Crescent Books/ Mitchell Beazley (New York, 1990). [A very well illustrated work that covers all aspects of the oceans in a detailed, scholarly fashion.]

Cherfas, J., *The Hunting of the Whale: A tragedy that must end*, Penguin (Harmondsworth, 1989). [A brief history of whaling and the IWC to 1989.]

Group of Experts on Scientific Aspects of Marine Pollution, (GESAMP) *The State of the Marine Environment*, Blackwell (Oxford, 1990). [The Group includes representatives of IMO, FAO, UNESCO, WMO, WHO, IAEA, UN, UNEP: the report thus covers a wide range of topics.]

Grubb, M. et al., *The Earth Summit Agreements: A guide and assessment*, Earthscan (London, 1993). [An authoritative summary and analysis of the conference by the Royal Institute of International Affairs, UK.]

Knight, G. and Chiu, H., *The International Law of the Sea: Case, documents and readings*, London/New York, 1991. [A technical legal work and thus only for those particularly interested in this topic.]

May, J., *The Greenpeace Book of Antarctica: A new view of the seventh continent*, Child & Associates (Sydney, 1988). [Another good introduction to the continent and related environmental concerns.]

Triggs, G.D. (ed.), *The Antarctic Treaty Regime: Law, environment and resources*, Cambridge University Press (Cambridge, UK, 1987). [A more academically rigorous collection of papers on various aspects of Antarctica — a very good background to the CRAMRA debate.]

Turbayne, D., *To the Summit and Beyond: A community guide to the Earth Summit and its outcomes* (ACOA Development Dossier No. 32), Australian Council for Overseas Aid (Canberra, 1993). [An Australian non-governmental organisation's perspective on the Earth Summit.]

NOTES

1   Hardin, G., 'The tragedy of the commons', *Science*, **162** (1968), 1243–8.

2   Resource Assessment Commission *Coastal Zone Inquiry: Final report*, Australian Government Publishing Service (Canberra, 1993).

3   UN Non-Governmental Liaison Service, *Briefing for NGOs on UNCED* #31, 28 July 1992.

4   Gore, A. *Earth in the balance: forging a new common purpose*, Earthscan, (London, 1992). Preface to reprint of late 1992, ix–x.

5   Gro Harlem Brundtland, quoted in UN Non-Governmental Liaison Service, *Briefing for NGOs on UNCED* #31, 28 July 1992.

6   *Report by the Hon. R.J. Kelly . . . on the Earth Summit . . .* AGPS (Canberra, 1992), Foreword, v.

7   Ibid., 12.

8   *Sydney Morning Herald*, 20 June 1992.

7

SOME WAYS FORWARD

HIS CHAPTER further develops some of the concepts introduced
earlier in the book, but places an even greater emphasis on
the future. While it builds most obviously on Chapter 6, refer-
ring in particular to issues raised in the *Rio Declaration* and *Agenda 21*,
it also picks up on a number of other themes running through earlier
chapters. Although the Earth Summit documents and discussions are
referred to frequently, all of the concepts and themes discussed here
were commonly spoken and written about many years before the
Summit. Furthermore, they are central to this book as a whole.

7.1 INTEGRATION

Perhaps the most obvious features of *Agenda 21* are its broad scope and
a keen awareness of the need to integrate the biophysical and social
sciences. The need to involve workers from all fields is stressed, as is
the need for people who can span discipline boundaries to take a
synthesising or holistic approach and work on the complex issues
involved in the intersecting environmental and developmental areas
(Section 1.2 stressed the role geographers can play in this regard).
Complexity is almost the chief catch-phrase of the document.

Decision-making in environmental and resource management is
necessarily complex, involving as it does such a wide range of issues
and perspectives. It should also involve a wide range of participants,
bringing different experience, expertise, attitudes, and values to the
task in hand. Furthermore, environmental decisions are never value-
free, yet another reason to take a wide range of views into account and
to go well beyond the biophysical or economic 'experts' in seeking
input to decision-making processes.

Many causes of the environmental crisis are structural, with roots in
social institutions and economic relationships. With the best will in the

world, a 'technological fix' cannot be made to work unless political, social, and economic factors are considered as well. It is, after all, people who have to put any plan into action. Plans have to be acceptable to the key people involved in that action — industrialists and other business people, bureaucrats, politicians and local 'grass roots' groups. Furthermore, in a democracy it is the mass of voters who, collectively, ultimately demand action on environmental concerns and who determine that they are willing to bear the costs and inconveniences involved in that action.

It seems almost a truism to say that economic rationalists by themselves cannot offer successful solutions to environmental crises. But neither can those offering only extreme points of view from ecology, nor those advocating any narrowly defined philosophical or ideological approach. The problems and any potentially viable solutions are much too complex for any single-strand, simplistic approach to adequately encompass. Besides, people are very different and all deserve to be heard. We need to be particularly wary of 'fundamentalists', whether they be economic, ecological, political or religious. Despite the enormous difficulties, it is essential that a widely based consensus involving as many viewpoints as possible is reached.

SCALE 7.2

Like much of the earlier debate and writing about the environment and development, *Agenda 21* acknowledges the need to address issues at various scales (Figure 7.1). The overriding tendency is to recommend referral of all decision-making to the most local level possible: grassroots participation is stressed over and over again.

Local and national communities need to 'own' decisions and thus need to feel that they have been involved, through their representatives if not individually. Programs imposed from above or from outside generally will not be well received, however well intentioned they might be. In more practical terms, local knowledge and experience can often save the 'experts' from acutely embarrassing and environmentally disastrous mistakes. A solution for one set of circumstances or a particular locality cannot be simply transferred to another set of circumstances or another locality. Furthermore, local involvement ties in with the often-stated desire to include as wide a range of participants as possible in both decision-making and practical activities (Section 7.1).

One very successful variant of local planning in low-income nations has been participatory rural appraisal, which is firmly based on the

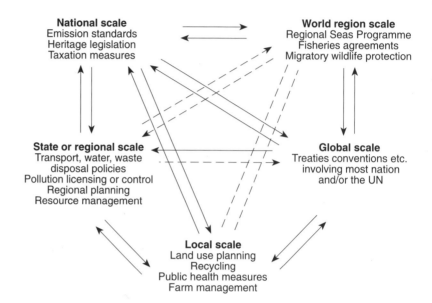

National scale
Emission standards
Heritage legislation
Taxation measures

World region scale
Regional Seas Programme
Fisheries agreements
Migratory wildlife protection

State or regional scale
Transport, water, waste
disposal policies
Pollution licensing or control
Regional planning
Resource management

Global scale
Treaties conventions etc.
involving most nation
and/or the UN

Local scale
Land use planning
Recycling
Public health measures
Farm management

Figure 7.1
The scales at which environmental decisions and actions take place.

assumption that local people with local knowledge and experience are more often than not the best ones to solve local problems and manage local environments. The Australian **Landcare** movement is a good working example of a similar approach (Section 2.6). The Cleanup Sydney Campaign, which became Cleanup Australia and has now been taken up in many other nations, is an excellent example of a local movement, led by a highly motivated individual, gaining momentum and spreading but retaining its grassroots character. More formally, there is a call in *Agenda 21* for global networking of local authorities and for local 'Agenda 21s' by 1996.

On the other hand, there is also a clear awareness that many issues need to be addressed at national, regional and global scales. *Agenda 21* is somewhat different, however, in the degree of stress it places on the sovereign rights of states. While much decision-making will obviously occur at the national level, despite the cross-boundary nature of many environmental and developmental issues, there may well be times when global considerations need to outweigh national decisions. The previous chapter contains many examples of just how difficult this is to achieve.

7.3 INEQUALITIES

Manifest inequalities exist at various scales: between nations, within nations and within communities. The relative poverty of entire nations and, in fact, entire world regions is widely acknowledged, as is the need for wealthy nations to help financially and in many other ways. International debt is commonly seen as one important manifestation of such inequalities on a national scale. A strong link between poverty at various scales and environmental misuse and degradation is central to many sections of *Agenda 21* and has already been introduced in Section 1.4. One key call for action in the UNCED document, repeated a number of times, is for programs to reduce the incidence of poverty, for both social justice and overtly environmental reasons, through the promotion of sustained and sustainable economic development.

Poverty is important in the context of the global environmental debate because many poor people, especially the rural poor in the low-income nations, cause serious and perhaps irreversible environmental damage simply to remain alive. Sparse tree cover is removed to use as fuel, for building purposes, or to sell to urban areas or even overseas (Section 3.4). Overgrazing occurs to support the meagre flocks maintained for subsistence purposes by local tribes (Section 2.3). Cropping spreads into more and more marginal areas as urban development, plantation agriculture or large-scale landowners displace small-scale farmers. And, in any of these examples, growing population numbers further increase the pressure on resources and on the environment. The only humane way to decrease those pressures is to find alternative incomes and livelihoods for those living in poverty. In addition, it is being increasingly accepted that poverty leads to high rates of population growth, rather than the converse.

Inequalities at the international level are also important, but best dealt with under the heading of 'international trade and finance' (Section 7.4). Suffice it to say that whole nations can be relatively poverty-stricken and forced into a situation where they overexploit their natural resources in order to ensure their survival, at least in the short term. In fact, the UNDP claimed in 1992 that the polarisation of global wealth had doubled between 1960 and 1989; Africa, as on so many other indicators, generally fares worst. Again, they need to find alternative, sustainable incomes, and this will inevitably involve some outside assistance, both financial and in terms of what *Agenda 21* consistently refers to as capacity building. Capacity building involves education and training, development of **appropriate technology** (Section 7.6) and building of infrastructure to enable the nation itself to cope with its present and future social, economic, and environmental problems. Aid may be valuable in the short term, but only has long-term benefits if it does contribute to capacity building, another point developed later in this chapter.

7.4 INTERNATIONAL TRADE AND FINANCE

One conclusion from reading *Agenda 21* must almost inevitably be that international politics is still much more the politics of trade than the politics of the environment, the Earth Summit notwithstanding. Free trade is placed on a pedestal and given a higher priority than environmental issues. It is clearly stated, for example, that only under extraordinary circumstances should restraints on trade be used to achieve environmental goals. Unlike the various **non-governmental organisation** (NGO) documents to come out of Rio, *Agenda 21* contains no questioning of the basic nature of the world economic system, though a few mild caveats are placed on its operation. By contrast, some prominent environmental economists have suggested that environmental considerations should become integral in future deliberations of the **General Agreement on Tariffs and Trade** (GATT) and similar organisations. One encouraging sign is that, during discussions in late 1993 aimed at recasting GATT as the **World Trade Organization**, greater emphasis did seem to be placed on environmental issues. The Director of the **United Nations Environment Programme** (UNEP) stated: 'For environmentalists the Uruguay Round [of GATT trade negotiations] represents the first step forward in recognizing that international economic policies will remain unsustainable unless they take full account of environmental realities.' It is doubtful, however, if anything positive has been achieved in development terms, and representatives of low-income countries have claimed that the concluded Uruguay Round will result in lower commodity prices and still further widen the gap between high-income and low-income nations.

Trade

Many global and, for that matter, local environmental issues are inextricably linked to trade, simply because so many of the key environmental concerns involve resource exploitation and manufacturing for export as well as local markets. High-income and low-income nations are linked in a complex web of trading linkages, something clearly illustrated in Chapter 3. In many cases, environmental damage through deforestation, mining, over-exploitation of fish populations or unwise agricultural practices occurs in the exporting nation (usually a low-income nation), but the greatest benefits in terms of either financial return or use of the finished products occur in high-income nations. Low-income nations are caught in a 'vicious circle' of dependency from which many cannot escape, especially when they are also burdened by crippling international debt.

Low-income nations are also often desperate to attract manufacturing as a means of diversifying their economies and as a supposedly necessary step on the path to development. They argue that they should be allowed to go through the industrial development experienced by the high-income nations without the burden of the tight environmental regulations those nations only thought of at a much later stage. Why should they bear the brunt of ameliorative procedures when, in a sense, it was the high-income nations that held back their development and painted them into the corner of dependence? Indeed, some leaders and academics from low-income countries have spoken of a new form of colonialism — environmental colonialism.

On the other side of the relationship, high-income countries by and large want to keep international trading arrangements favourable to their economies and industries. So too do transnational corporations. Many conservationists see them as the villains, whereas Stephen Schmidheiny, Chairman of the Business Council for Sustainable Development (an international body established in the run-up to UNCED) claims that 'economic growth is an essential prerequisite for sustainable development' and Maurice Strong, Secretary-General of the Earth Summit, told the same gathering of leading business people: 'You are a cadre of the world's leading practitioners of sustainable development.'

Even when governments do want to address environmental or social issues through controls on trade in certain products or goods produced in certain ways, they run into other obstacles. That free, unhindered trade is one of the prime necessities of life seems to be accepted by the international community — at least, by those powerful high-income nations in the **G7 Group** or the **OECD** that make the rules. The result is that GATT will not accept any individual nation placing barriers on trade for even the soundest of environmental reasons. The USA discovered this when it threatened to ban the importation of Japanese fisheries products if Japan did not cease driftnetting in the northern Pacific (see Section 6.2). Nor could Indonesia easily gain GATT approval to ban the export of rainforest logs because it preferred to have primary processing take place at home. Furthermore, discrimination on the basis of the method of production is not allowed. It appears that the only way to use trade to change actions that adversely affect the environment is to achieve international agreement, preferably through the United Nations and its agencies. Using that route, bans on trade in products derived from certain endangered species, for example, have been achieved, albeit slowly and not without difficulty.

Perhaps an award for openness and honesty should go to the Head of Environment at GATT, who warned in the week before UNCED that 'free trade would bring no automatic environmental dividend'. He went on to say: 'Trade is a magnifier. If you are trading in things that are destroying the environment, free trade will mean you destroy more.'[1] Perhaps free trade in environmentally friendly products and processes will help save the environment, but that needs a lot of business people doing the right thing. And freer trade *could* give low-income countries better access to the markets of high-income countries and hence the means to improve their environments and alleviate poverty. But on past indications, it might not.

International financial issues

Debt

Susan George, in a book published in 1992,[2] stresses feedback loops that make debt and its multiple consequences mutually reinforcing. From the onset of the debt crisis in 1982 (it had been brewing for much longer, of course) until 1990, debtor countries paid creditors in high-income nations US$6500 million per month in interest alone. Debtor countries found themselves 'cashing in their resources to foot the repayment bills'. They sought **International Monetary Fund** (IMF) loans to accumulate foreign exchange to repay other debts: the IMF insisted the money be spent that way until repayments were substantially met. Debtors then attempted to fulfil their obligations to the IMF by exporting natural resources such as minerals, rainforest timber, tropical plantation crops (very often grown on land that once produced food for the local people) and products produced by transnational corporations lured by cheap labour and lax environmental regulations. Nigeria, for example, used 31 per cent of its foreign exchange earnings to repay debt in 1990, money desperately needed for health, education and many other forms of capacity building. Today many low-income nations have large per capita debts still awaiting repayment, which destabilises national budgets and retards development programs (Figure 7.2).

On the other hand, George claims, the commercial banks of the high-income nations have lost very little because they have been subsidised heavily through tax relief and direct government subsidies. Because the IMF has insisted on repayment, low-income countries have been left too poor to import goods from high-income nations which have consequently foregone jobs and foreign earnings. Instead, they have subsidised the banks. In fact, the bulk of debt owed by low-

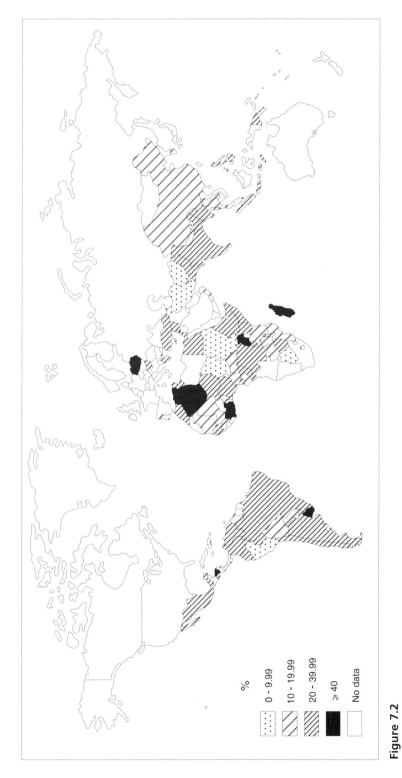

Figure 7.2

Per capita public and state-guaranteed private foreign debt, c. 1990. (Source: data from Bissio, R.R. (ed.) *Third World Guide 93/94*, Instituto del Tercer Mundo (Montevideo, 1992).)

%

0 - 9.99

10 - 19.99

20 - 39.99

≥ 40

No data

income nations has been repaid, but at what cost to all nations and to the smooth functioning of the global economy?

In the 1980s and early 1990s the IMF and the **World Bank** made a habit of placing stringent conditions on loans to developing countries. These certainly have not been conditions aiming to protect the environment, although there were some signs that this might be changing in the mid-1990s. In fact, many projects financed by the World Bank have been overtly harmful to the environment. It had a penchant for backing 'mega-dams', for example, but this may have now changed, as in early 1993 it finally withdrew its support from the highly controversial Narmada Dam project in India because of environmental and human rights controversies surrounding it (see also Section 2.2). Rather than stressing environmental factors, conditions commonly have been in the nature of demands for structural adjustment programs (economic restructuring) along the lines preached by economic rationalists. Requirements have usually included reduced roles for government (especially in providing welfare and essential services), and privatisation of many functions. Such an approach could suit high-income countries but, as with technology, it cannot simply be transplanted to an entirely different cultural context. Nor do the conditions seem to benefit recipient nations where the wealthy elite often become even richer and the poor even poorer. In 1990, the *New Internationalist* claimed that: 'The economies of 19 African countries with "strong" adjustment programmes contracted by an overall average 1.5% a year between 1980 and 1987, while 12 countries with "weak" or no programmes expanded by an average 1.2% a year'.[3] In early 1994 the World Bank remained unmoved despite the evidence, still insisting that its approach through 'structural adjustment' was the right one, arguing that the evidence on a world-wide basis showed the situation to be almost the exact opposite to that claimed by the *New Internationalist*. Whatever the truth on a national level, it is agreed by the vast majority of commentators that the poor are suffering in virtually all nations undergoing structural adjustment.

Aid packages

According to Maurice Strong, speaking some ten months before UNCED, 'poor countries must be given the means to develop with minimum environmental impact. We must shed the notion that aid is charity'.[4] The UN General Assembly meeting in late 1989 requested that UNCED 'identify ways and means of providing new and additional financial resources, particularly to developing countries, for environmentally sound development programmes and projects in ac-

cordance with national development objectives, priorities and plans'.[5]
This was to be a new form of international aid to be used for development, the alleviation of poverty and the amelioration of environmental problems. It was to be without the ties and conditions of most past
aid. Apart from anything else, if such aid were administered internationally rather than by any one nation it would be much less likely to
provide advantages to the donor that might outweigh those to the
receiver. While some of this aid was to help overcome immediate
environmental and social crises, capacity building to enable recipient
countries to reach the point where they can deal with their own
problems without continuing to rely on outside financial aid is much
more important in the long term.

Debt-for-nature swaps

Between 1987 and late 1992 about nineteen so-called debt-for-nature
swaps were concluded, mainly in Latin America. Some involved a
'donation' by the bank or banks involved in the original loan to a low-
income nation, but most took the form of the debt being purchased by
another party for less than face value (as lenders have often given up
hope of full repayment), but with funds greater than the purchase
price being made available for agreed conservation and environmental projects in the debtor nation. For example, the US group
Conservation International bought US$650 000 of Bolivia's debt at
the discounted rate of US$100 000 — the debt was then written off
in return for the Bolivian Government setting aside 1.5 million ha of
rainforest adjacent to the Beni Biosphere Reserve in Amazonia. By
1992, US$98.9 million in debt had been retired worldwide at a cost of
US$17.3 million under such swaps, with Costa Rica by far the largest
beneficiary.

How successful has this new approach been? So far debt-for-nature
swaps have relieved only less than 0.2 per cent of total world debt, but
they have been valuable in stabilising the situation in some countries
and preventing them sliding still deeper into debt by getting further
behind with their repayments. In a very few countries, such as Costa
Rica, it has meant a doubling of the funds available for environmental
projects. But the priorities of the sponsoring organisations are followed rather than local priorities. Much work needs to be done to
democratise the process and involve local people, including indigenous peoples, to a much greater extent. It is also difficult in some
nations to ensure that the funds are actually spent on environmental
projects. Despite the small scale of the swaps so far, and in spite of the
difficulties involved, this is an approach worth pursuing.

Post-UNCED institutional arrangements

Not surprisingly, the UN and its various arms are seen as having key roles in future international financial arrangements. The General Assembly and its Economic and Social Council are to arrange for regular reviews of progress in implementing the programs of *Agenda 21*, largely through the Commission on Sustainable Development. Expanded roles are envisaged for UNEP and the United Nations Development Programme (UNDP), while the **United Nations Conference on Trade and Development** (UNCTAD) is also given a key role, quite appropriately in the light of the importance of trade relationships. Furthermore, many other UN agencies and programs will be crucial to specific sections of the overall program.

Discussion on which agencies should administer funding were much more acrimonious at Rio. Low-income nations and environmental NGOs have a deep-seated mistrust of established international financial institutions like the World Bank, the IMF and the then newly formed **Global Environment Fund** (GEF) — (now called the Global Environment Facility). While there does need to be a co-ordinating body at the international level, it also definitely needs to be one that is sympathetic to environmental issues as well as development ones, and to the needs and aspirations of low-income as well as high-income nations. The GEF, the IMF and the World Bank need to be reformed and made to meet these requirements, or a new body must be formed. Since UNCED has decided to continue the GEF, the first alternative must now be followed through. An independent 200-page report release in November 1993, however, recommended fundamental changes to the GEF to allow it to reach its objectives, a call strongly backed by representatives of low-income nations at the GEF meeting at the end of 1993. In March 1994 donor countries agreed on a US$2 billion annual replenishment fund target: if reached, this would give the GEF 2.5 times the money available in its three-year pilot phase, but a sum still well short of the estimated requirements to fulfil the programs of *Agenda 21*.

A major disappointment of the Earth Summit was the failure to come to grips, in any practical sense, with the interconnected matters of debt, world trading patterns and financing of environmental initiatives. The Summit certainly discussed these matters at length, and they feature prominently in the documents that resulted. But there seems to have been very little real commitment on the part of high-income nations to deal with the inherent problems. Before the Summit, the Pakistani chairman of the **Group of 77** (low-income nations) called for 'a credible commitment on financial resources so that we do not leave

Rio with a mere statement of good intentions'. The Group wanted the creation of a fund to 'administer the greening of the planet'.[6] There was much argument about whether or not the GEF should carry out that task, many developing nations feeling that it was too dominated by wealthy nations and the World Bank. As the authors of an editorial in an academic journal state,

> The structure of environmental debates and the 'solutions' to the environmental crises of the [tropical] world remain embodied in an ideological framework about conservation and development which is largely divorced from the historical and economic realities of most of the Third World.[7]

That brings us back to the inescapable linkages between global financial and political structures on the one hand and global environmental crises on the other. If nothing else, UNCED brought home the crucially important nature of those linkages.

RESOURCE USE AND MANAGEMENT 7.5

Resource and environmental management

The need for careful and thorough planning of all actions affecting resource use, including the treatment and disposal of wastes, is another recurring theme throughout *Agenda 21*, as it is in this book. There are strong suggestions that clean production principles, involving the 'birth-to-death' life-cycles of products and reduced throughputs of energy and materials, should be adopted wherever possible. Furthermore, resource and environmental management must be based on sound data and sound analysis of that data. There is a need to think seriously about ecological consequences as well as economic ones, of the future as well as the present, of long-term outcomes as well as short-term ones, and of others as well as of ourselves. In other words, we need to carefully manage resource use.

No-one is suggesting that we stop exploiting resources altogether, as resource use is essential for our survival. Many people are, however, suggesting that we think carefully and in an unselfish way about how we use or exploit each resource, and whether we really need to exploit the resource to the extent that we do. In some cases there may be compelling reasons to cease using a particular resource altogether, while in others we may need to modify our use. We also need to consider very carefully the environmental effects of our actions, not only in terms of resource use but also in terms of the ways in which we are altering the environment. Management, then, is not diametrically opposed to exploitation, but it is most definitely opposed to careless exploitation and overexploitation.

Sound management has at least three fundamental requirements: sound, comprehensive data; a sound knowledge of the processes involved; and well-developed abilities in analysis and planning. Lack of data has been a recurrent problem in tackling environmental issues: we need the best possible data and continual monitoring in order to fine-tune management plans. But we also need to be able to accurately predict the outcome of actions and, for this, a thorough knowledge of processes is needed. An understanding of the processes necessitates the continued support of basic science (Section 7.6). A fourth requirement is the ability to take a broad view of each issue, as most environmental issues involve a complex series of interactions and feedback loops, something alluded to many times in this book. An environmental manager, then, needs to look well beyond the immediate problem and to consider the broader ramifications of his or her proposed actions.

Consumption, waste and recycling

Despite the US opposition to reference to overconsumption, *Agenda 21* does contain a chapter titled 'Changing consumption patterns', though it is very muted in its criticism of the high and often very wasteful resource consumption patterns in high-income nations. The focus is on attaining sustainable patterns of consumption. It is stated that 'special attention should be paid to the demand for natural resources generated by unsustainable consumption and to the efficient use of resources consistent with the goal of minimizing depletion and reducing pollution'. Further, 'changing consumption patterns will require a multipronged strategy focused on demand, meeting the basic needs of the poor, and reducing wastage and the use of finite resources in the production process'.[8]

This interconnection between demand, consumption, production process, resource use, waste generation and environmental degradation is vitally important. *Agenda 21*, in a very restrained and understated way, even questions the traditional acceptance of a necessarily positive link between consumption and economic growth and raises the need to take 'account of the full value of natural resource capital'.[9] Furthermore, we suggest in the next section that technology can help reduce the demand for resources, minimise waste, and maximise recycling and reclamation, all without necessarily impeding the economy or lowering anyone's standard of living.

SCIENCE AND TECHNOLOGY 7.6

Understanding and knowledge

To be successful, attempts at avoiding or ameliorating global crises or repairing environmental damage must be based on a sound knowledge of both biophysical and social sciences; neither the biophysical nor the social sciences alone will suffice, but neither will a reliance on technology while neglecting basic science. We desperately need greater depth and breadth in our collective knowledge of our world. We need above all to understand the processes operating within the Earth system and the complex web of interconnections between its component parts.

We need to gain so much knowledge so rapidly that we cannot afford to work in competition and replicate the work of others unnecessarily, though that is not to say that a high degree of specialisation is the answer. What is needed is international co-operation in research and the easy and unselfish exchange of ideas, data banks and other information. This has become increasingly easy with the advent of international computer-based networks.

Two examples will illustrate the fruitful way in which scientists from many nations can work together. The International Geophysical Year in 1957–58, involving scientists from many countries and many disciplines, considerably advanced the frontiers of knowledge on the geophysical aspects of the Earth and, at least indirectly, led to the Antarctic Treaty (see Section 6.3). More recently, the Intergovernmental Panel on Climate Change (IPCC) (see Chapter 5) has brought together atmospheric scientists from many nations to co-ordinate research on the enhanced greenhouse effect. IPCC's Working Group 3, consisting of social scientists, is now probably its most active group, following up on the basic atmospheric science with work on the impacts of the enhanced greenhouse effect on people.

Technology

Technology has a crucial role to play in any attempt at finding solutions, but we have seen that technology by itself will not fix anything. Technology is a social construct responding to social, cultural, political and economic demands and priorities. These factors determine not only whether technology is used positively or negatively, but which forms of technology are developed in the first place. Technology, then, must be seen in a social, economic and political context.

There are five separate but closely related ways in which changes in technology can assist in avoiding global crises: by reducing our dependence on diminishing resources; by helping develop more effective ways of managing resources such as soil and water; by avoiding or reducing pollution of the environment; by giving us better data on our activities, the environment, and the interactions between the two; and providing more powerful means of analysing that data. In the long run, the last two of these may turn out to be the most important, as one very real barrier to managing environmental issues has been inadequate data and the inability to analyse it, build models and develop management plans.

Many types of instrumentation will help increase the amount of information available. Satellites provide the capacity to record enormous amounts of information for every point on the Earth's surface, an ability alluded to earlier in discussions on land degradation (Chapter 2) and forests (Chapter 3). Information can also be updated at very frequent intervals, providing a unique opportunity to analyse processes and to heed early warning signals of impending problems. However, we have to be extremely careful in interpreting the data. Pretty maps on a screen are one thing; making practical use of them is another thing altogether. We will still need to collect a lot of ground or ocean surface data to verify our interpretations of the satellite data, but once we have 'cracked the code' and really know what the pretty pictures mean, we will suddenly acquire an enormous amount of extremely useful data. What is more, we have (or are developing) the super-computers needed to store and analyse that data.

Transfer of information and technology

Chapter 34 of *Agenda 21* deals at length with the international transfer of basic data, scientific knowledge and environmentally sound technology. It states that the basic goal is to place all nations in a position where they can make informed choices as to which technology is most appropriate in their particular circumstances. This will then strengthen each nation's own technological capabilities, especially in the case of low-income nations. Both information and technology are vital if global environmental catastrophe is to be avoided. Much of both will necessarily have to be transferred from high-income to low-income nations. There are two essential questions to be answered, however. On what terms will such transfers occur? What kind of information and technology should be transferred?

Transfers of technology and information frequently involve questions of ownership, patent rights and commercial advantage. Much of the technology needed by low-income nations to ameliorate or over-come serious environmental problems is too expensive for them to buy at market rates. Some is certainly in the public domain and therefore freely or relatively cheaply available, but what of emerging 'state-of-the-art' technology being developed commercially? Those developing it have definite rights to profit from its sale, so ways must be found to subsidise costs to poorer nations. There is an obvious role for aid in this area, as both parties can benefit: the low-income nations obtain subsidised access to desired technology, and the commercial developers are appropriately rewarded.

Just as important is the question of the appropriateness of techno-logy transferred to low-income countries. The high-income world is not the fount of all technological wisdom, nor are excellent techno-logical solutions to environmental problems in the high-income nations necessarily appropriate for similar problems in poorer coun-tries. The belief that they are could only be maintained if one believed that all other circumstances were also the same, including levels of education, technological expertise, ability to pay, social and cultural traditions, and so on. But the context clearly differs. High-income nations and their transnational corporations may well try to impose their solutions because they see profit in doing so, but such attempts must be resisted and more appropriate local solutions sought wher-ever possible.

Agenda 21 stresses the need for co-operative research and the shar-ing of information on an international scale. Again, national and commercial interests can be at odds with the need to assist poorer nations. But it is also essential that as much relevant information as possible, including information obtained by satellite, is available so that each nation can make its own informed decisions on environ-mental issues. Careful and thoughtful planning is essential, and that must be based on a sound data base.

POPULATION ISSUES 7.7

The greatest single barrier to ecologically sustainable development is, arguably, the demand for resources and the pressure on the global environment that inevitably follow increases in the number of people on the planet (see Section 1.3 for counter-arguments). The human population must be stabilised at a sustainable level, and that level may well be somewhat lower than the present world population.

One of the greatest disappointments of UNCED was the way in which this crucial issue was effectively side-stepped because of political pressure. *Agenda 21* is strong on rhetoric but very weak on suggestions for action on population. While it is good to see recognition of the links between environment and development issues and population, there is clearly a reluctance to grasp the nettle and put forward a viable international program of action, although one might argue that other UN programs concerning population go as far as they can, given the social sensitivity of demographic planning. According to a program for sustainable living prepared jointly by the IUCN, UNEP and WWF, 'Earth's survival depends on a global commitment to stabilise population growth within 20 years', a commitment that cleary was not forthcoming at UNCED.

The linkages we have referred to were made much more clearly in an early draft of *Agenda 21*. At that time it was proposed to link poverty, overconsumption in rich countries and rapidly growing populations in poorer nations as interconnected barriers to sustainable development. However, in March 1992 the USA attempted to veto any mention of overconsumption. In retaliation, several low-income nations refused to allow discussion of population control, while the Catholic Church also brought pressure to bear along similar lines. A great opportunity was missed, as the final document would have been much stronger and much more credible if such connections had been made with frankness.

Fortunately there continue to be promising signs of a decline in population growth rates globally, as well as in particular nations feeling acute pressures from population numbers. As recently as March 1993 *New Scientist* headed an article 'Births plummet as contraceptives sweep Third World', reporting that the average family size had shrunk from six in the 1960s to four today.[10] A crucial finding is that the reduction in family size is running ahead of the various development measures with which it has usually been linked by demographers and population geographers. African nations still appear to be resisting this trend, though there are even indications of change there as demand for contraceptives outstrips supply.

An International Conference on Population and Development held in Cairo during September 1994 addressed this crucial issue, though the important links with environmental questions were not stressed sufficiently. A scientific meeting held in Delhi in October 1993 to set the agenda for the Cairo Conference gave an indication of the difficulties ahead. The closing statement called for 'zero population growth within the lifetime of our children' and warned that otherwise science and technology might be powerless to prevent widespread poverty and irreversible damage to the environment. This statement was not endorsed by the representatives of the Vatican or Irish science bodies, while the African Academy of Sciences maintained that Africa needs a larger population to enable its natural resources to be developed and that alleviation of poverty must come before significant reductions in population growth rates.

While the outcome of the Cairo Conference was much more positive than many expected, it still fell well short of calling for strong demographic planning at a national level. There were, though, major gains for family planning and health programs and for the position of women. It also seems likely that US$17 billion will become available for related programs.

SUSTAINABLE DEVELOPMENT 7.8

The concept

The concept of sustainable development was introduced in Section 1.5 and is a recurring theme in this book. It is also central to *Agenda 21*. This section is not concerned with the technicalities or the economic theories of sustainable development, but with the general concepts involved.

An Australian Commonwealth discussion paper (1990) defined ecologically sustainable development as:

> using, conserving and enhancing the community's resources so that ecological processes, on which life depends, are maintained, and the total quality of life, now and in the future, can be increased.[11]

The paper recognises community concern that 'in pursuing material welfare, insufficient value has often been placed on the environmental factors that also contribute to our standard of living'.[12] The paper then goes on to talk about the linkages between economic and ecological factors, and the fact that ignoring those linkages can lead to environmental damage. The task ahead is summarised in the following manner:

> The task confronting us is to take better care of the environment while ensuring economic growth, both now and in the future. Ecologically sustainable development provides a conceptual framework for integrating these economic and environmental objectives, so that products, production processes and services can be developed that are both internationally competitive and more environmentally compatible.[13]

Five key elements of ecologically sustainable development are outlined in the paper:
- integrating economic and environmental goals in policies and activities;

- ensuring that environmental assets are appropriately valued;
- providing for equity within and between generations;
- dealing cautiously with risk and irreversibility; and
- recognising the global dimension.

The authors of this paper deny that economic and ecological goals are always incompatible, or even usually so despite the fact that they have often been portrayed in that way. They say that it is not true that only negative economic growth can save the environment, though some other writers disagree. Ideally, they say, both economic growth and environmental protection should be optimised. Resources need to be used as efficiently as possible and great care needs to be taken to ensure that manufacturing and other processes are 'environmentally friendly'. At times, the two sets of goals will be irreconcilable. In those cases, *both* a good knowledge of human and physical processes *and* a sound and comprehensive data base are necessary if the best choices between alternatives are to be made.

One particular problem identified in the discussion paper is that resources are very frequently under-valued because environmental values are not taken into account. Under-valued resources are often over-exploited, something that might well be avoided if costs were to rise in line with 'true' values, both economic *and* environmental. (Sections 2.5 and 4.6 both discuss this argument in the context of water supplies). Many environmental economists are now calling for an expansion of national accounts in all countries to include a realistically derived environmental capital account that monitors any decline in the stock of resources.[14] They also point out that gross national product (GNP), a common measure of how well a nation and its economy are doing, only serves to hide environmental costs (Box 1.2).

Equity between sectors and between generations is another major issue to be considered. Are the environmental costs being borne by a group or generation other than the one deriving the benefits? Or are they being borne disproportionately compared to the benefits gained? Are some of us running down resource stocks faster than they can be replenished? And what about those resources that are non-renewable? Does this mean that future generations will necessarily have a lower standard of living? Are some of us now taking more than a reasonable share and thus adversely affecting the living standard of others, now or in the future?

One central theme of writings on sustainable development is that development and economic growth can no longer be seen as limitless. If they continue to be viewed in this way, there must inevitably come a time when the system collapses and, for reasons partially covered in this book, that point of collapse is probably rapidly approaching. If that is the case, it would seem only sensible to change our whole approach to development. Ecologically sustainable development means that our goal is a system that is in a **steady state**. Such a state is not static and unchangeable, but it is characterised by a dynamic equilibrium (see Section 1.3) between economic activities and environmental factors. Any changes that do occur are carefully monitored, and interventions are only made as a result of full consideration of the consequences of proposed actions.

If there is obvious risk of uncertainty, then we should proceed with great caution and allow a wide margin of safety. This approach is often referred to as the precautionary principle, and is embodied in Principle 15 of the *Rio Declaration*. For example, we should not wait until we are *sure* that a particular form of toxic waste causes serious environmental damage, but take appropriate precautions in handling it and disposing of it if we consider it is *likely* to cause such harm. Such an approach also has the major benefit of reducing the likelihood of both ecological and economic collapse. This is easier to demonstrate in the narrower context of a sustainable yield of a particular natural resource. If a fishing or timber industry is based on maximum yields, there is a very high risk indeed of the industry collapsing when stocks become severely depleted. Such a collapse might well have disastrous effects on local, regional and national economies, as well as on the environment. But, if operations are based on sustainable yields, the future health of both the industry and the environment is more assured. Short-term gains may be smaller, but longevity is much more probable.

All aspects of our daily lives will be affected by any serious attempt to embrace the introduction of ecologically sustainable development. We will have to seriously consider, and probably extensively change, such diverse areas as the food we eat, the extent to which we recycle wastes, the forms of transport we use and the manner in which the goods we consume are produced.

Australian implementation

Australia was one of the nations to sign the 1980 World Conservation Strategy (see Section 6.6) and in 1984 adopted a National Conservation Strategy: both strategies contained most of the building blocks that have more recently come together as the concept of ecologically sustainable development (ESD). However, in Australia the concept only gained political and public exposure and a fairly large degree of acceptance after the release of the 1990 Discussion Paper referred to in the previous section. The paper followed from Federal Government environment statements in 1989 and 1990.

In 1991 the Federal Government established nine Working Groups to study the implications and implementation of ESD in nine industry sectors: agriculture, energy production, energy use, fisheries, forestry, manufacturing, mining, tourism and transport. Each group contained academics and representatives of state and federal governments, industry, unions, conservation groups, consumer groups and social welfare organisations. In addition, a number of 'cross-sectoral' issues, such as biodiversity and climate change, were also addressed. Community consultations occurred in the second half of 1991. Nine issues of the *ESD Newsbrief* appeared between mid-1991 and mid-1992 in which various interest groups set out their views in brief articles, while other articles were aimed at educating the public on environmental issues and alerting them to the consultation process. In 1992 the Earth Summit and related issues gained increasing prominence. Draft reports were prepared and comments called for before the final reports, including an Intersectoral Report and one specifically on the enhanced greenhouse effect, were published in December 1991. The entire process, then, took less than six months, but did at least attempt to involve all sectors, including members of the general public.

Following the release of the reports, the Inter-governmental ESD Steering Committee was formed to consider the 500-plus recommendations and draft implementation strategies. A draft national strategy was released in mid-1992 and submissions and comments were called for, leading to publication of the final document in December 1992.[15] It is impossible to deal with the Working Group recommendations or the National strategy at length here, but the goal, core objectives and guiding principles of the latter are set out in Box 7.1.

The Steering Committee produced its first annual report in December 1993.[16] In the overview section, the report claims that a wide range of initiatives were promoting an 'Ecologically Sustainable Development ethos', and that the strategy had 'played a significant role on focusing attention on certain issues, in accelerating action in others and in ensuring that greater priority is accorded a particular action . . . ' Particular areas of progress mentioned include the following:

- the National Landcare Program (see Section 2.6);
- adoption of 'best practice environmental management' by the manufacturing and service sectors;
- moves toward more integrated urban and transport planning;
- the National Greenhouse Response Strategy (see Section 5.7);
- a National Water Quality Management Strategy;
- moves to establish the National Environment Protection Authority;
- a program to achieve a 50 per cent reduction in waste going to land fill by 2000;

National Strategy for Ecologically Sustainable Development — Key Concepts

BOX

7.1

Goal

Development that improves the total quality of life, both now and in the future, in a way that maintains the ecological processes on which life depends.

Core objectives

- to enhance individual and community well-being and welfare by following a path of economic development that safeguards the welfare of future generations;
- to provide for equity within and between generations;
- to protect biological diversity and maintain essential ecological processes and life-support systems.

Guiding principles

- decision-making processes should effectively integrate both long and short-term economic, environmental, social and equity considerations;
- where there are threats of serious or irreversible environmental damage, lack of full scientific certainty should not be used as a reason for postponing measures to prevent environmental degradation;
- the global dimension of environmental impacts of actions and policies should be recognised and considered;
- the need to develop a strong, growing and diversified economy which can enhance the capacity for environmental protection should be recognised;
- the need to maintain and enhance international competitiveness in an environmentally sound manner should be recognised;
- cost-effective and flexible policy instruments should be adopted, such as improved valuation, pricing and incentive mechanisms;
- decisions and actions should provide for broad community involvement on issues which affect them.

Source: Australian Government, *National Strategy for Ecologically Sustainable Development*, AGPS (Canberra, 1992), 8.

- consideration of ESD principles in international aid programs;
- promotion of environmental education in schools and in educational sectors;
- involvement of local communities and peak (or national co-ordinating) bodies; and
- commencement of work to develop appropriate economic instruments and sustainability indicators.

Introducing the sustainable development ethos into the many and varied facets of public and private activity would obviously take more than a year. It was certainly obvious that acceptance of that ethos had, by the end of 1993, been very patchy. Furthermore, particular sectors and groups, not surprisingly, tended to interpret ESD in their own, sometimes quirky, ways. Even so, Australia did see more serious attempts to achieve consensus and to address environmental issues in the early to mid-1990s than at any previous time. But there is still a long, long way to go. The impetus has to be maintained — indeed, the pace of change needs to be accelerated. Instead, enthusiasm seemed to be flagging in 1994 and economic considerations were clearly dominating environmental ones in political and media circles. One cause for optimism, though, is that public opinion polls in 1994 showed that Australians, by and large, saw the environment as one of the most important issues facing them — perhaps the most important.

7.9 ENVIRONMENTAL INTEGRITY *AND* DEVELOPMENT FOR ALL?

Many of the most radical 'green' activists strongly believe that '*environmental well-being*' and '*development*' are mutually exclusive concepts. Are they so, or can both occur as the whole ethos of UNCED and *Agenda 21* implies? Put more colloquially, can we have our cake and eat it too? We probably can, but only if we switch from the wicked Carmen Miranda rum-chocolate-and-cream special to the carrot cake. But, after all, carrot cake is delicious, satisfying, and much better for us. It also uses fewer and less expensive ingredients and undoubtedly costs less when you order it. Perhaps the ambience of the café and the company you keep are more important than the type of cake, at any rate.

The implication, then, is that we cannot have environmental health and development if we define development in the way that the high-income nations now do. We certainly cannot go on increasing energy use, resource use and waste generation; so if further development implies such increases, we cannot have both development and environmental health. But there are surely other ways of developing, or of at least maintaining, a fulfilling and satisfying way of life that is sustainable.

Does that mean that low-income nations must be satisfied with their present standard of living and level of development? That position is not tenable, either morally or practically. One of the main reasons that high-income nations must become less energy and resource hungry is to allow modest but meaningful increases in consumption in poorer countries. There is no way, though, that the entire population of the world can ever consume and pollute at the present US or Australian levels. Earlier sections have referred to the complex inter-relationships between poverty and environmental degradation. Peoples of the poorer nations must be given a way out of the vicious circle of poverty in which they find themselves, and that might well mean a reduction in the *material* standard of living of the richer nations.

If ecologically sustainable development is to be achieved locally, nationally, or globally, then a great deal of very careful investigation and planning will be needed. It seems most unlikely that it could be achieved by market forces alone, whether those forces be international trade along the lines advocated by GATT or WTO, or a local, un-fettered market place. There will need to be direction, persuasion and coercion from national governments and international bodies like the UN and its Commission on Sustainable Development. A wide variety of people and groups will need to be involved, ranging from indig-enous peoples and NGOs to transnational corporations. Many indi-viduals, groups, firms and governments will need to make major changes in their thinking and their actions. In fact, it goes further than that. There will need to be major changes in basic philosophies, goals, objectives and belief systems. Now, for the first time, a significant proportion of people and organisations around the globe do see that necessity.

Ultimately, each person on Earth needs to make a commitment to play their part, however small and insignificant that may seem, in reversing the environmental deterioration of recent decades. We must face the global crises head on, resisting any temptation to feel utterly helpless in the face of the magnitude of the task. Individuals must play their part, however, small. Above all, we need to reassess our consump-tion and waste generation and to think deeply about our own relation-ships with nature and the global environmental system.

296 | **FURTHER READING**

Australian Government, *Ecologically Sustainable Development: a Commonwealth Discussion Paper*, AGPS (Canberra, 1990).

Australian Government, *Ecologically Sustainable Development Working Groups: Final Report — Executive summaries*, AGPS (Canberra, 1991).

Australian Government, *National Strategy for Ecologically Sustainable Development*, AGPS (Canberra, 1992).

Australian Government (ESD Steering Committee), *Summary Report on the Implementation of the National Strategy for Ecologically Sustainable Development*, AGPS (Canberra, 1993). [These four mainly short publications usefully trace the development of the ESD concept in Australian Government circles.]

Beder, S. *The Nature of Sustainable Development*, Scribe (Newham, Victoria, 1993). [A sound, clear and comprehensive introduction to sustainable development written by an Australian from an Australian perspective.]

Carley, M., and Christie I. *Managing Sustainable Development*, Earthscan (London, 1992). [This book introduces the concept of sustainable development but, more importantly, suggests a practical means of implementation at various scales by using action-centred networks that involve a wide range of affected and interested parties.]

Daly, H.E., and Cobb, J.B., *For the Common Good: Redirecting the economy towards community, the environment and a sustainable future*, Green Print (London, 1990). [The title encapsulates the main themes of the book.]

George, S., *The Debt Boomerang: How Third World debt harms us all*, West Viewpress (San Francisco, 1992). [The definitive work on low-income nation debt.]

Gore, A., *Earth in the Balance: Forging a new common purpose*, Earthscan (London, 1992). [A typically US approach from the environmentally aware Vice President: contains some good background material if you can ignore the politics and religion.]

Jacobs, M., *The Green Economy: Environment, sustainable development and the politics of the future*, Pluto Press (London, 1991). [Concerned with 'how industrialised economies can be redirected to meet the environmental imperative'.]

MacNeill, J., Winsemius, P., and Yakushiji, T., *Beyond Interdependence: The meshing of the world's economy and the Earth's ecology*, Oxford University Press (New York, 1991). [A compelling economic and environmental case for reform.]

Ophuls, W., and Boyan, A.S., *Ecology and the Politics of Scarcity Revisited: The unraveling of the American dream*, W.H. Freeman (New York, 1992). [Defines the ecological crisis and deals with its political, social, and economic implications.]

Pearce, D.W. (ed.), *Blueprint 2: Greening the world economy*, Earthscan (London, 1991). [An innovative environmental economics approach to dealing with global environmental crises.]

Pearce, D.W. and Warford, J.J., *World Without End: Economics, environment, and sustainable development*, Oxford University Press (Oxford, 1993). [A comprehensive review of the relationship between economics and environment, including a substantial section on sustainable development.]

Schmidheiny, S. et al., *Changing Course: A global business perspective on development and the environment*, MIT Press (Cambridge, USA, 1992). [The views of the Business Council for Sustainable Development.]

Weiner, J., *The Next One Hundred Years: Shaping the fate of our living earth*, Bantam Books (New York, 1990). [Details evidence that planetary dangers are real and offers a prescription for the future.]

Young, M.D., (1992) *Sustainable Investment and Resource Use: Equity, environmental integrity and economic efficiency* (Man and the Biosphere Series, Volume 9), Parthenon (Park Ridge, USA, 1992). [An approachable introduction to environmental economics with many suggestions for future action.]

NOTES

1 *New Scientist*, 6 June 1992, 5.
2 George, S., *The Debt Boomerang: How third World debt harms us all*, West Viewpress (San Francisco, 1992).
3 *New Internationalist*, June 1990, 23.
4 *New Scientist*, 10 August 1992, 12.
5 Quoted in *Agenda 21*, paragraph 33.1.
6 *New Scientist*, 11 April 1992, 13.
7 Hecht, S.B., and Cockburn, A., 'Realpolitik, reality and rhetoric in Rio' (Editorial), *Environment and Planning D: Society and Space*, **10** (1992), 367–75.
8 *Agenda 21*, chapter 4, both quotations are from paragraph 4.5.
9 *Agenda 21*, chapter 4, paragraph 4.6.
10 *New Scientist*, 13 March 1993, 7.
11 Australian Government, *Ecologically Sustainable Development: A Commonwealth discussion paper*, AGPS (Canberra, 1990), Preface.
12 ibid., 1.
13 ibid., 1.
14 See Young, M.D. *Sustainable Investment and Resource Use: Equity, environmental integrity and economic efficiency* (Man and the Biosphere Series, Volume 9), Parthenon (Park Ridge, USA, 1992).
15 Australian Government, *National Strategy for Ecologically Sustainable Development*, AGPS (Canberra, 1992).
16 ESD Steering Committee, *Summary Report on the Implementation of the National Strategy for Ecologically Sustainable Development*, AGPS (Canberra, 1993). [All material quoted is taken from the 'Overview of progress during 1993' on pages 4 to 6.]

GLOSSARY

DEFINITIONS

Aerobic Organisms which utilise oxygen in respiration; environments where oxygen is available for such life forms.

Aerosol Colloidal particles (those between 10^{-5} and 10^{-7} cm in diameter) dispersed in the atmosphere, important in forming raindrop nuclei.

Albedo The ratio of the solar radiation reflected from a surface to that received by it.

Anthropogenic Created or originated by humans.

Appropriate Technology Technology appropriate to its context, not only in economic terms but also in environmental, social, cultural and developmental terms.

Biodiversity The diversity of plant and animal species in specific regions or throughout the world. More specifically, the US Office of Technology Assessments defined it as 'the variety and variability among living organisms and the ecological complexes in which they occur. Diversity can be defined as a number of different items and their relative frequency . . . the term encompasses different ecosystems, species, genes and their relative abundance'.

Biogas Gases generated by anaerobic decay of organic material (particularly manure and crop residues) in a digester and used as an energy source, typically comprising about 60 per cent methane and 40 per cent carbon dioxide.

Biological Control Control of pests and weeds by the use of natural predators, parasites or pathogens; most readily applied to exotic pests and weeds.

Biological Magnification Increase in the concentration of certain substances (often toxic) in the tissues of organisms at successively higher levels of the food chain.

Biomes Complex biotic communities with distinctive plant and animal forms, covering large areas and often paralleling areas of distinctive climatic types; for example, deserts, tundra, tropical rainforests.

Biota   The total plant and animal life present in a region or environment.

Biotechnology   All aspects of technology which use or manipulate living organisms for industrial, agricultural or medical purposes.

BP (Before present)   Defined for the purpose of carbon dating as the number of years before 1950.

Buffering   The capacity of a system to limit the impact of a major disturbance; specifically, the ability of a soil to maintain its composition and pH within narrow limits.

Carrying Capacity   The maximum population of a species (natural or otherwise) that an environment can support without damage.

Catalyst   A substance that causes or accelerates a chemical reaction without itself being permanently affected.

CFCs *see* Chlorofluorocarbons.

Chlorofluorocarbons (CFCs)   A family of manufactured inert gases containing chlorine, fluorine and carbon, which have been widely used since about 1940 as refrigerants, aerosol propellants, foaming agents (e.g. for plastics) and cleaning agents.

Community   A group of plants and animals living together in an ecologically related fashion in a definite environment or region.

Continental Shelf   The shallow ocean floor immediately adjacent to a land mass, often defined as being less than 200 m deep. The substrate is continental crust and not oceanic crust.

Cycle   Any series of changes in a system which brings the system or the relevant section of it back to its original state.

Denitrification   Bacterial breakdown of soluble nitrates in the soil and the return of nitrogen to the atmosphere without passing through plant tissue.

Disturbance Regime   The range of environmental disturbances to which a particular community or ecosystem is subjected.

Dobson Units   Units used in measuring the amount of ozone in the atmospheric column above a particular place.

Ecosystem   A community of organisms occupying a given area together with their physical and chemical environment and the interactions between the organisms and their environment.

EEZ *see* Exclusive Economic Zone.

El Niño–Southern Oscillation (ENSO)   A periodic warm-water outbreak in the eastern Pacific off Peru which causes a cell of circulation in the atmosphere (the Walker Cell) to reverse direction and to ascend over the eastern Pacific and descend over eastern Australia. Such a reversal increases rainfall on the Pacific coasts of North and South America and brings extended drought conditions to Australia, South-east Asia and even Africa.

Endemic, Endemism   Limited to a particular region or geographical environment; *endemism* is a measure of the proportion of endemic species present.

ENSO *see* El Niño–Southern Oscillation.

Entropy A measure of disorder or randomness in a system — the higher the entropy, the greater the disorder; also a measure of the unavailable energy in a thermodynamic system.

Environmental Impact Assessment (EIA) A formal process of investigating and documenting the likely environmental effects of a development proposal and assessing their significance as an aid in decision-making.

Eutrophication The enrichment of a water body with an excess of plant nutrients (especially nitrogen and phosphorus compounds), thus enabling a rapid increase in phytoplankton and plant populations which may deplete available oxygen and render the water and bottom sediments anaerobic.

Exclusive Economic Zone (EEZ) Region of the ocean within 200 nautical miles of a coastline, within which a coastal state claims exclusive rights to fish and exploit other marine resources; rights of passage by shipping are not affected.

Expert System A computer program based on the combined input of a number of experts in a field, which can be applied to predict outcomes and assist decision-making in novel situations.

FAO *see* Food and Agriculture Organization.

Flux The rate of flow of a substance or of energy, or the rate of change in a property.

Food and Agriculture Organization (FAO) An organisation within the United Nations dealing with international issues in the broadly defined area of food and agriculture, including forestry.

Freedom of the Seas The right of unhindered navigation guaranteed by international law, both on the high seas and in zones claimed by individual nations.

G7 (Group of Seven) A grouping of the world's seven most industrialised nations (Germany, Canada, the USA, France, Italy, Japan and the UK), founded in 1975.

Gatt *see* General Agreement on Tariffs and Trade.

General Agreement on Tariffs and Trade (GATT) An international organisation founded in 1948 to oversee world trade and to free it as much as possible from national regulations. It has over 100 members, but is dominated by the USA, Japan and the European Union. (*See also* World Trade Organization.)

Genetic Engineering The use of laboratory, medical and industrial techniques to alter genetic characteristics. Recombinant DNA technology is one form of genetic engineering.

Genus A group of closely related species that resemble one another but do not normally interbreed to produce fertile offspring.

Green Revolution Agriculture changes introduced in the 1960s and 1970s based on the breeding of new, high-yielding grain varieties and increased inputs of water and fertilisers. Such changes were widely applied in low-income nations, sometimes with adverse social or environmental impacts.

Group of 77 Formed in 1964 at the first UN Commission on Trade and Development Conference, this grouping of low and medium-income nations now has over 100 members and fights for a more equitable trading role for its members.

High Seas   The oceans beyond the furthest claims to national jurisdiction by coastal states: under UNCLOS III this means ocean areas more than 200 nautical miles from the nearest coastline.

Humus   Dark organic matter in soils produced by the decomposition of vegetable and animal matter; it is essential for maintaining fertility and favourable water supply.

Hydrocarbons   A class of compounds containing only hydrogen and carbon and including many common fuels.

Ice Age   A period of time during which glacial ice spreads over regions not normally ice-covered; the last such period, the Pleistocene Ice Age, ended about 11 000 years ago.

IMF   *see* International Monetary Fund.

International Monetary Fund   An organisation founded in 1944 as a parallel to the World Bank, primarily to promote international economic stability through co-operation. More recently, a major function has been to assist member nations (173 by 1992) with balance-of-payments difficulties, often resulting in benefits to high-income nations more than to those nations receiving 'assistance' or to their people.

IUCN — The World Conservation Union   A non-governmental organisation founded in 1948 to monitor and evaluate the status of nature and natural resources; to encourage sound management practices; to conserve biological diversity; and to promote the development of human communities toward a life in harmony with the biosphere.

Landcare   A 10-year program initiated by the Australian Government in 1990 to encourage and fund landscape restoration, reduce land degradation, and achieve ecologically sustainable development. The program is driven by local Landcare groups formed to deal with common problems.

Leachates   Solutions of chemicals leached out by water percolating through mine wastes or landfills and entering local streams or groundwater reservoirs.

Lithosphere   The crust of the Earth; rocks and related material.

Lithospheric Energy   Energy within the Earth's crust (lithosphere), naturally expressed in volcanoes and earthquakes, which can be tapped in regions with high geothermal activity, e.g. the North Island of New Zealand and Iceland.

Microclimate   The climate of a very small area, such as a single paddock, creek valley or street.

Monoculture   Cultivation of a single crop species on a large area of land, typical of agriculture in high-income nations.

Mutualistic   Relating to a symbiotic relationship between two or more organisms through which all benefit.

Niche   The position or function of an organism in a community of plants and animals.

Non-governmental Organisation (NGO)   A group with interests in specific issues (for example, environmental, development, aid or social issues) and not formally associated with government at any level.

Non-Renewable Resources   Resources which are not regenerated or replaced by natural processes within human lifespans. Also known as stock resources.

OECD (Organization for Economic Co-operation and Development)   Formed in 1960 and with 25 high-income nations as members by 1994, the OECD aims to assist member nations formulate economic and social policies and co-ordinate their positions as high-income nations.

Oxidation   Any chemical reaction in which a substance loses electrons. Originally used to refer to reactions in which oxygen is combined with another element.

Perturbation   A significant disturbance, usually by a force or event external to the system under consideration.

pH   A measure of the acidity or alkalinity of a substance, which uses a logarithmic scale: acidic substances have a pH of 1–6, neutral substances pH = 7, alkaline substances pH of 8–14.

Photochemical Smog   Complex of atmospheric pollutants from industrial and urbanised areas produced by reactions between hydrocarbons, nitrogen oxides and sunlight.

Photodissociation   The splitting of a molecule into atoms or smaller molecules by the absorption of radiation (especially solar radiation).

Photolytic Reaction   A reaction involving the breakdown of materials under the influence of sunlight.

Photosynthesis   The process by which plants use solar radiation to extract carbon from the atmosphere (in the form of CO_2). This permits the plant to create organic materials from inorganic forms and to store energy within its tissues.

Phytoplankton   Microscopic organisms that float or drift in surface waters and fix energy through photosynthesis.

Polyculture   Complex system of crop cultivation where several or many species are grown together for mutual support and sustained production over long periods; typical of agriculture in many low-income nations where particular microclimates may be exploited on small parcels of land.

Propagules   Those parts of organisms that can give rise to new individuals, such as seeds, cuttings or embryos.

Rangelands   Areas of extensive grazing land used by native or domestic animals consuming natural vegetation.

Ratify   Confirm an agreement, especially when a government confirms an international agreement reached by its representatives. Ratification also involves recognition that national legislation and practice will be altered where necessary to give effect to the provisions of the agreement.

Recombinant DNA Technology   Processes of genetic engineering which involve the excision of particular gene sequences from the DNA or RNA of one organism and their incorporation into the embryos of another. Also called gene splicing.

Residence Time   The average time that a component of a system or cycle remains in one place or condition.

Riparian Zone   Area of land adjoining a stream; the banks and flood plains.

Shifting Cultivation   A system of agriculture involving clearance of small patches of forest, crop cultivation for a few years, then abandonment and removal to new plots. Also known as 'slash-and-burn' agriculture after the normal method of forest clearance.

Siltation   Accumulation of sediment (of any size) in a stream, lake, estuary or reservoir.

Sink   That part of a system where energy or matter is consumed or drained away.

Speciation   Process of evolution of new species.

Steady State   A system is in a steady state when it is operating without (major) changes to inputs or outputs and the nature and structure of the system does not change.

Store   Part of a system where energy or matter is held for some time and where inputs and outputs are relatively small compared to the dimensions of the store.

Stratosphere   That part of the atmosphere between 17 and 48 km above the Earth's surface; temperatures increase with height in this layer and hence there is little mixing of air masses.

Stratum   A layer of material with distinctive and recognisable properties; a layer of vegetation, such as the canopy or groundcover.

Sustainable Yield   A level of harvest of a renewable resource which can be maintained indefinitely without damage to the resource base. Maximum sustainable yield does not always give maximum economic returns.

Synoptic Wind   A wind driven by a large-scale pressure field, as distinct from local winds such as sea breezes; known by meteorologists as a gradient or geostrophic wind.

System   A combination of parts and connections between them working together as a coherent whole. Open systems have discrete inputs and outputs via a 'porous' system boundary, while closed systems have 'non-porous' boundaries and recycle all matter and energy within themselves.

TCM   *see* Total Catchment Management.

Thermal Mass   The ability of a material to absorb (or lose) large amounts of energy with little gain (or fall) in temperature.

Threshold   A critical level of input or output to or from a system. Once the inputs or outputs pass that level, a substantial and often permanent change in the system may be triggered.

Total Catchment Management (TCM)   The integrated management of all land uses within a catchment by all involved bodies and individuals in such a way that none adversely impinges on the hydrologic values of the stream basin.

Transgenic New animals or plants which have been created by recombinant DNA techniques and whose genetic composition includes gene sequences derived from entirely different species.

Transhumant Involving seasonal migration of people and domestic herds between lowlands and mountains.

Transpiration The emission of water vapour to the atmosphere through the stomata ('pores') of plant leaves.

Troposphere The lowest 17 km of the atmosphere, in which most clouds are formed and most weather processes occur.

Tundra Vast, nearly level, treeless plains of the Arctic regions of Europe, Asia and North America, often with vast marshy areas over frozen subsoil (permafrost).

UNCTAD *see* United Nations Conference on Trade and Development.

UNDP *see* United Nations Development Programme.

United Nations Conference on Trade and Development (UNCTAD) A United Nations body concerned with trade issues, but largely superseded, in practical terms, by the GATT. UNCTAD has, however, been particularly active in the area of commodities such as agricultural products and timber, especially as exported by low-income nations.

United Nations Development Programme (UNDP) Founded within the UN in 1965 to promote development in low-income nations, stressing the building of nations' capacities to manage their own economies and environments, but also promoting international partnerships and co-ordination of efforts.

Urbanisation The process by which the proportion of a global, national or regional population living in urban areas increases; or the increasing dominance of human societies by urban influences.

Water Table The upper boundary of the zone of groundwater saturation.

WHO *see* World Health Organization.

WMO *see* World Meteorological Organization.

World Bank More formally known as the International Bank for Reconstruction and Development, it was established in 1944 and now incorporates the International Development Association. Its major focus has been on providing large loans, loan guarantees and other assistance for capital investment, particularly in low and middle-income nations.

World Conservation Union *see* IUCN — The world conservation union

World Health Organization (WHO) An intergovernmental organisation formed in 1948 to promote and co-ordinate international advances in human health.

World Heritage List A listing of sites of global significance nominated by national governments and accepted by the Convention Concerning the Protection of the World Cultural and Natural Heritage (World Heritage Convention), administered by UNESCO.

World Meteorological Organization (WMO) Formed in 1950 as an intergovernmental organisation and a specialised agency within the United Nations to promote international co-operation in meteorology, especially the gathering and exchange of data.

World Resources Institute   An independent, non-profit research and policy institute concerned with a wide range of environmental and development issues. A central aim is to generate and disseminate accurate information on those issues.

World Trade Organization (WTO)   Formed in 1994 as a successor to the GATT. The WTO incorporates into its responsibilities intellectual property rights and trade in services, agriculture and fibres, areas all previously outside the ambit of the GATT.

World Wide Fund For Nature (WWF)   A non-governmental organisation founded in 1961 to promote the conservation of nature, the use of sustainable resources, and the reduction of pollution and waste generation.

WTO *see* World Trade Organization.

WWF *see* World Wide Fund for Nature.

ACRONYMS AND ABBREVIATIONS

ACT	Australian Capital Territory
AFZ	Australian Fishing Zone
BP	before present
CBD	central business district
CFC	chlorofluorocarbon
CITES	Convention on International Trade in Endangered Species of Wild Fauna and Flora
CRAMRA	Convention on Regulation of Antarctic Minerals Resource Activities
CSD	Commission on Sustainable Development
CSIRO	Commonwealth Scientific and Industrial Research Organization
DDT	dichlorodiphenyltrichloroethane
DNA	deoxyribonucleic acid
EEZ	exclusive economic zone
ENSO	El Niño–Southern Oscillation
EPA	Environmental Protection Agency (USA)
ESD	ecologically sustainable development
FAO	Food and Agriculture Organization
FFA	(South Pacific) Forum Fisheries Agency
G7	Group of Seven
GATT	General Agreement on Tariffs and Trade
GCM	general circulation model
GDP	gross domestic product
GEF	Global Environment Facility (formerly, Global Environment Fund)
GNP	gross national product
IAEA	International Atomic Energy Agency

IGY	International Geophysical Year
IMF	International Monetary Fund
IMO	International Maritime Organization
IPCC	Intergovernmental Panel on Climate Change
IPM	integrated pest management
ISA	International Seabed Authority
ISEW	Index of Sustainable Economic Welfare
ITTA	International Tropical Timber Agreement
ITTO	International Tropical Timber Organization
IUCN	International Union for the Conservation of Nature (now the World Conservation Union)
IWC	International Whaling Commission
MARPOL	Convention for the Prevention of Pollution from Ships
MDBC	Murray–Darling Basin Commission
NASA	National Aeronautics and Space Administration
NGO	non-governmental organisation
NNP	net national product
NRMS	Natural Resources Management Strategy
NSW	New South Wales
OECD	Organization for Economic Co-operation and Development
PCB	polychlorinated biphenyl
RAC	Resource Assessment Commission
RMP	revised management procedure
RNA	ribonucleic acid
SAP	structural adjustment program
SCAR	Scientific Committee on Antarctic Research
SPM	suspended particulate matter
TCM	total catchment management
TFAP	Tropical Forest Action Plan
TOMS	Total Ozone Mapping Spectrometer
UK	United Kingdom
UN	United Nations
UNCED	United Nations Conference on Environment and Development (the Earth Summit)
UNCLOS	United Nations Conference on the Law of the Sea
UNCTAD	United Nations Conference on Trade and Development
UNDP	United Nations Development Programme
UNEP	United Nations Environment Programme
UNESCO	United Nations Educational, Scientific and Cultural Organization
US(A)	United States (of America)
USSR	(former) Union of Soviet Socialist Republics
UV	ultraviolet
WCED	World Commission on Environment and Development
WHO	World Health Organization
WMO	World Meteorological Organization
WTO	World Trade Organization
WWF	World Wide Fund for Nature (formerly World Wildlife Fund)

UNITS OF MEASUREMENTS

SI UNITS

The Système Internationale (SI) is based on seven independent, fundamental units: metre (length), gram (mass), second (time), kelvin (temperature), ampère (electric current), mole (amount of a substance) and candela (luminous intensity). SI units of other quantities, such as force (newton), pressure (pascal), power (watt), and energy (joule) are defined in terms of the fundamental units. Multiples or fractions of units, in powers of ten, are designated by the following prefixes:

p	pico-	one trillionth	10^{-12}	0.000 000 000 001
n	nano-	one billionth	10^{-9}	0.000 000 001
μ	micro-	one millionth	10^{-6}	0.000 001
m	milli-	one thousandth	10^{-3}	0.001
c	centi-	one hundredth	10^{-2}	0.01
d	deci-	one tenth	10^{-1}	0.1
da	deca-	ten	10^{1}	10
h	hecto-	one hundred	10^{2}	100
k	kilo-	one thousand	10^{3}	1000
M	mega-	one million	10^{6}	1 000 000
G	giga-	one billion	10^{9}	1 000 000 000
T	tera-	one trillion	10^{12}	1 000 000 000 000

OTHER NOTES

A **nautical mile** (nm) is equivalent to 1852 metres. This unit is still commonly used in marine and aeronautical contexts, including the Law of the Sea Convention.

A **teragram** (Tg) is equivalent to 0.001 Gt (gigatonnes). Both units are used in the literature on atmospheric pollution and global warming.

ppmv, **ppbv**, **pptv**: parts per million (billion, trillion) by volume.

INDEX